HAYLE IN WORLD WAR TWO
"A TOWN NOT A VILLAGE"

BRIAN SULLIVAN

All rights reserved. No part of this publication may be reproduced, converted or archived into any other medium without a relevant permission first being obtained from the publisher. Nor should the book be circulated or resold in any binding other than its original cover.

Hayle in World War Two – A Town Not A Village

© Brian Sullivan

First Edition published 2011

Cover: © M.M. Sullivan. – The image shows two FW190's having bombed St Ives as they make their escape over Hayle firing their cannons and machine guns, and in turn being engaged by the Hayle anti-aircraft defences.

Frontispiece: © Imperial War Museum – J&F Pool's employees firing a 3in mortar on Hayle Towans as a reward for completing one million mortar bombs by 1943.

Rear Cover images: © Imperial War Museum – Workers at the J&F Pool works, Hayle, boring out shell cases.

Designed & Typeset: Tobi Carver
Printed & Published by:
The St Ives Printing & Publishing Company,
High Street, St Ives, Cornwall TR26 1RS UK.

www.stivesnews.co.uk

ISBN: 978-0-948385-53-7

HAYLE IN WORLD WAR TWO
"A Town Not A Village"

by

Brian Sullivan

Dedication

This book is dedicated to two splendid but unsung teachers, Mr Michael Kirby of London, and Mr Francis Thomas of Porthleven.
 They encouraged the study of language and literature at Hayle in the difficult days of the Second World War.
 'It was the best of times, it was the worst of times . . .'

CONTENTS

Acknowledgements 9

Preface 10

Chapter One:
Lacuna 11

Chapter Two:
Prelude & Sitzkrieg 13

Chapter Three:
'We Shall Fight Them On The Beaches' 17

Chapter Four:
Garrison Town 29

Chapter Five:
The Home Guard & the Auxiliary Units 33

Chapter Six:
Civil Defence – A.R.P. 39

Chapter Seven:
The Firefighters – *A.F.S. & N.F.S.* 45

Chapter Eight:
'Starfish' & Other Decoys 51

Chapter Nine:
Bombs on Hayle & District 53

Chapter Ten:
'Suffer the Little Children' – *The Evacuees* 57

Chapter Eleven:
The *Rossmore* & The *Marena* – *The Battle of the North Coast* 63

Chapter Twelve:
The Red Duster – *Merchant Shipping in Hayle* 67

Chapter Thirteen:
The Mystery of the French Crabber 71

Chapter Fourteen:
Social Life – *The Light in the Darkness* 73

Chapter Fifteen:
Air Crashes – *Hayle Area* 81

Chapter Sixteen:
The B-17 That Didn't Quite Get to the War 83

Chapter Seventeen:
'They're Just Like Us' – *The US Army in Hayle* 89

Chapter Eighteen:
'Rhinos' on the Weir 93

Chapter Nineteen:
Cadets – *Teenage Life* 99

Chapter Twenty:
National Savings – *The Weeks* 105

Chapter Twenty-One:
The Short & Unhappy Life of a British Restaurant 111

Chapter Twenty-Two:
Flight Lieutenant Meyer D.F.C. 113

Chapter Twenty-Three:
Everday Life in Wartime Hayle 115

Chapter Twenty-Four:
Aftermath – *The Break-Up of Ships* 123

Chapter Twenty-Five:
'Lest We Forget' – 1939 – 1945 125

Appendix I:
Chapter Notes & References 127

Appendix II:
Associated Octel 135

Appendix III:
Civil Defence 136

Appendix IV:
Police 141

Appendix V:
Aid Posts and Nursing 142

Appendix VI:
Fire Service & Water Supplies 144

Appendix VII:
After the War 146

Index 147

ACKNOWLEDGEMENTS

MY SINCERE THANKS are due to those who helped in so many ways with information and guidance in the compilation of this history. Notably the *Cornishman* newspaper and its network of unknown, but faithful local correspondents, ably led by the father and son proprietors and editor in those days, Mr Herbert Thomas and Mr H. Hartley Thomas. Without the efforts of all these dedicated persons and their newspaper this book would have been very much smaller.

I would also like to thank Capt. Hogg of the Falmouth Maritime Museum Library for his assistance and advice on matters nautical, especially for vital information in respect of the D-Day operations, and the 29th Infantry Division's involvement.

Much help was given by David Chinn of Newlyn, the leading expert on the local press of yesteryear, who never once failed to answer a query, however obscure, unearthing correct and detailed information from the original published source. Vital data on a little-known subject, the decoy towns and airfields, was supplied by Mr Huby Fairhead in his books and in personal correspondence.

In respect of the photographic content many thanks are due to Mrs Maureen Southcott for the publication of her late husband Adrian's dramatic and highly important unique photographs of the wartime barge and shipbuilding in Hayle.

My thanks also to Nigel J. Clarke Publications for the waiving of reproduction charges for the German aerial reconnaissance photograph and likewise to the Imperial War Museum for similarly not charging for the inclusion of images purchased from their collection. Detailed aviation data was supplied by Mr Bob Andrews of Newquay.

Many eyewitness details of everyday life in the barge-building shipyard were given by Mr Alfred Williams of Hayle; and his brother Gerald supplied unique information on the victim disposal arrangements for Hayle in the event of heavy air raids. Useful data and helpful contributions were also forthcoming from Mr Cedric Appleby, Mr Ted Lever and Mr Donald Waters.

Appreciation and thanks are due to Mr Brian Stevens for help and assistance, and to Cornwall Archaeological Unit, especially Mr Nicholas Johnson. Help was also forthcoming from Hayle Town Council via Mrs Vivienne Parsons the former Town Clerk. Many others have been most helpful with their recollections and anecdotal evidence; where possible they have received due acknowledgement in the text. To them also many thanks.

My brother Mervyn, a skilled aviation artist is to be congratulated and thanked for his superb cover painting of the Luftwaffe aircraft crossing Hayle after attacking St Ives. SAM Publications (*www.Sampublications.com*) were the source of accurate data on the livery of these aircraft.

Finally I must thank the Morrab Library, Penzance, in the persons of Annabelle, Margaret and Alex for their help, assistance and encouragement over countless Saturday mornings when they sustained me with coffee and biscuits, as I progressed through the manuscript in the peaceful ambience of the Jenner Room – my second home.

BJS 2010

PREFACE

THIS BOOK CAME about as the result of a draft outline for a general history of Hayle. I decided to start with the WWII chapter because having lived throughout the period in Hayle, a number of events were still fresh in my memory, many of which were details not available in the sources to which one could go for research. The WWII section, however, began to become so large and self-contained that it far outgrew the possibility of its being merely a component of a general history, so the decision was made that it become a separate book in its own right.

Apart from the personal recollections and the detailed research into specific events such as aircraft crashes etc., much of the general information regarding social activities, political manoeuvres, and other local affairs has been culled from the pages of *The Cornishman* newspaper which, despite being restricted by the heavy hand of state censorship, managed to record faithfully the day-by-day life of West Cornwall at war. In most cases I have given the specific publication date in the reference section of each chapter.

For some facts and comment, I have quite deliberately gone outside the strict confines of the town of Hayle. This has been necessary to give an overall picture of conditions and social/political attitudes in the area at the time. I make no apology for this as some of the decisions taken then, such as the precipitate withdrawal of fire and rescue services, have had repercussions detrimental to the people of Hayle and their safety, lasting to the present day and which have still not yet been resolved.

Lastly, it must be said in all humility, that this account of World War II could not have been written, had it not been for the sacrifice of those men of Hayle who gave their lives for their country; and, indeed, all those others, men and women, who wore the uniforms of the three services, the merchant fleets, and the civil defence organisations during those dangerous years.

Chapter One:

LACUNA

IN THE EIGHTEENTH and nineteenth centuries, Hayle had been in the forefront of the British industrial revolution and the worldwide ramifications and developments of that significant happening. The two great iron foundries of Harvey & Co at Foundry, and Sandys, Carne & Vivian at Copperhouse led the world in the engineering aspects of hard-rock mining, municipal water supplies, canal management and many other applications of advanced steam power. This pre-eminence had, for various well-recorded reasons outside the scope of this book, passed from Hayle by the turn of the 19th/20th century. In the years leading up to the onset of the Second World War Hayle, like most of Cornwall, was experiencing a prolonged slump in economic activity and prosperity apart from the nascent peripheral holiday industry.

However, to those who lived through the nineteen-thirties in Hayle, and, indeed, the southern half of Britain, it must sometimes have seemed to have been a golden age compared with the standards and ethos of today.

Most people were quite poor to be certain, but in their own way somehow relatively happy. The sun, in recollection, seemed to shine unceasingly across a succession of long, hot summers. There were jubilees and coronations to celebrate. Convoys of brightly-painted fairground and circus wagons trundled across Cornwall on their itinerant journeys, bringing enjoyment and temporary distraction to lighten the lives of the populations of the small towns and little villages.

The people of Hayle did the best that they could within their severely limited incomes to nurture their children and their old people. They tended their sick and ailing with kindness. They buried their dead with dignity. In their turn they courted, became engaged, married and had their children. They supported their chapels and churches. They funded their ambulance service and hospital to the best of their ability and finances.

The Hayle of the 1930s/40s was of an interesting social mix. Overwhelmingly it was working-class as defined in those days, and most people were relatively poor, even if in full-time employment, which not many were.

Given this situation many employers, encouraged by the harsh 'means test' policy of the time, were able to pay the lowest wages in the country. Dock labourers, for example, received just 5s.10d (29p) per day; and the Thomas W. Ward ship-breaking undertaking paid their men 30 shillings (£1-50) per week for doing that dangerous work.[1]

Hayle's population growth had arisen in the mid-eighteenth to mid-nineteenth centuries with the importation of industrial workers from other places in Cornwall and Britain, and who having no inborn tradition of subservience to the local hierarchy of landowners, clergymen and farmers, developed an independence of outlook and attitude, that has always been regarded as 'awkward' or even downright 'cussed' by the authorities, and viewed with the utmost suspicion by the populations of the so-called more select adjacent areas. This independence of outlook is often referred to as 'Hayle'.

Thus in the 1930s/40s the top layer of society in Hayle consisted of a few landowners and wealthy farmers, some directors and managers of local companies who still preferred to live near to their factories, although many had begun to migrate across the estuary to the more elegant surroundings of Lelant. All the medical practitioners still lived in the town, amongst and accessible at all times to the people to whom their professional responsibilities lay, as did the policemen.

The next social layer, if such it could be called, for they were never regarded with any great awe, even if they were the 'pillars' of the chapels or the 'lodge', and relatively well-to-do, were what the heavy-industry workers alluded to as the 'shopmen' and their families. Supporting these upper layers was the great homogeneous mass of the good people of Copperhouse and Foundry. All of these groups could be found represented on the various committees and other organisations including sports clubs, regatta committee, The St John's Ambulance Brigade, and other social bodies. It was always said in the past that nobody could get above themselves in Hayle. Anyone attempting to do so would be brought up sharply.

The people were, of course, not unaware of the war clouds building on the horizon. As the great leaders and eminent personages of twentieth century history planned their moves; signed their protocols; built their armies; tore up their treaties and threatened their neighbours, the people of Hayle could only look on powerless, and quite unable to have any influence on the politicians and warlords whose actions and decisions controlled their lives and destinies, they did what countless ordinary folk have done before them, and can only do when confronted with circumstances utterly beyond their control.

They rose as usual early each morning and tackled their daily tasks, or went off to their job if they had one, in order simply to live. They washed, fed, and clothed their children and sent them off to their schools. At weekends they supported their local rugby or cricket teams each in its season with enthusiastic and vociferous partiality. On Sunday there was chapel to be attended, morning and evening, with the children despatched in their turn to Sunday School. When bereavement came, as it must to every family, they buried their dead with due respect and ceremony.

To lighten the burdensome routine of everyday life there were the special social occasions; the chapel anniversary tea-treats, the annual carnival and regatta; and in the dark evenings of the winter months there were home-grown concert parties together with the whist-drives and other functions leading up to Christmas and its delights. So the nineteen-thirties passed into history in a long-to-be-remembered haze of pleasant recollections, while far away from the people the approach of war was slowly and inevitably coming ever closer to the residents of Hayle.

A thousand miles to the eastward of Cornwall, Adolf Hitler was formulating the war plans that would change the way of life in Hayle for ever, although he himself almost certainly knew nothing at all about the town. As the last years of the decade approached, reports in the local press began to indicate ominous signs of the war that was nearing. A number of small discrete items which when looked at together, from the viewpoint of over half a century later become definite pre-cursors of the onset of World War II.

Chapter Two:
PRELUDE & SITZKRIEG

AS EARLY AS 1922 with the experience of the Great War of 1914 – 18 and its consequences still fresh in their minds the authorities were showing remarkable prescience with regard to future conflicts as a local newspaper report on Hayle shows: 'The footpath between the P.O. at Foundry and that at Copperhouse is being excavated and a telephone cable laid down in lieu of the overhead line, thus obviating accident and risk from aerial attack.'(1)

In 1935 at Penzance the St John's Ambulance Brigade was concerning itself with a national appeal for volunteers with experience in anti-poison gas treatments (presumably ex-WWI medical orderlies).(2)

In April 1937 the countrywide Air Raid Wardens Service was set up, and in July 1938 a meeting was held at Connor Downs to discuss air raid precautions. The Chairman of Gwinear-Gwithian Parish Council appealed for volunteers to be air raid wardens. This prompted a response, one wag remarking: 'Why bother about air raids in the tail-end of England, down here?' The reply is not recorded, but one hopes that the questioner did not have to eat his words just two years later, when the German army swept through France to the Atlantic coast, and the Luftwaffe established bases from where their aircraft could very easily reach Connor Downs; and later, indeed, did severely bomb Roseworthy, the very next village.

Mr E.G. Shovel, the West Penwith Rural District Council (RDC). councillor remarked that: 'Hayle might get a packet, Connor Downs would not unless the enemy had a few bombs left over.' This remark was greeted with much laughter. Mr H.W. Turner, the ex-Hayle police sergeant who had been appointed Hon. Organiser Air Raid Precautions (ARP) Eastern District, West Penwith RDC, stated that a ratio of three wardens to every forty houses would be required. Hayle would be the ARP centre for the eastern district.(3)

In August 1938 it was reported that Germany, which had occupied Austria six months earlier, announced that 750,000 reservists were to be called up ,manoeuvres were to commence and that no man of military age could leave the country.(4)

At the Hayle Carnival of Saturday 31st August 1938 there was a tableau depicting the work of the ARP volunteers. A year later and the 1939 carnival shows a heavy military/civil defence component including a detachment of the Hayle section of the No. 203 Heavy Anti-Aircraft (HAA) Battery of the 56th Regiment, Royal Artillery (TA), and two detachments of the Penzance Auxiliary Fire Service, in uniform and with two types of trailer pumps, in charge of Sgt Fulford, and were reported as, 'looking efficient.'(5)

At the Penzance Carnival in August 1939 there was an 'air raid simulation' by the Penzance section of 203 HAA Battery Royal Artillery (TA), under Lt R.J. Rogers with Major W. Smith in general command. There were two detachments of No. 4 Anti-Aircraft Searchlight Company, Falmouth, with 2nd Lt Hicks in command, and also on parade were the ladies of the 1st Cornwall Company ATS (Auxiliary Territorial Service), commanded by Mrs Crosbie Garstin.(6) With the general mobilisation that followed the outbreak of hostilities, Penzance was presented with a stirring military spectacle as Mrs Garstin, ever an imposing figure in her own right, at the head of the column marched her girls, in full uniform and in regimental order, down the length of Market Jew Street to Penzance Station and off to the war.(7)

Slightly earlier at the July 1939 meeting of West Penwith RDC., Mr J.H. Woolcock, a Hayle councillor, protested that the gas masks allocated to Hayle had not yet arrived. However, on the 30th of August, it was reported that over seven thousand gas masks had been assembled in the Hayle Drill Hall in the space of ten hours, and were being distributed.(8)

With the outbreak of war only three days away we find that Hayle Parish Council is, quite rightly, becoming concerned about certain aspects of the civil defence of the town. The Clerk said that the Minister of Health had replied to his letter concerning a First Aid Post for Hayle, in which he stated that the Minister felt he could not depart from his previous decision in the matter. Mr H.W. Turner (Chief ARP Warden for Hayle) said that they should be better served. He had consulted a doctor in the town (Dr W.H. Palmer),and they had decided to form a First Aid Post privately for Hayle. Hayle was a town of large proportions and they had 8000 people to cater for. They were told that they would be served by a mobile post, which was a motor bus converted into an ambulance. He moved that a letter be sent to the Ministry protesting against their decision, and pointing out that Hayle was 'a town not a village.'(9)

On Sunday 3rd September 1939 war with Germany was declared, and life in Hayle was to change dramatically over the coming years, both in physical terms, and in the social aspect. The Hayle component of the Territorial Army had been mobilised on the 24 – 28th August joining their fellow gunners of No. 203 HAA battery 56 Cornwall Regt RA from Penzance, St Ives and St Just, and had departed to 'somewhere in Britain' – in fact, to Weymouth; and later to engage the enemy in the 'Battle of Britain,' before being sent to the cold coasts of Iceland.(10) Army, Navy and Royal Air Force (RAF) reservists were called to the colours; and as in the rest of the country a one hundred per cent blackout of all buildings and street lighting was imposed, and would stay in place for the next four years.

The expected mass air raids on the civilian population did not occur, and the panic measures by the authorities were eventually relaxed, the Ritz Cinema in Penzance, for instance, had been closed since the outbreak of the war.(11) So the cinemas, theatres and public halls were allowed to re-open and carry on business as usual. This lull in belligerent activity except at sea, for the remainder of 1939 and the first half of 1940 was referred by the Americans as the 'Phoney War,' or to quote one bored British soldier in France: 'instead of the Blitzkrieg we got the Sitzkrieg!'

In Hayle life carried on much as before. The younger men, however. were conscripted or volunteered for the armed services, leaving their families and homes, many for far-distant places across the world; some of them, sadly, never to see Cornwall again. The rationing of certain foods, slowly at first, made only a gradual impact on the lives of the population, the delicious Carwin Dairy ice cream, for instance, could still be enjoyed well into 1940 at Owen Clemence's shop in Foundry Square, or the Carwin Cafe on Hayle Terrace. Public involvement in the war effort was well under way. By February 1940 the St Erth Working Party for Hospital Supplies and Comforts for the Troops bi-weekly meetings up to date had sent away 149 garments including 11 bed jackets, 5 nightshirts, 6 day shirts, 30 helmets (presumably Balaclavas) and other comforts.(12)

Also in February a major food scandal was reported – 'The Great Meat Muddle.' It appears that local-grown beef had become almost unobtainable. People were unable to bake their pasties or cook their Sunday roast. Frozen mutton, however, it was reported, was very much in evidence. Presumably the rapidly-expanding armed forces were commandeering the bulk of the available beef. Local butchers were having to close for three days a week, while at the same time Truro market sent ninety-one bullocks away to London. When finally a shipment of beef did arrive in West Cornwall, the robust and outspoken councillor and prominent Hayle pork butcher, Mr Arthur Kevern was outraged to discover that the meat was being delivered to Hayle and St Just in the West Penwith RDC refuse wagon.(13)

An indication of the approaching seriousness of the food supply situation, now becoming dangerously threatened by the German U-boat activities was when Mr H.W. Turner resigned his seat on Hayle Parish Council, having joined the Ministry of Food as the Food Enforcement Officer for the area.(14)

The almost cosily relaxed mood of the Phoney War was to come to an abrupt end with the news of the German attack on Holland, Belgium and France on the 10th of May 1940. All of Britain including the far west of Cornwall would now be within the range of aircraft from the Luftwaffe's newly acquired bomber bases. In addition the entire coastline of southern Britain was in danger from imminent sea and airborne invasion.

At this crucial period of the war the safety of the civilian population was the responsibility of the local authorities throughout Britain. In the case of Hayle this meant that the public's protection from the Luftwaffe, the world's largest and most efficient air force, rested entirely in the hands of the bucolic councillors and officers of West Penwith RDC, in their cosy Penzance offices, a situation which in the light of eventual experience, proved to be dangerously detrimental to the people of Hayle and their safety until central government was forced to step in, take control, and impose and enforce national standards of efficiency throughout the country.

A Type 24 Pillbox, in the dunes above the mouth of Hayle harbour on the Lelant side.

Photograph: the author

Chapter Three:

'WE SHALL FIGHT THEM ON THE BEACHES'

DURING THE 'PHONEY War' or 'Sitzkrieg' period, Cornwall was relatively unprotected against air attack as it had been considered well out of range of the aircraft based in Germany. Modern airfields were almost non-existent in the county. A large Coastal Command base was nearing completion at St Eval, and there was a small fighter detachment at Roborough, Plymouth.

Following the conquest of France and with the Luftwaffe units settling on their newly-captured bases in Normandy and Brittany, hurried plans were drawn up to build Fighter Command airfields at Portreath which opened in March 1941, and its smaller satellite at Perranporth. Later a large multi-use RAF airbase was constructed at Predannack on the Lizard peninsula. Radar stations were to be provided at Drytree (Goonhilly), and Trerew near Newquay.

At Hayle, Riviere House and the Penmare Hotel together with many bungalows and huts on the Towans were commandeered to house the influx of troops. The Bluff Hotel and Taylor's Tea Rooms were also taken over. Anti-tank and anti-personnel mines were laid in the soft sand between the cliffs and the mouth of the river. The whole of the beach and cliff tops were strung along with coils of barbed wire entanglements, and slit trenches. The entire beach area which was exposed at low tide was criss-crossed with large tree-trunks set vertically in the sand to prevent German troop-carrying aircraft from landing. Strong points were established at the ferry and along the cliff tops, consisting of concrete-block pillboxes and mortar

Type 24 pillbox, over looking the Hayle channel from the Ferryhouse, Lelant.
Photograph: Mr Beckett Cook via Mrs Dorothy Cook.

platforms. The pillboxes from the Hayle River to Godrevy were built by the late Mr Percy Jacka of St Erth who had one labourer to help him. He was given two weeks to build each one to a standard government specification using local concrete blocks.(1)

Many of those defences can still be seen on the cliffs at Hayle, although misguided persons still campaign for the removal of what they consider to be 'eyesores' defacing the countryside. Recently the authorities at the highest level have become seriously alarmed at the wholesale destruction of the physical remains of the war, and have ordered steps to be taken by county councils to survey, record and protect the remaining items.

An anti-tank roadblock, zig-zag in outline and obstructed with 'dragon's teeth' concrete blocks was constructed on the Causeway Road, near to the present Tempest building. Further pillboxes were positioned on the Gwithian road and on the A30 main road. The one on the Carwin Rise to Connor Downs had a wood and corrugated iron shed built around it to disguise it as a petrol filling station, complete with enamel advertising plates.

Large circular emergency water tanks, approx. 20ft (6m) diameter, 5ft (1.5m) deep, were placed at Penpol Terrace opposite where the Post Office now is, and on Merchant Curnow's Quay roughly opposite St Elwyn's Hall. Another important water reserve which could be used at times of low tide, was what is now called Wilson's Pool at Copperhouse. The pool was permanently flooded at all times for the duration of the war, providing a huge reserve of non-tidal water.

The importance of North Quay was noted, housing as it did the only major power station in Cornwall feeding the National Grid; and a large bulk storage and distribution petrol complex which in addition to supplying local area civilian and army users, was responsible for the provision of aviation fuel to local airfields, including RAF Portreath and RAF Perranporth. Also on North Quay was a recently-built 'shadow' factory designed and operated by ICI to produce 'anti-knock' additives for aviation fuel, not available anywhere else in the UK in wartime, by extracting bromine from the sea water.

Outlines of a World War II anti-tank roadblock.
This roadblock was on the Hayle Causeway, and in the distance is the former Hayle NHS Fire Station.

Photograph: the author

At the end of July (1940) the 53rd (London) Medium Regt Royal Artillery was moved in to thicken up the defences of the West Country. 209 Headquarters (HQ) was set up at Feock with an assortment of static guns at Padstow, Hayle, Marazion, Porthleven, Gunwalloe, St Austell, Par and Fowey. The regiment's period defending the beaches officially came to an end on 1st January 1941 when it handed over to the newly-formed 11th Defence Regiment At this time the batteries were re-equipped with 6 inch howitzers.(2)

In August 1940 North Quay was classed as a 'Protected Area'. Armed guards were posted there, and admission was by official pass only. The Admiralty ordered three booms to be deployed at North Quay, one at East Quay and two at Foundry Quay, to prevent enemy craft getting alongside the quays. The three booms at North Quay were removed in August 1941.(3) Demolition charges were placed ready under the swing bridge, and slit-trenches were dug at Clifton Terrace, and along the cliff tops around the cove.

With the onset of total war J & F Pool Ltd, the long-established metal perforators and general engineering works in Hayle, had converted to full wartime production. Their main output was concentrated on finishing the outer casings of 3in mortar bombs. The rough castings would be unloaded at Hayle goods sidings and conveyed to the factory for the precision work necessary before the bombs were ready to be sent on to be filled with explosives.

By mid-1943 J & F Pool had completed over 1 million bomb casings. The workers were rewarded by the government by being taken to the army mortar range then on Hayle Towans, and were shown and took part in the live firing of a 3in mortar. They were also given rides on Bren Gun Carriers over the sand hills. Photographs were

---

The remains of the concrete base for a 3in mortar platform (upside down).
This area of Hayle Towans was used as a mortar training ground.

Photograph: the author

taken by an official photographer. A number of the colour photographs were published at the time in a national magazine. In addition to the mortar bombs, among many other items, J & F Pool made armour plate protection for aircrews, aircraft engine cowlings, other components for aircraft, gun mountings and even such mundane, but essential items such as ammunition boxes and mess tins for the Army.

With all these vital facilities concentrated in one town, the major defensive effort at Hayle, was protection against air attack. The Cornwall County Council website *Defended Cornwall* states that in WWII Hayle was, 'of immense strategic importance'. A stirring sight one morning in 1941 was the sudden appearance of a long line of mobile anti-aircraft guns parked along the roadside of Penpol Terrace. Later that same day they were deployed around the outskirts of the town on twelve sites carefully surveyed to give maximum cover against high and low-flying aircraft coming over the estuary and town. Hayle was now officially designated a 'GDA' (Gun Defended Area), second in size and strength to Cornwall's other town GDA, Falmouth.

Heavy AA sites were established at Gwinear (SW 595 372), Calais (SW 580 352), Trevarrack (SW 522 374) and Gunwyn Farm (SW 537 382) The major gunsite at Gwinear was developed to become what in the official Royal Artillery terminology is referred to as a 'half-battery' ie 4 x 3.7in heavy AA guns. The Calais, Trevarrack, and

---

Facing page:
Staff of J & F Pool enjoying their ride in a British Army Bren Gun Carrier.
Photograph: Imperial War Museum

Twenty-one year old Dorothy Couch, of Hayle, assembles the nose and tail sections of a 3in mortar round at the J & F Pool's factory, Hayle, 1943.

Photograph: Imperial War Museum

Gunwyn Farm sites were also equipped with 3.7in (94mm) guns. A total of eight 3.7in AA guns ringed Hayle on these sites.(4)

The 40mm (1.6in) Bofors light AA guns were situated on the Towans behind Clifton Terrace (SW 556 380) and consisted of 1 gun, two pits (one predictor?) and one Nissen hut. The site on Bodriggy Fields (SW 567 373) was an extensive Bofors complex, consisting of seven circular emplacements with four guns plus predictors, ammunition stores and two Nissen huts. This site has now been completely built-over by the Harvey and Ellis Way estates.

Another Bofors gunsite was at Griggs Hill (SW 546 361) in the field to the left of the road to Penzance. This site was destroyed when the dual carriageway was built. A further Bofors site was above Porth Kidney Sands (SW 548 383) and another at Lelant Bend (SW 543 374). One on Mexico Towans (SW 559 387) was later relocated to Lelant Towans (SW 541 382). Aerial photographs show locations of light AA guns at Lelant Quay (SW 551 375). There were circular emplacements with two Bofors and possibly one predictor. Another site is recorded on Hayle Towans (SW 554 386) again one Bofors or possibly a machine gun.

There were three machine gun posts (Lewis Guns) on the roof of Block 3 of the ICI chemical works. These machine guns were under the supervision and maintenance of Mr Harry Thomas, an 'Old Contemptible' veteran of World War I.(5)

The Hayle AA guns were manned by Battery 462 of 137 Regt, 8 AA Division (later 3AA Group) R.A. Some idea of the strategic importance of Hayle at this time can be gathered from the memoirs of General Pile: 'At the beginning of May 1942 we had only 43 Bofors guns deployed on the whole south coast'.(6) At that time nine Bofors guns were positioned at Hayle.

Although the remains of many of these important sites in the history of Hayle have largely disappeared or have been built over, there are still traces to be found of their previous existence. At the site above Clifton Terrace, the gunpits can clearly be seen,

---

Bofors gun pit behind Clifton Terrace, Hayle.

Photograph: the author

and the outlook across the town and estuary is excellent showing the superb field of fire that the site afforded. At Porth Kidney, Lelant, the regular flattened areas in the dunes, where the huts etc once stood are still plainly recognisable, but most significant of all is the special level crossing, complete with gates, that crossed the St Erth to St Ives railway line. This was the only access to the site for vehicles carrying supplies and ammunition from the main road and across Lelant golf course. After being locked and out of use for over 60 years this crossing has been re-opened to give access to the new beach lifeguard hut overlooking Porth Kidney Sands.

At the major gunsite behind Gwinear Church just a few random concrete blocks remain to show what was a most important heavy AA deployment. The loss of many of these wartime sites is to be regretted. Modern methods of warfare have changed so greatly over the last fifty years, that these gun positions, along with the old concrete pillboxes and air raid shelters are now obsolete yet as historically important as the Norman castles and Roman defensive walls that are treasured so much.

A dramatic event occurred on Friday 28th August 1942 when two FW190 fighter-bombers from 10 Staffel/Jagdgeschwader 2 (10/JG2) in Normandy[7], attacked St Ives dropping two bombs, one of which destroyed the gasworks, the other damaged residential property in Belmont Place. Mrs Elisabeth James, was killed, 13 persons were seriously injured and 27 were slightly injured, The gasometer was destroyed and the gasworks was put out of action. 4 houses were seriously damaged and

---

The special level crossing on the St Ives Branch Line.
The crossing was built to service the gunsite at Porth Kidney Beach.
Closed for sixty years it has recently been re-opened
to allow access to the Lifeguard's Hut.

Photograph: the author.

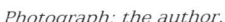

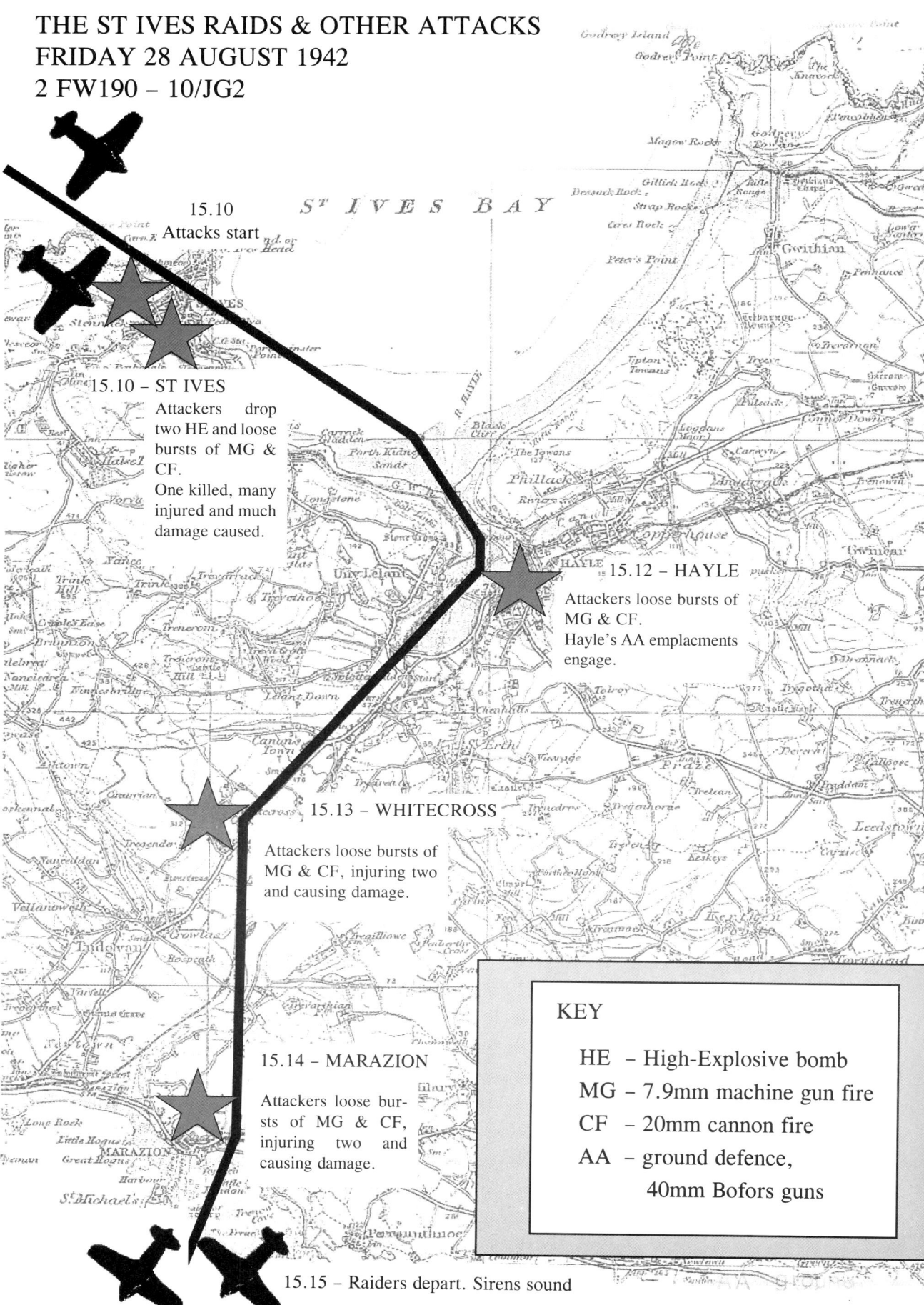

approx. 90 slightly damaged. There was damage to electric and telephone lines, and water mains. Machine-gunning of streets also occurred during the attack.(8)

The two machines then made their getaway at high speed across Hayle Estuary shortly after 3pm firing their machine guns and cannon at targets of opportunity(9) (unconfirmed reports suggest that after coming over the bar they flew under the high-tension cables strung across the harbour from the power station to Lelant). The anti-aircraft guns at Hayle opened fire with a tremendous noise, but were unable to hit the planes as they flashed by at 400mph. On their way across the isthmus of Penwith the German pilots cannon-shelled and machine-gunned a Western National bus between Canonstown and Whitecross Bend, severely injuring two Penzance children; eight year old Diana Willoughby was hit on her leg, and Anthony Allen aged 5 had a bullet wound to his knee. He was removed to hospital where he was said to be 'very ill'. Four others were slightly injured including the driver who had a lucky escape when a bullet scraped past his ear, and made a hole in his uniform cap. Roofs and windows of 20 houses in the locality were damaged. Finally before departing the Cornish coast the same aircraft opened cannon-fire on a council estate at Marazion causing roof and ceiling damage to 4 houses. An ARP warden was seriously injured and another person was slightly hurt.(10)

St Ives Bay, and the entrance to Hayle Harbour were protected against surface vessel invasion forces by a battery of guns positioned in the cliff under Porthminster. Many and varied have been the myths and legends spread concerning these guns: One St Ives historian even claiming that they were of 11inch calibre. They were, in fact, a pair of ex-French Navy 100mm (3.9in) guns recovered from a French destroyer sunk in World War I. It has been said that they were never fired in WWII because there was no suitable metric ammunition available in the UK. This seems highly unlikely as the ordnance factories were quite capable of producing metric shells. 20mm and 40mm ammunition was supplied in thousands for aircraft cannon and Bofors AA guns. It is also unlikely that the authorities would have constructed the extensive gun emplacements and installed the weapons if they had no possibility of being fired.

A senior REME (Royal Electrical & Mechanical Engineers) officer who travelled down to correct a fault on the guns recollected that they were quite badly corroded having spent many years at the bottom of the sea. The inside of the barrels were very pitted and he said he would not fancy being around when they were fired.

An interesting sidelight on this occasion was that when the REME officer's transport broke down at St Erth, he and his equipment were carried on the St Ives branch line where the GWR engine driver obligingly stopped the train at the gun site for him to get off, and picked him up again for the return journey.(11)

It is highly probable that these guns at St Ives (and Gwithian?) were installed by the 53rd (London) Medium Regt RA mentioned above, since their database mentions, in passing, that among the guns that they installed in 1940 were a number of ex-French Navy 4inch guns.

For most of the wartime period there was established on Hayle Towans a commando-style battle course. One of the exercises called for both British and GIs to lie flat

---

Facing Page
The flight path of the German raiders of Friday 28th August 1942

BJS 2010, Map: courtesy of Ordnance Survey

on the Hayle beaches at Gwithian while marksmen on the Towans above fired live ammunition, the bullets falling short three feet of them. This was to see how they would react under fire.(12)

In the early days of WWII with the possibility of imminent air attack the Superintendents of the UK power stations were instructed to contact local artists to advise on and devise camouflage paint schemes for their respective power stations. The Hayle Supt Mr Fred Peller called in an artist friend Mr Harry Rountree (1878-1950) who lived just across the Bay and was prominent in the St Ives artistic circles. Unfortunately, Mr Rountree was a well-known and accomplished caricaturist so for the duration of the war Hayle Power Station sported a distinctive camouflage scheme that bore scant relation to the surrounding environment; in fact it consisted of striking black and white scrolls in a random pattern that covered the entire building which stood out as a prominent feature of the North Quay location. When he had finished his task, Mr Rountree ever an eccentric, did a caricature of Mr Peller which had on a wall a tongue-in-cheek drawing of his rejected first suggestion to string lines of washing between the chimneys of the power station to fool the German airmen that it was a cosy Cornish waterside cottage! It was all really quite unnecessary for very early in the war the Luftwaffe had taken an excellent target photograph showing Hayle Power Station and the pylons feeding the National Grid. The Germans would have been highly amused by Mr Rountree's efforts – perhaps the washing lines idea might have been more effective! Interestingly, the adjacent ICI bromine works was more sensibly camouflaged in colours compatible with its surroundings, and as far as is known the plant went undetected by the Luftwaffe.(13)

On the civilian side, a Hayle Invasion Committee was formed on Tuesday 17th November 1942. The Chairman was Mr S.S. Spray; the Deputy Chairmen were Mr

---

The Hayle Power Station and ICI plant on Hayle's North Quay.

Photograph: the author

A caricature by Harry Rountree of Mr Alfred Peller, manager of the Hayle Power Station. During World War II Harry Rountree designed the unorthodox camouflage scheme for the power station. The painting on the wall is Harry Rountree's joke suggestion that the power station be disguised as a Cornish cottage with washing strung across the chimney

via Marion Peller

C.R. House and Mr J.P. Moffat; the Secretary was Mr G.H. Start, and his assistant was Mr A. Thomas.(14)

Sometime at the height of WWII, the precise date so far unknown, a curious story emerged, firmly held at the time and still recalled today, that a German Navy *Leutnant* came ashore at Gwithian presumably in uniform and for some reason or purpose not revealed. He was, it seems, apprehended by a farmer and handed over into the custody of a local Home Guard NCO. From then on, almost certainly the result of wartime security regulations, the trail goes cold and the story stops there. It is to be hoped that at some future time the true details of this mysterious incident emerge; and interested speculation will at last be satisfied.

Riviere House, Hayle.
One of the billets for the US Army 29th and 35th Divisions in World War II

Photograph: the author

Chapter Four:

GARRISON TOWN

THERE WERE SOLDIERS stationed at Hayle almost to the end of hostilities. It is not difficult to see the reasons why. There was ample accommodation both in the town, such as the Drill Hall, Penmare House, Riviere House etc, and in the holiday huts and houses on Hayle Towans, The Bluff, Taylor's Tea Rooms, Chyreene Warra among others. As early as mid-1940 a dance was organised by the women soldiers of the ATS (Auxiliary Territorial Service) stationed in Hayle. The dance was at the Drill Hall, with music by the Blue Rhythmics.(1)

The Towans provided excellent battle-training areas, and a desert warfare training school was set up early on, to accustom troops to fighting in the desert conditions of North Africa.

Because of wartime security measures it is difficult to discover all the regiments based at Hayle, and particularly the periods when they were there. The following is a possibly incomplete list of the units known to have been stationed at Hayle. The longest-staying and most familiar around the town were the men and women of the Royal Artillery who manned the anti-aircraft guns that encircled the town. These soldiers and ATS girls could be distinguished by the red patch on the uniform sleeves showing a drawn bow with the arrow pointing vertically skywards. They were part of Hayle town life from December 1941 until they were quite suddenly diverted to South-East England in July 1944 as part of the 'Diver' operation to counter the V1 flying bomb menace.

The United States soldiers, popularly known as G.I.'s or more universally as 'Yanks' although those at Hayle were mostly from the Southern States or the West. They were the next longest to stay in the town, later on in the war, prior to D-Day; and are dealt with in a separate chapter.

The main British regiments are listed below, the information being culled from a possibly not-too-reliable memory; and by the quite open reports in the local press. At a time when almost every spare shop window and notice-board was covered with posters exhorting the public to 'Be like dad – keep mum,' and told that 'Careless talk costs lives' or 'Telling a friend may mean telling the enemy' we see the newspapers being allowed to print reports of cricket or football matches between Penzance and so-and-so regiment, or dances at Hayle Masonic Hall, music supplied by the dance band of this or that body of soldiers. It is highly unlikely, however, given the now-known dearth of enemy agents in the UK at the time, that the German intelligence services had any regular access to British local newspapers.

Early in the war the Drill Hall was occupied by the Duke of Cornwall's Light Infantry during which time shower bath facilities were built behind the building. The soldiers slept on camp beds lined-up in rows in the hall. The main bulk of the DCLI were on Hayle Towans, at first living under canvas and later accommodated in the chalets, bungalows and hotels overlooking the sea. These troops had an uncomfortable time when during an invasion scare they spent up to six days in the cliff-top pillboxes awaiting an enemy landing that did not happen. Later they served with the Eighth Army from El Alamein through to the north of Italy.

The next body of troops to arrive were detachments of the West Yorkshire Regiment who laid out the beachside minefields, and placed the mines in position in the sand. In May 1941 there was a report on a boxing match programme at St. John's Hall, Penzance, featuring the West Yorks.(2) Later in the year there was a photograph of the West Yorks Dance Band playing locally.(3)

The West Yorks were followed by the King's Own Regiment. The local press carried a number of reports indicating the location of this regiment. In May 1942, around possibly the lowest point reached in the war, we are informed that at a dance in St John's Hall, Penzance music was supplied by the 'King's Own' Dance Band.(4)
Again on the 20th May the band played at Saturday's dance at the Drill Hall (Hayle). On the 10th June we are told the band played at St Just Drill Hall.(5) In August 1942 a cricket match was played at Penzance, one of the teams being from the King's Own Regiment(6); and in September 1942 at the Masonic Hall, Hayle, the Hayle First Aid Post organised a dance for the Hayle District Nursing Association, music by the King's Own Dance Band.(7)

In August 1942 the troops situated on Hayle Towans were the 'Green Howards,' who assisted at the Whitley bomber crash (see Chapter 17)(8)

A corroded cap badge of the Devonshire Regiment,
uncovered in the sand of Hayle Towans by Paul Frost.

Photograph: the author

In late 1942 the public were made aware of the identity of another replacement body of troops, the Royal Inniskilling Fusiliers. In October 1942 a report was published of a football match at Hayle with the 'Inniskillings' one of the teams.(9) In December the boxing team of the Royal Inniskilling Fusiliers fought a team from the Northamptonshire Regiment at Penzance.(10)

The Inniskillings at Hayle were mainly soldiers from the Catholic areas of Northern Ireland. On Sunday mornings they would march as a body through the town and up to the small Roman Catholic chapel at St Michael's Hospital, that served both the nuns of the convent, and the local Roman Catholics as a parish church. Correctly known as the Church of the Holy Ghost, it would be full beyond capacity with the normal congregation supplemented by this large body of troops; the situation not being helped at all by the addition of another large body of men, this time the Italian prisoners of war marched over under escort from their camp at St Erth.

The Royal Inniskilling Fusiliers departed in early 1943 and were replaced by the Durham Light Infantry, and the town now got used to the 'Geordie' accent after that of Northern Ireland. One incident that occurred during the stay of the 'Durhams' happened when a sea mine which had broken loose, was at high tide washed against the cliffs under The Bluff Hotel and exploded. The detonation blew in the windows of the hotel severely injuring many of the soldiers billeted there. It also badly damaged the Cove Cafe. The DLI were followed by the King's Own Royal Regiment; and later in 1943 the last large body of British troops to be stationed in the town before the arrival of the US Army was the Devonshire Regiment. Each of these groups of military sojourners enlightened the life of the town in many ways before going off to engage the enemy in locations across the world. A number of them courted the local girls and married them during the war, or soon after if they survived. Each departure was a sad occasion, and all were missed in their turn.

The people of Hayle, in a number of ways, looked to the welfare of the troops during their stay as best they could given the wartime shortages and circumstances. In August 1940 it was felt by a large number of people in Hayle that some form of entertainment could be provided for the servicemen; a committee was formed, and on September 1st 1940 the Hayle Services Canteen was opened in the Baptist Church Hall (now St Joseph's Catholic Church). The Organising Secretary was Mr R.J. Reynolds. It was independent of any body or organisation, and it relied upon the good nature of several ladies to keep it running. Table Tennis was provided along with darts and cards; the piano was accessible, and there were writing materials, books and magazines. The ladies acted as mothers to the 'boys,' undertaking any darning or sewing required; they were also responsible for baking the cakes each day. They assisted the troops to secure lodgings for their wives to come and stay, and even undertook to do any shopping for them. When funds became low, whist drives and dances were organised; to which the servicemen were invited free. The canteen was open from 6pm to 10pm daily; and 3pm to 10pm at weekends.

The canteen was open every day until November 25th 1944. During this time it served 101,588 cups of tea; 14,181 meals, and 125,535 hot beverages. The canteen never closed once during the whole time. Hundreds of troops used the canteen, and a grand collection of regimental badges, given by each unit as a token of friendship, was given to the Baptist Church suitably inscribed for their splendid help and co-operation in allowing the canteen committee to have the use of their schoolroom. In addition a wall clock given by the Royal Inniskilling Fusiliers to the canteen in recognition of the many happy evenings, and the kindness shown to them during their stay was also later given to the Baptist Church.

The balance in hand on winding-up was distributed in the following manner:

Cornwall Troops Welfare	£10
Hayle Troops Christmas Fund	£10
Prisoners of War (Red Cross)	£5
Hayle British Legion	£5
Hayle Troops Welcome Home Fund	£5

A sum of £30 was presented to the Baptist Church in recognition of their kindness and help. *The Cornishman* summed up the Hayle Canteen's efforts as: 'A magnificent record for a band of voluntary workers.' (11)

An indication of the work of the volunteers is given in a newspaper report that Hayle Services Canteen under Mr R.J. Reynolds gave the servicemen unable to go home a party on Christmas Day (1943) with free meals, cigarettes and games.(12) Mr R.J. ('Jack') Reynolds was well-known and popular in Hayle. He was a salesman for the Cornwall Electric Power Co. and later SWEB. He lived in the flat above the Electric Shop in Copperhouse. In addition to his voluntary work in the canteen mentioned above, he was the Warrant Officer of the Hayle Flight, Air Training Corps. Later he became the Commanding Officer. He died in March 2001, aged 93.

Chapter Five:

THE HOME GUARD & THE AUXILIARY UNITS

IT IS IMPOSSIBLE these days to speak or write about the Home Guard without reference to the term 'Dad's Army'. This, however, is the only time it will be used in this book. It was not a wartime usage.

Reducing the image of these brave men to a bunch of incompetent buffoons, no matter how brilliant the writing, acting and production, and how enjoyable the programmes, does the gravest disservice to the thousands of ordinary, decent, family men who at a crucial time became Britain's first line of defence against an invasion by hostile forces. Unlike every other branch of the fighting services the Home Guard could not retreat; for they alone had no transport facilities to withdraw in; if the situation became hopeless, they simply had to stand and fight. They had no artillery cover, no tanks or armoured cars, no trucks.

In the early days, they were spread thinly across the cliffs and countryside, in small sections armed with shot-out old US and Canadian rifles from the Great War of 1914 – 18. They were deployed, quite cynically, simply to delay the crack German forces long enough for the full-time army divisions held hundreds of miles inland, behind Field Marshall Lord Ironside's 'stop lines' (aka 'GOC' lines or 'HQ' lines) to come to full readiness to launch a massive hoped-for counter-strike. In the case of the south-west peninsula a line was drawn from Axminster to Bridgwater. West of this line, Devon and Cornwall and their valiant defenders were quite simply, under this plan, to be yielded to the German forces.[1] Given the nature of armed conflict, and the brilliant generalship and training of the German army, there could have been only one outcome; the Home Guard units would have been totally overrun and eliminated by the awesome power of the Wehrmacht airborne and panzer divisions.

The earliest volunteers, especially, were prepared to defend their homes, towns and country against the finest spearhead striking force in the world at the time. These gallant gentlemen, for such they were, many of them no longer young, nonetheless went out night after night in 1940, poorly armed and in the full knowledge that they would, eventually and inevitably, be overwhelmed. Almost all of them dead now, they should not be mocked, for as Dr Johnson said: 'Every man thinks less of himself for never having been a soldier'.[2]

The Home Guard originated when a request from London was published on the 14th May 1940, only four days after the invasion of France and the Low Countries, asking for volunteer 'sky watchers' to deal with possible landings of parachute troops. It also announced that 'A home-front force to be known as the Local Defence Volunteers (LDV) is being formed and will be open to British subjects between the ages of 17 and 65.' Volunteers began to present themselves at Penzance Police Station as early as seven o'clock the next morning, and by 3.30 the number had reached 120.[3] On the 22nd May the numbers had topped 200 and the volunteers were being called 'parashooters'; a silly national media name that soon died away. The appointed district leader of the LDV for the Borough of Penzance and the West Penwith District was Capt. C.E. Venning. He was to work under Major Watson-Smyth whose area of control embraced both the East and West Penwith Districts and the Borough of Penzance. Capt. Venning desired all motorcyclists who could use their machines for the purpose of acting as messengers to apply to him forthwith at 58 Morrab Road, Penzance.(4)

An article in *The Cornishman* announced that the County Organiser for Cornwall LDV was Brig.-Gen. W.D. Croft, and that the Bishop of Truro was an early volunteer. Local clergymen also joined in. The Rev. C.H.S. Buckley formed the Gulval LDV, and at St Just the Rev. J.T. Jenkin was also a prompt volunteer.(5)

At Hayle as the Home Guard evolved from the early LDV into a formal recognisable military unit, it was originally part of the 12th (Land's End) Battalion, commanded by Lt Col. Watson-Smyth of Lelant. He resigned through ill health in 1942 and was replaced by the next officer in seniority, Major C.N. Norman MC, and the headquarters was moved from Lelant to Hayle. The Home Guard in Cornwall was affiliated to the county regiment, the DCLI whose cap badge they were entitled to, and proud to wear.

In September 1941 it was reported that on the National Day of Prayer, that the 'Hayle Home Guard under Capt. C.V. Wills, Lt. Pearce and CSM Holland marched from the Drill Hall to Phillack Church for a service conducted by the Rev. Moysey.(6) (C.V. Wills JP, the chairman of Harvey & Company, was at this time 64 years of age.) Later in the same month representing the Home Guard at the funeral of Mr Gregor the Hayle barber, were Lt. Pearce, Sgt Major S.J. Kennedy, Sgt Palk and Sgt Streete.(7)

By August 1942 Hayle Company of the Home Guard was still part of the 12th (Land's End) Battalion now commanded by Lt Col. Norman who lived at Waverley, Hayle. There were changes in command at Hayle.

The Commanding Officer was now Major Wynne-Harley. Other personnel named were: HQ Section; Lt Jenkins; Lt Maddern; Lt D. Pearce, Lt Trewhella, 2nd Lt Wickens, 2nd Lt Casley, 2nd Lt Carveth, Sgt Barker, Sgt Bonner, Sgt. Taylor, Sgt Derrick, Cpl Stone. Others included Lt Hodgson, Sgt Biggleston, Sgt Palk and Cpl Young.(8) In June 1943 a report on the retirement of Mr W.F. Bew, headmaster of St Erth school said that he had been the Acting QMS of St Erth Home Guard from May 1940 to Christmas 1942.(9)

In a court case regarding non-attendance at Home Guard parades, the witnesses for the Hayle Home Guard are given as Major H.J.P. Venn, Lt G. Wickens, Sgt. Major W.J. Holland and Sgt G.W.H. Dowrick.(10)

Almost certainly due to the effect of the introduction of compulsory Home Guard service, the number of men enrolled from Hayle and its surrounding areas, was large enough to constitute a separate battalion designated the 14th (Hayle) Battalion commanded by Lt Col. P.J. Chellew, an ex-mayor of St Ives.

The 14th (Hayle) Battalion consisted of:

'A' Company (Marazion)	Major Tyacke
'B' Company (Gwinear)	Major Wynne-Harley, later Major Read
'C' Company (St Ives)	Major L.D. Fuller, later Major Woolcombe Major Wickens and Major White
'D' Company (Hayle)	Major Venn – ('Bill' Venn was the works manager of the British Ethyl Corporation, ICI Bromine Works, North Quay, Hayle.)(11)

At its maximum strength the 14th (Hayle) Battalion mustered 1,300 officers and men, and guarded a coastline of approximately twenty miles, from Godrevy to Gurnard's Head and inland to the centre line of Cornwall.

The Medical Officer was Major Hadfield; the Ammunition Officer was Mr William Payne and the signals section officials were Mr T. Bryant, Mr B. and Mr C.P. Harvey. Senior NCOs included RQMS Streete (Hayle), RSM Wills (Hayle) and store man Sgt Stratton.(12) Cecil Palmer Harvey at this time was the deputy chairman of Harvey and Company, Hayle. Although he had been Captain Harvey in the First World War, he served as a private in the Lelant Home Guard. The reason being that when the Lelant volunteers reported, it seems that there were far too many ex-officers and not nearly enough other ranks, so, presumably, lots were drawn or some other method used to decide who were to be officers and who were the private soldiers. When he was down for early evening duty, Mr Harvey would drive to Hayle in the morning, and sit in his office and conduct his business all day dressed in the uniform of a Home Guard private.(13)

No. 21 Platoon of 'C' (St Ives) Company manned the Royal Artillery Coast Battery at Porthminster Point. No. 6 Platoon of 'A' (Marazion) Company was made up of the

---

A pass issued on Cornwall Electric Company note paper authorised by the Hayle Company Officer Commanding Major Wynne-Harley and bearing the HQ stamp to allow the bearer to travel to his shift unhindered, almost certainly during a county-wide invasion exercise.

Photograph: the author

staff of the Primrose Dairy Ltd, St Erth, and the GWR station St Erth. 'B' Company (Gwinear) had a 'brilliant' cyclists patrol; as did the J & F Pool's platoon at Hayle.

The 14th Battalion was also renowned for its military band formed in March 1943, mainly from ex-members of the pre-war Hayle Town Silver Band. Known as the 'Band of the Hayle Battalion Home Guard' the Bandmaster was Mr Stanley C. Coombe, of Hayle. The band was very popular, and was called-for to play at many Home Guard occasions in the west of Cornwall; and for numerous civilian functions at fetes in the district. In January 1944 the band was invited by the BBC to record a concert for The Overseas Forces Programme.

The West Cornwall Sector Home Guard consisted of: the 7th (Falmouth) Battalion; the 8th (Helston) Battalion; the 12th (Land's End) Battalion and the 14th (Hayle) Battalion. The Commanding Officer of the West Cornwall Sector was Col. W.D. Croft, CB, CMG, DSO, with Lt Col. Norman, Hayle as second-in-command.(14)

In August 1943 the Fraddam Platoon held a Gala Day. Led by Hayle Home Guard Band (under Bandmaster S.C. Coombe) the parade marched from 'No Man's Land'. Fraddam Home Guard were under 1st Lt F.W. Trewhella. Others taking part were Leedstown under Lt P.R. Walker; Gwinear under Lt B. Casley and Wall under 2nd Lt B. Carveth. The salute was taken by Lt Col. P.J. Chellew, 14th (Hayle) Batt. Home Guard supported by Maj. H. Reed, Capt. A. White and Lt Hodson. An 'end of day' dance was held in the Fraddam Army Hut with music by the Crewenna Dance Band.(15) In January 1944 a Hayle Home Guard shooting team is listed as: L.C. Allen; Sgt Orchard; Pte Nicholas; Pte. Callaway; Pte Roach; Pte Semmens Cpls Burrows and L.C. Southcott. At the funeral in January 1944 of Mr T. Murley, the Home Guard was represented by Lt W. Faulkner and 2nd Lt A.S. Macgeorge.(16)

By 1944 nationally the Home Guard had been transformed into an efficient disciplined civilian standing army of over 1,700,000 men and women, fully-trained and well equipped. It was no longer regarded as a joke – even by the German High Command. This high standard is borne out by a contemporary list of the weaponry available to the Hayle Battalion in 1944. It included Vickers, Lewis and Browning machine guns; Browning Automatic Rifles (BARs);

An example of an early Home Guard arm-band

Photograph: the author

Northover Projectors; Spigot Mortars, Sten Guns; anti-tank rifles; mines, grenades and bombs of all descriptions. Up-to-date radio and telephone systems were also in use.(17)

All this firepower, however, happily was destined never to be used in anger. Following the successful D-Day invasion of France, the Home Guard throughout Britain proved extremely valuable in replacing the full-time army in many duties such as guarding important sites and installations, and manning AA guns where they helped to fight off the flying bomb onslaught. But as the Allied armies pushed eastwards towards Germany, the threat of an invasion of Britain dwindled to non-existence, and the time came for the Home Guard to disband.

In November 1944 a 'stand down' dinner was held at St Ives, when Certificates of Service were issued to the Home Guards. In the same month, No 10 Platoon, 'B' Company (Gwinear) held a farewell dinner and dance in Gwinear Church Hall.(18) In December 1944, the *Cornishman* was reporting on the progress of the return of Home Guard equipment.(19) The force remained in this 'stood down' condition for a year, being finally disbanded on the 31st December 1945. So ended the honourable saga of the Home Guard and its readiness to defend the British Homeland.(20)

The professional opinion of the Regular Army senior officers was expressed in the fortnightly pamphlet *WAR*, published by ABCA (The Army Bureau of Current Affairs) issue No. 70 entitled: *The Other Army* dated May 13th 1944. They state:

> *In some ways the Home Guard have had to suffer more from their friends than from their enemies. There are the friends who think the Home Guard still the jolly romp with pikes and shotguns that they imagine it was in 1940 (although that was not the general reaction at the time). There are also the friends who claim, by implication, that the Home Guard is twice as efficient as a field force unit and three times as keen.*

THE AUXILIARY UNITS

It was announced in January 1943 that a Certificate of Good Service had been awarded by the Commander-in-Chief to Capt. W.H. Abbis in connection with his market garden business helping to feed the population.(21) Capt. Abbis was at that time also the County Horticultural Superintendent, and Horticultural and Supplies Officer to the Cornwall Agricultural Committee. Two years later he was awarded a more substantial honour: 'Capt. H.W. Abbis DCM, MM of Truro, awarded the MBE (Military Division) for meritorious service in connection with a "specialist branch of Home Defence"'(22)

What could not be referred to in any way in 1943 and was barely hinted at two years later, was the nature of the 'specialist branch' mentioned in the latter award. In addition to his overt comprehensive horticultural duties at county level, Capt. Abbis was in charge of a top secret organisation, even today shrouded in mystery and only partially revealed in guarded reminiscences. He was the organiser and commander in Cornwall of a clandestine bunch of dedicated potential cut-throats and saboteurs, who recruited locally and secretly by word of mouth and formed in discrete cells throughout the county, were highly trained in the black arts of sabotage and destruction. In the event of a successful German invasion they would disperse into prepared underground bunkers, known officially as 'operational bases' (OBs)(23) which were fully stocked with explosives, weapons, food and fuel. They would later emerge by night to create mayhem and disruption among the occupying force and its communications.

Even today it is difficult to ascertain the top levels of this secretive organisation. It seems to have been designated officially as the 'British Resistance Battalion' and the '203 (South of England) Auxiliary Unit' although if Cornwall came under the last named formation one cannot confirm. Cornwall was part of No. 4 Region. The Controller for Cornwall in 1940 is given as John Dingley, a local banker. Nominally included on the enlistment rolls of the Home Guard, they were not in full-time service with their local units and many persons alive today do not know that their quiet friendly neighbour was one of these deadly irregulars. Each area had its secret bunker well stocked in advance with explosives and weapons; but at this distance of time they are extremely difficult to locate. The only one to be confirmed in the Hayle area was located in the old long-abandoned Wheal Merth mine on the northern side of the valley at Heather Lane, Canonstown. If there are any others in the vicinity of Hayle, they remain a total mystery and probably will do so for the future. As regards the Hayle unit personnel we have only the name of the leader, who was listed as a Lieutenant W.R. Sandow.(24)

We know of at least one occasion when the Auxiliary Units in Cornwall were secretly called out to test their efficiency. On a large Invasion Exercise when the invading force, 77 Division, was advancing through Cornwall: *. . . some headquarters vehicles were attacked and captured by Resistance men. The attack which had been ordered by General Morgan, VIII Corps Commander (VIII Corps was the Army Command for the Cornwall area at the time), was much more effective than even he had anticipated, and in the end he had to call off the Resistance so that 77 Division could continue its training.*(25)

Chapter Six:

CIVIL DEFENCE – A.R.P.

WITH THE BREATHTAKING development of aviation technology in the 1920s and 30s, and evidence of the dreadful application of modern airborne weapons, especially upon defenceless civilian populations in China and Spain, had led to serious thinking about how to protect the public in an all-out air war over Britain. In Hayle as in the rest of the country, public protection became a matter of great concern. As the war advanced in seriousness, the town began to assume its wartime appearance. Surface air raid shelters of a standard pattern were built at various places throughout the town, including almost every street; and in the school playgrounds.

They were located at the following sites. The figures indicate the number of shelters built at each location.

St John's Street	7	Bodriggy Street	4
Hillcrest Road	1	Trelawny Place	10
Commercial Road	6	Hayle Terrace	4
Passmore Edwards Institute	1	Penpol Terrace	4
Penpol Avenue	1	Chapel Terrace	2
Foundry Square	1	Bay View Terrace	1
Harbour View Terrace	1	West Terrace	1
St Elwyn's Place	1	Clifton Terrace	2
Mount Pleasant	2	Undercliff & Steam Packet	1

Penpol Council School – Bodriggy Council School – Copperhouse (evacuee) School and Hayle Grammar School. All for pupils and staff. Shelter accommodation was provided for approx. 3000 adults and children.[1]

The attitude of Cornwall County Council in regard to protection of schoolchildren is interesting. Its advice was that if bombs fell without warning, children should lie on the floor away from the windows. At rural schools it was not considered that shelters on a scale appropriate to the more vulnerable areas could be justified. Those schools were advised to dig shallow trenches or if houses were nearby, children could run to them. One wonders, in retrospect if the shelter provision for staff at County Hall, Truro at that time consisted of shallow trenches; or did they rely on neighbouring houses to which the officers might hurry in an 'alert'.

It was also noted that many houses had Morrison indoor table shelters. A heavy steel cage type, which was positioned in the living room. By early 1943 West Penwith RDC had Morrison shelters for issue free to persons with incomes less than £350 per annum.[2] Unfortunately they were far too large to fit into the average Cornish cottage or terraced dwelling house.

There was much concern at the time, that the public air raid shelters provided throughout Cornwall including those at Hayle, were poorly designed and constructed. Lime and sand mortar had been used, and they had gable roofs of thin interlocking pre-cast slabs. After the failure of their design in the massive air raids on Plymouth, they were considered unsafe in their original form. Col. E.H.W. Bolitho commented that it was, 'more dangerous for people to go into them than to remain outside.'[3] Later as a result of this, most major street shelters in Hayle were re-roofed by adding an approximately eighteen-inch flat roof of reinforced concrete.

Until quite recently a perfect set of the typical public street shelters, interestingly of the early unmodified pattern, still stood at the rear of the Passmore Edwards Institute (see photo), the last remaining example in Hayle. This unique historic structure was, quite wantonly, demolished without any prior consultation or advice, simply to provide parking space for one car.(4)

In November 1941 West Penwith RDC received a letter from the County Architect offering two hurricane lamps for the Hayle air raid shelters.(5) At this time there were over forty shelters in the Hayle district.(6)

The main Air Raid Wardens' Post was situated in Lloyds Bank, Foundry Square in the part of the building that is now the main entrance and banking hall. In December 1940 Hayle Parish Council was informed that the Ministry of Home Security had approved an ARP Rescue Party at Hayle. The number of men required was 15, ie a rescue party of 10 and a reserve of 5.(7) A photograph published in the *Cornishman* in June 1991 lists some of the Hayle Civil Defence Corps including Edgar Roberts, Nicholas Couch, Archie Biggs, Bill Muir, Simon Jory, Albert Pascoe, Fred Williams, Billy Simons, Fred Peller, Robert Bond, Bill Wakeford and Morris Morgan.(8)

The First Aid Post originally proposed in September 1939 was finally set up in April 1941. It was situated on the west side of Foundry Square in the ground floor area beneath Harvey & Company's head office (now John Harvey House, 24 Foundry Square). This space had previously been occupied by the C R House grocery shop. Strong reinforcing was carried out by rebuilding with concrete blocks. The post was manned on a 24hr basis by staff consisting of Sister Dempsey and Nurse Farthey plus additional supplementary volunteer nursing assistants. The ambulance drivers on call were Mr J. Fitzgerald of Hayle, and Mr Gall of St Erth. The First Aid Post proved an extremely useful additional facility throughout the war years as a centre for the provision of public health services such as children's check-ups, bulk vaccinations

---

The air raid shelter situated in the grounds of the Passmore Edwards Institute. The shelter was destroyed in the 1980s.

Photograph: the author

and inoculations, and contagious disease screening and treatment, on an out-patient basis.

A section of St Michael's Hospital was set aside and equipped as a casualty clearing station, should a large number of injury cases occur from enemy action. The Casualty Officer for Hayle was Mr Edwin G. Newton, a builder and undertaker, appointed in July 1940. He was issued with a large quantity of hessian body-bags, which were stored in his builders yard, now the Millpond Gardens. He was also allocated 40 coffins for possible Hayle casualties. The coffins were kept stored at Truro. These details were not, of course, released to the general public at the time.(9)

In February 1941, nearly 18 months after the declaration of hostilities Hayle still relied on a siren that was privately owned and on private property installed for the benefit of employees of the power station.(10)

In April 1941 it was reported that Cornwall Emergency Committee did not see its way clear to granting Hayle an extra siren. The Hayle Parish Council clerk stated that 50% of the population including those in the most crowded part of the town could not always hear the 'alert'. ARP officers and the police inspector had voiced their objections to this refusal and agreed that an additional siren was needed. The cost would have been £10.(11)

In June 1941 Hayle was offered a siren of a ½ horse power. The private siren on the Hayle Power Station, that could hardly be heard in Copperhouse, was of 5 horse power. In August 1941 a correspondent reported that 'Some excitement' was caused in Hayle when residents thought they heard the 'all clear' siren sounded twice. The mystery was cleared up when it was found that the earlier 'all clear' was a siren in

The interior of the Passmore Edwards Institute air raid shelter, which was demolished in the 1980s.

Photograph: the author

St Ives.(12) For some reason throughout the war, the St Ives siren always sounded earlier and could be heard more clearly in Hayle, than the one at Hayle itself.

By September things had still not improved. At Hayle Parish Council concern was again expressed that a public air raid siren had not yet been provided, and the town was still relying on a private siren on the power station.(13)

At the same meeting, elected from Hayle to the Local Defence Committee were Messrs W.L. Barnes, W.J. Drew, G. Wilkes, J. Ellis, J.B. James and J.H. Woolcock. Mr G.J. Kennedy, the coordinating officer, wished to have his position defined, as West Penwith RDC were 'not helpful.'(14) That month there was an exercise for Hayle Casualty Service including, AFS, Home Guards, Hayle Ambulance Squad and St Michael's Hospital. The exercise was organised by Mr Kenneth Uren (Commander of Hayle Casualty Service) and Mr Blackmore (Chief Warden).(15) In February 1943 an ARP exercise was held on Saturday night the 14th. The Rescue Squad was under officers Rookley and Prisk; and the wardens were led by Mr J.K. Blackmore.(16)

Even at this late stage in the war, the friction and distrust between Hayle and West Penwith RDC. continued to fester on. A report in the *Cornishman* records a grave feeling of injustice in Hayle, when at a meeting of the Parish Council, 'A confidence vote was proposed on West Penwith RDC, by Mr J.H. Woolcock: "Hayle is being treated by WPRDC officers as a second class village. Hayle's resolutions were always referred back or turned down . . . officials override members in all matters and it was time to put Hayle's foot down"'(17)

This sense of utter frustration on the part of the Hayle parish councillors at their treatment by the bucolic bunglers in their Penzance offices can be understood, when as was revealed later that Hayle supplied over half the funding of West Penwith RDC, and yet was allocated only 15 of the 48 seats on the council.(18) Hayle with a population of 4 to 5,000 paid £12,975, while the other 17,000 ratepayers contributed £12,927. The water-rate difference was even more startling. Hayle paid £1,008 and the rest paid just £362.19.

An indication of the increased strength in the manning of Hayle First Aid Post (FAP) is given in a report on the county heats and semi-final when Hayle beat Penzance and Redruth FAPs. The Hayle team consisted of Nurses P. Farthey (leader), M. Symons, L. Shelton, J. Symons, K. Galloway, V. Love, and N. Orchard. Also Messrs R.H. Bridger and D.V. Young. The Medical Officers were Dr W.H. Palmer and Dr E. Atkinson.(20) It is uncertain when exactly the Hayle FAP ceased its useful ARP and civil functions, but in February 1945 the closure of the St Ives FAP was reported.(21) Presumably the Hayle post would have closely followed or preceded it. The Fraddam – St Erth Praze First Aid Post was disbanded in July 1945 when a large amount of equipment which was obtained by local funds, in August 1942, for war emergencies had been shared among St Michael's Hospital, Hayle, Hayle and Fraddam Ambulance Cadets. A First Aid box had been left in each village and £3-14s had been sent to the Salvation Army at Hayle.(22)

By late 1945 with the war over, thoughts were turning to a normal way of life. At a meeting of West Penwith RDC Mr J.H. Woolcock raised the question of the removal of air raid shelters, especially those at St John's Street, Hayle.(23)

A little-known and long-neglected aspect of civilian defence in Hayle is highlighted in a report in *The Cornishman* in November 1945 on the work of the Women's Voluntary Service (WVS). Hayle branch was asked to staff a maternity home; and Hayle WVS assisted in the staffing of the British Restaurant at the time official parties of evacuees left to return home; Hayle and St Hilary arranged the food for the journey, while several members accompanied the children to London. Six village

Hayle in World War II   43

leaders were in office from the start of the WVS until the stand-down including Mrs Ellis and Mrs Norman (Hayle) and Mrs Hale (St Erth).(24)

In summation and looking back over the fifty-plus years, it is a fascinating paradox that while the local authority, West Penwith RDC Emergency Committee, responsible for civil defence was almost totally ignoring, or indeed sometimes actively opposing the needs of Hayle and its people, at the same time at national level the authorities were showing the utmost concern about the military defence of Hayle, so vital was

---

Luftwaffe aerial reconnaissance photograph, c1940/41.
Hayle Power Station and high tension National Grid line and pylons
are clearly outlined. As is the site of the ICI works, but not the ESSO depot.
The German code number for power stations was 50.

Photograph: Nigel J. Clark Publications

it strategically to the war effort in Cornwall. In the period July 6th 1940 to June 13th 1944 in West Cornwall there were 713 'alerts' when sirens were sounded.(25) In February 1945 the retiring Regional Commissioner for the South West, Sir Hugh Ellis said that for two months in 1941 Cornwall was the most bombed county in the whole of the British Isles.(26)

Faced with this desperate emergency situation, records show that West Penwith RDC's responses to have been niggardly, penny-pinching and wholly neglectful of its responsibilities to the civilian population of Hayle. The council's lethargic attitude and lack of action appears at this distance of time to have been utterly reprehensible and, indeed, verging very close to what the Americans would term: 'Dereliction of Duty'.

Chapter Seven:

THE FIREFIGHTERS – A.F.S & N.F.S.

THIS CHAPTER IS more relevant today than most others in the book and, perhaps, the most important, for the reason that the problem of fire and rescue provision for Hayle after over sixty years up to the date of writing have still not been resolved, and the scandalous decisions taken prior to, and at the end of World War Two and more recently, seriously affect the safety and security of the ever-increasing population of Hayle.

For a number of reasons due to its vital facilities and its geographical position, Hayle at the outset of war became a town of major strategic importance, quite out of proportion to its relative size. Following the fall of France and the subsequent 'Battle of Britain' and the winter 1940/41 night 'blitz' many of the power stations, already operating at full stretch supplying energy to the expanding war production industries had been knocked out, or severely damaged due to enemy action. Hayle Power Station was the only major producer of electricity in Cornwall, and with the National Grid at this time seriously weakened and well overstretched, should the Hayle station be taken out by enemy bombing, the army camps, RAF stations and naval bases in the county would have been in serious difficulties, unable to carry on indefinitely using their emergency generators. This together with the presence of the ICI bromine factory, the fuel depot, the coastal shipping and with the war factories such as J & F Pool Ltd, all combined to make Hayle a prime target. Consequently the authorities at the national level were very concerned with the problem of defending the town. At the earliest opportunity Hayle was ringed with heavy and light anti-aircraft guns, and the approach by sea was covered by ex-French 100mm naval guns sited at St Ives and Gwithian.

While all this comprehensive protection of the town was being undertaken by central government, the responsibility for civil defence was allocated to the local authority; in Hayle's case West Penwith Rural District Council, based in Penzance. The contrast in approach was startling. Hayle considered to be of such vital strategic importance by the authorities at national level, was seemingly dismissed as a poor relation of little consequence by the paperclip paras and committee-room commandos of West Penwith RDC.

The first priority of civil defence in wartime is in the field of rescue and fire fighting. Throughout the country in the period prior to the outbreak of war, men were encouraged to form volunteer fire-fighting units, known collectively as the Auxiliary Fire Service (AFS) and were to be attached to their local regular fire brigades. An AFS unit duly formed itself quite early in the war at Hayle with 19 volunteers enrolled by September 1940, but with an estimated thirty-two men eventually required. From the very start problems began to arise with the overseeing authority West Penwith RDC.

After the fall of France in mid-1940, public feeling was running very high in Hayle. At a meeting of the parish council, the clerk Mr J.A. Harvey had received a deputation from clergymen of the town; and another deputation from the residents. Those deputations stressed that unless something was done regarding the matter of firefighting appliances for Hayle, they were going to take the matter up with the Ministry. Mr Harvey added that until they acquired a trailer pump of their own they would not be issued with any ARP appliances.[1] Later the same month (July 1940) there was reported a quite unbelievably scandalous statement by the Clerk to West Penwith RDC who is quoted as saying: 'The Home Office Commissioners had already recommended a fire brigade for Hayle, but when he (the Clerk) obtained information as to the cost involved, the Council did not proceed with it, and it was agreed that they should accept the protection of the St Ives Brigade.'(2) In August 1940 the Clerk to West Penwith RDC received a telegram to say a trailer pump was on its way and was to be sent to Hayle Station.(3)

The dispute smouldered on, with West Penwith not budging an inch. The *Cornishman* reported that: 'Mr Battrick, Clerk (WPRDC) pointed out that before Auxiliary Fire Service equipment could be provided at Hayle, it was necessary to satisfy the Home Office that there were adequate peace time firefighting facilities at that place. Not until that had been done would they receive AFS. supplies'. After Mr Kennedy had argued that a fire station should be set up at Hayle, Mr G.W. Fenton declared that it was high time the council realised the question of expense that was involved. A peacetime fire establishment meant a pump at Hayle. That together with equipment and fire brigade, would involve the outlay of a lot of money. If Hayle insisted on a fire engine costing about £1,400, it would have to be borne by the general rate.(4) In January 1941 when German bombers had devastated Britain's major cities, and Hayle, itself, had already received its first bombs, Mr Arthur Keverne the stalwart defender of Hayle's interests was reported as stating that West Penwith RDC had declined to give assistance to the ARP at Hayle, and that officers of the Council had twice declined to attend meetings without extra payment.(5)

Just when it seems that the situation could not become any more ridiculous, it then descended into utter farce when it was reported that a Compulsory Fire Watching Order had been imposed on the towns of Penzance and Hayle by the Government. Employees and managers aged 16 to 60 would have to stay certain nights in their factories or business premises to protect them from incendiary bombs. At West Penwith RDC, Mr Fenton (a company director) said he took it that the term 'managerial staff' did not include directors.(6) The introduction of this order caused a ludicrous situation down at West Penwith, and a classical dilemma. Hayle, because of its war industries and population, was the only place in the West Penwith RDC area with a Compulsory Fire Watching Order imposed, yet the Council still would not budge on providing the town with a fire service.(7)

Unashamed and unabashed, West Penwith RDC was still being as obstructive in March 1941 when the Council was reported as saying in respect of Hayle that, '. . . it was necessary to provide peacetime fire-fighting equipment to get AFS equipment.'(8) Despite this very dubious bureaucratic nonsense, the *Cornishman* of March 5th 1941 was able to report that, 'Hayle AFS under Mr Jones practiced extinguishing incendiary bombs.'(9) One can only wonder what equipment they used to do so. At a meeting of Hayle Parish Council in April 1941 it was reported that Mr Jones, AFS, complained about the lack of AFS equipment. They had at last received two cars but they had no uniforms, firemen's boots, oilskins or badges. Mr Jones (Headmaster of Hayle Grammar School) said that West Penwith RDC had treated him with contempt; his letters had remained unanswered.(10) Mr Jones might well have saved his time and his breath, for in the same week it was reported that West Penwith RDC had decided not to appoint a Fire Protection Officer at Hayle.(11)

Even some non-Hayle members of West Penwith were by now beginning to become concerned at the developing situation. At a meeting of the Council, Mr G.W. Fenton said that; 'the Hayle AFS men had been trained six, nine and even twelve months and went out on every "alert" and yet the council had provided nothing for them – no appliances, no tools, no axes and no overalls. The state of affairs at Hayle and Marazion was nothing short of shameful.' Mr S.J. Kennedy of Hayle said that, 'the Council did not know the meaning of the word "emergency". They had plenty of trained men at Hayle, but these men were becoming discontented through the lack of equipment. The whole trouble was due to slackness on the part of the Council.'(12) The temporary AFS station at Hayle, (housed in a corrugated iron structure at the level crossing) was described as a 'tin tabernacle'. The Clerk stated that the cars at Hayle Fire Station were insufficient for the work required.(13)

The publication of these severely adverse comments, or perhaps, foreknowledge via the 'grapevine' of the imminent huge shake-up of the fire services nationally, may have jolted West Penwith RDC and its officers out of their lethargy, for at the end of May 1941 the Council announced that Hayle would be allocated two trailer pumps but could not have a permanent fire station, and must rely on St Ives plus the trailer pumps.(14) The Council also may well have been shamed finally by a report from Chief Fire Officer, Mr W. Lanyon of Redruth which said that, 'Hayle AFS had a very serious grievance in not having had anything done for them in the way of uniforms or clothing or quarters. As members they have to report for duty every time the siren goes.'

The Emergency Committee resolved that Mr Langdon (Lanyon?) should arrange for the accommodation required by the fire station at Hayle including the provision of five bunks and twenty blankets and the provision of a lavatory and wash-up. The Council also resolved to purchase the necessary car for the trailer pump at a cost of £100 and to accept with thanks the offer of Mr W.B.C. Tregarthen and his brother for the loan of their horse-van for the duration of the war for the transport of men and equipment.

All this local council claptrap and nonsense was brought to an abrupt end at midnight Sunday/Monday 17th/18th of August 1941 when the National Fire Service came into existence organised by central government to standardise fire cover throughout the whole country.(15) Serious lessons had been learned during the heavy raids in the winter of 1940/41 when many country fire brigades brought in to assist and relieve their nearby cities under attack, found that their hoses would not couple to the hydrants, and other equipment was not compatible. Thus under the Fire Services (Emergency provision) Bill of the 8th August 1941 which established the National Fire Service (NFS), the Cornish fire brigades combined to become Fire Force Area 19. Almost at once we see a change of attitude to the position at Hayle. A Council sub-committee submitted for approval, '2 full-time firemen at Hayle, a gas meter and ring and provision of uniforms and oilskins.'(16)

Evidence of later full fire service presence at Hayle is noted in a report of a whist drive organised in February 1943 by NFS Capt. E. Johns for the NFS Benevolent Fund in Hayle Ambulance Hall.(17) Later that month Capt. Johns arranged a NFS dance at the Masonic Hall, Hayle. The M.C. was Column Officer H.G. Skinner. Also present were Divisional Officer H.D. Cassini, Coy Officer Fowler, Section Leader H. Roberts, A.G. Officer Mrs Brown who was in charge of the Women's Section of Sub-Division 2Z, and Leading Firewoman Spooner. Coy Officer Thomason, the Welfare Officer, was unavoidably detained. Music was played by the Arcadian Dance Band.(18) The names of most of the Hayle NFS men at its maximum wartime strength are given in the full list later. We do know of the Officer-in-Charge Mr A.E. Johns, a driver Mr Simon Jory, and two of the firemen, Mr Douglas Oliver and Mr Billy Rusden, all of Hayle.

In February 1943 serious activities were recorded when the NFS 2Z Division staged a static water test at Hayle. It was assumed that the Foundry area was 'blitzed' and water was brought from Copperhouse by the use of one mile of hose piping.(19) Real-time action occurred in August 1943 when Mr C.M. Hosking's fish & chip saloon on Penpol Terrace (now Hubbard's) caught fire. The Hayle and Camborne NFS parties soon had the fire under control.(20) Mr Hosking was taken to hospital for treatment to badly burnt arms. This reassuring newspaper report is rather misleading, for on 7th September 1943 Mr A.F. Johns, Officer In Charge Hayle NFS complained to the Hayle Invasion Committee that at a recent local fire, he was unable to tow his pumps to the outbreak owing to the state of the equipment. The committee undertook to take steps to put things right. Subsequently at the committee meeting of 2nd November 1943, Mr Johns was able to report that the NFS transport was now satisfactory.

By 1943 the Hayle NFS HQ Station was located at the Causeway Garage (now Tempest's depot), and the equipment consisted of 3 pumps including:

1 x major pump (Dennis) delivering 350-500 gallons per minute, and carrying 1000ft of hose.

2 x light pumps (trailer) delivering 120-150 gallons per minute, and carrying 500 feet of hose each.

The personnel on the 30th October 1943 consisted of 31 firemen; and a firewoman in the Control Room. There was also a pump at J & F Pool's works with a trained crew.(21)

The civilian involvement mentioned above under the fire-watching orders, meant that staff and workers had to form fire-parties, and were required to be on duty for 48 hours per month. They were supplied with a lighter-weight steel helmet and stirrup pumps. During May 1944 the Lelant Fire Guards organised an imaginary fire to which it was recorded that, 'Hayle NFS unit responded quickly to an urgent message for help to fight the . . . fire.'(22)

So at last, and for the first time in its history, Hayle had at least some degree of the long-promised fire and rescue protection based in the town. The population could, finally, sleep secure in its beds, aware that a trained force was on watch for them day and night. Sadly, as it seems is always the case in Hayle, it was not to last. With the retreat of the German forces from France and the lessening of the danger of air attack on western Britain, the authorities recommenced their bean-counting once more and began to scale down the civil defence and fire cover. At Hayle the bombshell was the announcement that the fire station was to be totally closed down forthwith, and the population once again left completely unprotected, relying upon the distant Camborne Fire Station to provide a response that was totally inadequate from the rescue aspect, and as a consequence Hayle residents were, once again, condemned to die trapped in house fires.

At that time the fire services were still under the control of the NFS which ultimately sanctioned the closure, but their centralised decision-makers could only have acted on local advice from County Hall and West Penwith RDC in Penzance. Their precipitate action to withdraw fire cover from Hayle was facilitated by the understandable request of the owner of the requisitioned Hayle Causeway Garage, Mr Wm Trevaskis for the return of his property, as he wished to resume his pre-war commercial activities. The authorities seized on this as an opportunity and a justification to act instantly on the closure.

The reaction in Hayle to this disreputable decision was immediate and hostile, but ultimately futile. Late in 1945 it was reported that the National Fire Service sub-committee had dealt with a communication from Hayle Parish Council stressing the need to retain a fire-fighting facility and that a new building to accommodate the service should be considered. Mr R.A. Keverne of Hayle suggested using the defunct British Restaurant premises (now the site of Hayle Library and Age Concern). He thought it would be suitable, but the Chairman of the West Penwith Finance Committee said, 'It is a question of expense.'(23) Not one notes a question of people's lives.

By this time Hayle Parish Council was becoming desperate in its attempts to persuade the central authorities to ignore the advice from the NFS sub-committee of West Penwith RDC. They passed a resolution urging all possible steps be taken to retain a NFS service as effective cover could not be provided from adjacent towns.

As a last-ditch effort to retain fire cover, it was suggested that the building rented by the Rural Council for storage (now Philp's Foundry Bakery) be made available as a headquarters for the firemen, and that in the near future, a suitable fire station should be built. Such hopes were finally dashed when Mr J. Chinn said: 'it did not look as if the retention of such personnel was likely, as he understood that the equipment at the temporary headquarters at the Causeway Garage had been sent to Bristol.'(24) Decisions and action had been taken, it seems, without reference to the people of Hayle or their elected representatives by West Penwith RDC and the Area Fire Force Commander, to abandon the town to extreme and totally avoidable hazards.

In a craven attempt to distance itself from any responsibility for the scandal, West Penwith RDC, through its Clerk, outlined its position in the matter with the following statement: 'Prior to the war no properly equipped service was provided by the Council . . . In February 1941 the Secretary of State intimated that a proper peace time fire service should be established at Hayle, as the Auxiliary Fire Service was not intended to deal with normal fires, but had been instituted to deal with firefighting on a war footing. In July 1941 the National Fire Service was created, and all local authority brigades were taken over by the Central Department. AFS and local brigades were then merged and no differentiation existed between peace time and war time services . . . a fully effective service (for Hayle) with suitable premises on a partial voluntary basis might cost a 7d rate over the whole district. After a discussion the sub-committee formed the view that . . . Hayle would receive most effective cover from Camborne . . .'(25)

In January 1946 *The Cornishman* reported that, 'A strong plea for the retention of a fire service unit is made by Mr A.E. Johns of Guildford Viaduct, Hayle who was in charge of the NFS at Hayle from 1940. First he disagrees that it would cost a seven penny rate to maintain an efficient brigade in the town, stating that he had prepared a report on equipment and personnel recently at an estimated cost equivalent to a 5½d rate . . . now we are in the position of being covered by one station or another, both of which have to travel between five or seven miles. In fire-fighting the first few minutes are the most essential.'

He goes on to describe a recent fire in Hayle when Camborne fire service took 30 minutes to reach a fire, 'The trouble arose through the officer commander being unable to find the fire . . . which was situated in a back alley. No guides were available as in the war days. Another difficulty was that they came right up against Hayle's bugbear, a complex water system. They ran right into the only hydrant of that type in Hayle and had not brought the standpipe required.' In conclusion he says: 'Before disbandment I had eighteen trained men standing by to form a volunteer brigade. Men trained in the use of equipment, who knew the town, and also had a filing system which gave information about water, hydrants, best route to take, and all over knowledge necessary for efficient fire-fighting.'(26)

On April 1st 1946 compulsory service in the NFS ceased and with the passing of the Fire Services Act 1947 control of fire stations went this time to the county councils; and Cornwall County Council continued the abandonment of the population of Hayle to cover from distant fire stations. At the time of writing 60 years later, Cornwall County Council, despite pressure from central government, after first deciding that Hayle should have a fire station, has reneged on its firm promise and refused to implement this decision.(27) One must wonder if there is another separate town of 6,000+ housing units, with a population of 11,000 residents; and summer holiday accommodation numbering over a thousand units, that has no permanent town Fire and Rescue station. Meanwhile the supposedly cash-strapped Cornwall County Council while holding 'road-shows' at Truro fire station to recruit seventeen new firemen, on the grounds of 'economy' instead of providing the promised fire and rescue facility, delivered to each house in Hayle a leaflet with which to fight fires or rescue trapped people.

Surely it must have been with a sick sense of 'gallows humour' that they had the breathtaking audacity to call this pathetic exercise 'Hayle Safe'.

In 2011 Cornwall Council announced their intention to sell the Camborne and Redruth fire station properties. They would substitute a new-build central station midway between the two communities. This would presumably leave Hayle well outside any Home Office response times. Previously unavailable funds have surfaced, and Hayle after sixty-six years could again have its own fire and rescue station. We await events.

THE HAYLE 'GDA' – gun defended area WW2

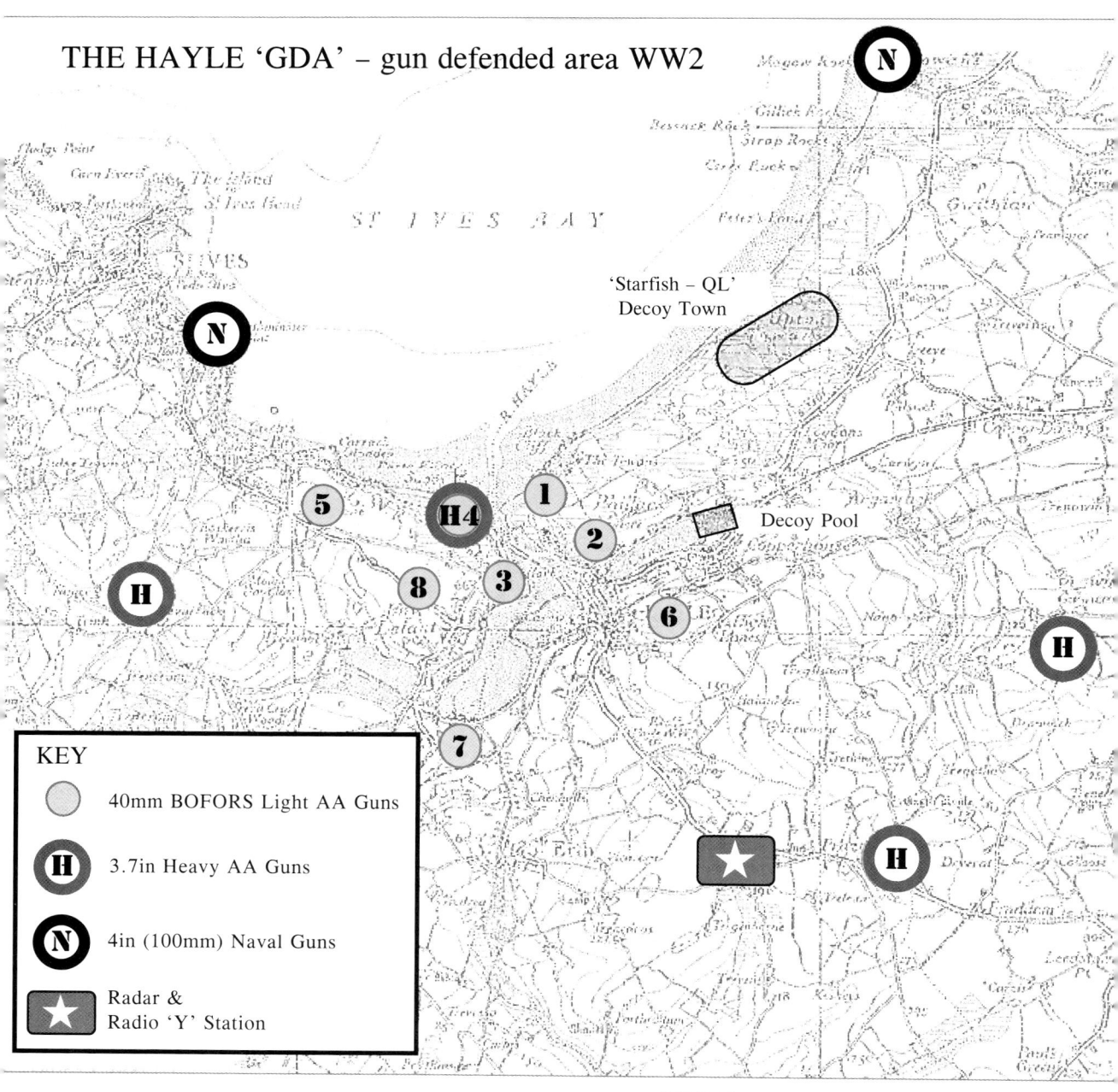

KEY
- 40mm BOFORS Light AA Guns
- **H** 3.7in Heavy AA Guns
- **N** 4in (100mm) Naval Guns
- ★ Radar & Radio 'Y' Station

'Starfish – QL' Decoy Town

Decoy Pool

BJS 2010. Map courtesy Ordnance Survey.

Chapter Eight:

'STARFISH' & OTHER DECOYS

IN EARLY 1942 the growing force of RAF Bomber Command carried out a series of area bombing raids on the historic German towns of Rostock and Lubeck. The attack on the latter town on Sunday 25th March 1942 was particularly severe, causing serious damage to the mediaeval buildings and resulting in 320 deaths with a further 400 injured. Hitler was infuriated, and in revenge he ordered his air force to attack English historic towns and cities, most of them of little military importance and largely ill-defended. Cathedral cities such as Canterbury, Norwich, Exeter and Bath among others, were heavily bombed in turn suffering severe damage and casualties. As the targets in Britain appeared to be those places marked with three stars in the well-known German guide book, the attacks became known at the time as *Baedeker* raids.(1)

General Sir Frederick Pile, GCB, DSO, MC (1884-1976) who was GOC-in-C Anti-Aircraft Command 1939-45 was faced with the problem of extending his already-stretched defences to locations which were previously not considered possible targets. In his autobiography he states: 'We selected for defence such places as Penzance, Truro, Hayle, Exeter, Bath . . .'(2) It would seem that when the General was writing his memoirs post-war, his recollection probably faltered slightly. Hayle being strategically important had already been heavily defended with his AA guns since December 1941. The reason for Hayle's inclusion in this list of largely non-military towns and cities stems from another project entirely. A component of the defence systems set up for vital cities, towns and airfields was a number of elaborate decoy sites adjacent to the target areas to mislead enemy aircraft crews to bomb the decoys instead. These decoys were known under the code name of 'Starfish,' or 'Starfish QL' if they included special lighting components. Starfish sites could simulate the night effects of towns, harbours, railway stations and sidings; and if a raid threatened false fires could be started and fake bomb explosions would be set off to divert enemy activity from the real town or airfield nearby. They were sited throughout the country mainly around large towns and important centres. Bristol, for example, had eleven Starfish sites in the countryside around the city.

At the time of the Baedeker raid defences the provision of a Starfish QL was laid out on Hayle Towans at map reference SW569 396. As a decoy for Hayle it covered an extensive area and appears to have extended well into the western end of the former National Explosives Works. References to this Hayle decoy can be found in Mr Huby Fairhead's excellent definitive book on the secret decoy sites of WWII, *Colonel Turner's Department* published in 1997. Mr Charles T. Sharp relates: 'From 1941 to 1943 I helped to build and later man and maintain Starfish/QL sites . . . In 1943 I was posted to Cornwall and served on three more Starfish/QL sites: The Towans two miles north of Hayle; Probus four miles north east of Truro; Mousehole three miles south of Penzance.'(3) Later in the same book, Mr Kenneth Comer recalls: 'At the age of fifteen I started work in 1940 on Starfish decoys . . . My first job was making "fire baskets" . . . These were timber-framed crates . . . filled with firewood and wood shavings soaked in creosote . . . laid out in various patterns and linked together with wicks . . . wired back to the operating bunker . . . The sites I can recall were at . . .

Hayle Sands and Kynance Cove . . . I must point out here that Starfish decoys were only designed for use at night and were operated by RAF personnel from a concrete bunker about a quarter of a mile from the actual site.'(4)

There were a number of other Starfish/QL sites in Cornwall including the decoy airfield layout for RAF Portreath, the concrete control bunker for which can be seen quite clearly today alongside the road from Hell's Mouth to Portreath, on the right-hand side. Mr Fairhead also states, in a personal letter, that there was another Starfish adjacent to Hayle in the Fraddam/Leedstown area.(5) As mentioned above, Starfish decoys were only effective at night. For daytime deception other means had to be adopted. At Hayle an elaborate scheme was devised to alter the appearance of the geography of the town and the layout of its harbour and waterways, and to draw attention particularly away from the vital industrial complex of North Quay. The subterfuge used was to displace the apparent position of Copperhouse Pool as seen from the air, by utilising the concrete dams and sluices under the Black Bridge. The dams were originally built in 1936 by Hayle Model Boat Club to form a boating pool by keeping the water in the upper pool. To reinforce the deception, the wartime visiting fun fairs were sited on the waste ground that is now the Co-op Hayle car park area instead of the usual Commercial Road car park, which once the war ended reverted to become again the usual fairground venue. A very similar and much more elaborate scheme was devised by the German authorities in Hamburg where a false embankment was built across the Binnen and Aussen Alsters thus altering the perceived relative positions of these large expanses of water in the centre of the city. One wonders if the Hayle scheme was based on the one at Hamburg, which had been detected by the RAF Photographic Unit quite early on. With no evidence either way we can only speculate.

Decoy towns and facilities were not ,as is often thought, a WWII innovation. From the onset of strategic bombing in the latter days of WWI attempts were made to conceal vital sites subject to attack. Germany, as usual, led the way. The aviation historian Stephen Budiansky states: 'a number of simple German countermeasures to aerial attack had proved remarkably effective. Dummy blast furnaces consisting of lights and "a certain amount of masonry" had been constructed a thousand metres or so from the real plants at Bous and Volklingen and had successfully drawn off British bombers.'(6)

Chapter Nine:

BOMBS ON HAYLE & DISTRICT

EVIDENCE OF THE nearness of German bombers to Hayle, and their menacing activity over Cornwall, came on the 7th August 1940 when four high-explosive bombs fell on Trevega Farm, Townshend. Hayle itself, after several false 'alerts' received its first bomb at 9.07pm on the 4th September 1940 at Ventonleague. It was believed to have been a parachute landmine, a most devastating weapon 2,200lb (1,000kg) weight; and the explosion was massive. It fell 200 yards North of the main GWR line, roughly where the entrance to Guildford Road Industrial Estate now is; and caused a crater 48ft (14.6m) x 20ft (6.1m) to a depth of 25ft (7.62m). This was described as the largest seen in Cornwall. The Police report states; 'No casualties. Damage to roof, windows of one dwelling house and damage to windows of 15 others. Telegraph wires down for 300 yards. GWR, GPO and Electric Company informed.(1)

The Cornishman report describing Hayle under wartime censorship as a 'southwest town' wrote: 'the bomb . . . fell on Mr Ingram's field near Mr Clarence Mungles' house only 50 yards (45.7m) from the crater.' Interviewed, Mr Mungles said: "We were sitting in the kitchen listening to the wireless when the explosion occurred – no we didn't hear the plane. I jumped up and caught hold of my wife, and got her and the children into a corner, but the force of the explosion hurled both of us against the wall. The dog was flung from the window against the door, but fortunately none of us suffered from anything more than a bit of a shaking-up. The worst part was when the stones from the crater were falling through the roof . . . If the walls had not been solid 2ft (61cm) thick the house would not have been standing now." The house was completely plastered with mud every window was broken. The roof was holed in several places and the back door had been torn right off its hinges. Near to the crater was a chicken coop in which the fowls were pecking their way about as unconcerned as if the bomb had dropped 100 miles (161km) away.

Amongst the chickens there were no casualties, the only loss of life being two grey-birds.

"I am in the Home Guard," said Mr Mungles, "and maybe one day I will have a chance to get my own back."(2)

On the 7th November 1940 in a major raid sixty-one bombs were dropped on Penzance. One of the casualties was Mr Nuttall the Hayle barber who had his shop in Foundry Square. He was severely injured, and ever after moved around his hairdresser's chair with a pronounced limp. On the 7th January 1941 the village of St Erth was machine-gunned, but the police reported that there was no damage and no casualties.(3) While throughout that year the visual effects of raids could be seen at night on the far horizons as the Luftwaffe attacked such targets as Falmouth docks and Portreath airfield.

Shortly after midnight (12.44 am) on the night of the 1st/2nd August 1941, the village of St Erth was rocked by the sound of explosions as four high-explosive bombs were dropped in the vicinity of Trewinnard Manor. They fell on the path that connects Trewinnard and Tredrea. Fortunately no one was injured and there was no damage to property. Damage was caused to telephone wires.(4)

The next direct assault on Hayle took place at seven minutes past midnight on the night of 17th/18th August 1941 when four high-explosive bombs fell on the area of Hayle Towans where the Haven Holiday Camp is now situated. The bombs fell spaced out in a straight line exactly in the direction of the adjacent Hayle Power Station and parallel to the National Grid power lines. It was thought at the time that the aircraft dropped its bombs at the wrong end of the white smoke trail that was streaming across the Towans from the works. Mr John Baumbach and his family had a very lucky escape when the last bomb of the stick dropped a few yards short of their wooden bungalow. Fortunately the force of the explosion was directed upwards by the soft sand from the bomb which had buried itself deeply.(5)

Later the same year four more bombs fell, this time at Guildford on the 30th October 1941. Dropped from a lone German aircraft, the bombs were spread in an area around approx SW573378. The *Cornishman* reported that: '. . . slight damage was done to an empty house, where the panes of glass were broken and a door burst. There were no casualties. Of the craters two were in a broccoli field belonging to Messrs Lello Bros; and two alongside the field. It appeared that two of the bombs were of a very small type, whilst the others must have been of a heavy calibre. A hole was torn in the roof of a barn and cow loft belonging to Mr W.J. Williams and some damage was done to the stables. Two heavy horses and a pony which would normally have been in the

Craters of the four High Explosive (HE) bombs dropped on Hayle Towans on the night of 17th/18th August 1941.

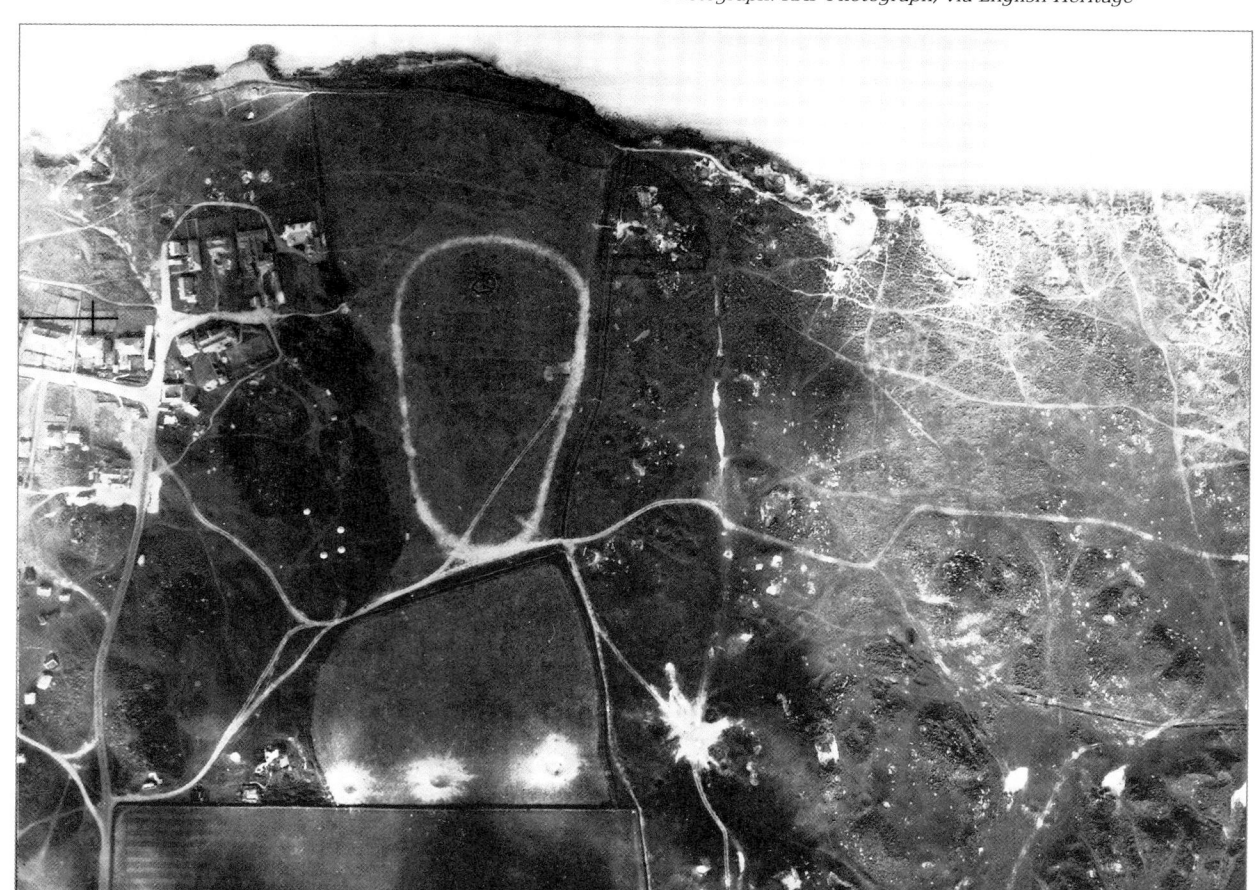

Photograph: RAF Photograph, via English Heritage

stables were across the road in a field and so escaped being killed. Mr Williams was outside in the yard at his home when the bombs fell. "As a matter of fact" he told the reporter "I had just got home. I heard the plane about and I didn't like it at all - I had an uneasy feeling . . . at last I heard the roar and saw the flash. I bolted upstairs and brought the kids down, and then came over here right away." Mr and Mrs Williams had two children at the time, a daughter aged seven and a boy of fourteen months. The boy had already experienced bombing. He was born at ten o'clock in the morning, and at nine o'clock on the evening of the same day a bomb fell near their house, shaking the floor as though someone had fallen heavily upstairs.' (This would have been the Ventonleague parachute mine of 4th September 1940 described above).(6)

What was not mentioned in this newspaper report, and could not be because of wartime censorship, was that two of the bombs fell in Copperhouse cutting and severed the GWR main line from Paddington to Penzance. Railway gangers and platelayers from all over the west of Cornwall were turned out of bed to fill the crater and re-lay the track. The line was repaired and through traffic restored by the next day.(7) The official police report on this incident goes: 'Supt Rowland reports that at 21.30, 30/10/41, four HEs dropped at Trevassack, Hayle = ½ mile east Hayle PS . . . two on main railway line – blocking both lines, 2 in adjoining fields. Damage to nearby cottages. No casualties. Railway company informed who have the matter in hand.' The following day Supt Rowland gives two follow-up reports that by 18.20hrs on 31/10/41 that: 'the up-line is now cleared' and by 21.05 'the down line is now cleared.'(8) An interesting sidelight on this raid is that a large splinter from one of

Bomb sites within Hayle and the greater St Ives Bay area.
BJS 2010. Map courtesy Ordnance Survey.

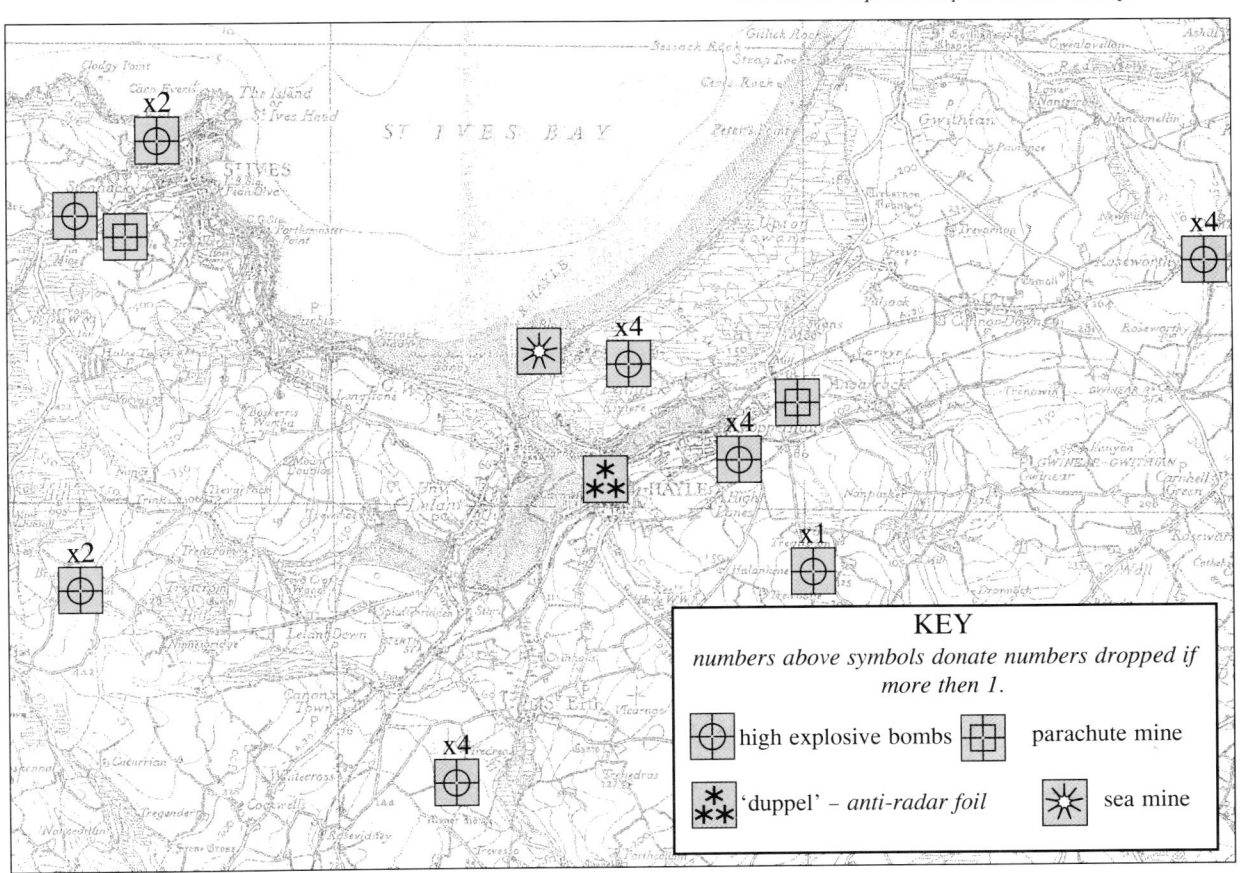

the bombs went clear across Copperhouse and penetrated the roof of the Stevens' fish and chip shop that was then in lower Church Street.(9)

On the 6th November 1941 at 8.15 in the evening an HE bomb was dropped on open fields at Lower Treglistian Farm, Hayle. No damage or casualties reported, but it made a very large crater.(10) On the same night it was reported that a large crater was caused at Phillack by a single large bomb. No further details were given but it is quite possible that this is the same incident.(11) On the 1st March 1942 four bombs fell on the little hamlet of Roseworthy, destroying the Cornish Shovel Works, owned by J & F Pool Ltd of Hayle. The official report states that: 'the bombs straddled four cottages, badly damaging them, and slightly damaging others. There were four casualties, one serious injury; Mr J. Williams, fracture of the thigh; Mr George Williams, broken collar bone; Mr J. Pascoe, minor injury to hand. All taken to hospital, Mrs W.H. Curnow was treated for shock.(12)

On the 8th August 1943 a sea mine that had broken loose from its mooring, floated in at high tide, and detonated on contact with the cliffs under the Bluff Hotel shattering the windows and causing injuries to a number of the Durham Light Infantry soldiers billeted in the building. Damage was caused to three houses, two having to be evacuated.(13)

An incident presumably not due to enemy action, but alarming and very mysterious occurred on the 12th January 1943. On Tuesday afternoon at about 1 o'clock whilst passing over Hayle Viaduct, one of the vans of a GWR goods train by some means exploded. The amazing thing about this incident is that, although blowing up to a height of thirty feet above the viaduct and then falling down into the middle of the town, right in front of Clark's Restaurant (now Warrens) the half-ton van failed to cause any damage to property or to injure any people.(14)

On the 27th March 1944, Hayle was showered with a massive number of black/silver aluminium strips. This material, later revealed to be the secret anti-radar device called 'window' by the RAF and 'chaff' by the US Air Force, was dropped over a large area of Cornwall. This incident was reported by the Police Superintendents of Penzance, Camborne, Falmouth, Truro and St Austell.(15) A rumour swiftly spread throughout Hayle, where masses were found on South Quay and the harbour area, that the strips had been dropped by the Nazis, and were contaminated with germs to spread disease; alternatively they were coated with poison to kill anyone who touched them. No epidemics ensued and the population did not drop dead in massive numbers, but it is interesting that lay-people seemed to have had an intuitive foreboding how chemical and biological warfare would develop fifty years later.(16)

No explanation of the origin of these foil strips was given at the time, or has since been forthcoming, and as it is unlikely that such massive quantities would have been dropped by the RAF or the USAAF over Cornwall and the UK it is highly probable that local people were quite correct that the source was enemy aircraft. It is significant that from January to May 1944 was the period of the 'baby blitz' (Operation Steinbock) a sustained attack by Luftwaffe bomber forces on London and other targets such as Bristol, Plymouth and Portsmouth.

On the very night that the foil fell on Cornwall (27th March 1944) Bristol was raided by aircraft coming up from France led by their pathfinder force who dropped masses of the German anti-radar foil, code-named 'Duppel' when approaching the area.

Chapter Ten:

'SUFFER THE LITTLE CHILDREN'
The Evacuees

WITH THE FALL of France and the Low Countries, London and other large cities of Britain became even more vulnerable to air attack; and a second mass evacuation of schoolchildren and some mothers with babies took place. Cornwall, along with other places was designated a 'reception area.' The county was expected to take 28,200 children; the numbers relating to the West Cornwall area were Penzance 2,500; West Penwith 2,000 (Hayle 1,000); St Ives 800 and Camborne-Redruth 3,000.

The effect of the sudden arrival of this large number of little strangers on local communities was quite varied and very interesting. The local press duly reported the reactions of the towns and villages affected. Hayle, perhaps because of its fairly level and equable social composition at the time, with a mainly ordinary decent working-class population, comes out very well when compared with some of its larger and more affluent near-neighbours.

The *Cornishman* in a report on the arrival on Sunday June 11th 1940, of the first batch of evacuee children states: 'Hayle is well-known for its hospitality, and one feels that these children will be treated with every kindness and consideration by the residents.'(1) A slight hiccup occurred when due to a misunderstanding, the coach drivers bringing them from Penzance Station to Hayle, deposited 150 children at the little village of Gwinear, much to the consternation of the tiny population. The situation was resolved, however, after the children were housed overnight somehow, and the missing waifs were duly returned to Hayle the next day Monday 12th June.(2)

There were no such happy outcomes at Penzance and St Ives. Previously at Penzance, the Town Clerk, ominously, had already laid down the guidelines and specified the social attitudes to the expected children when, back in March 1940 he said that: 'It was not fair to ask boardinghouse keepers to take children at the billeting allowance when they could let rooms at a profit.' The Penzance authorities then went into an 'angels on the head of a pin' mode to decide what was a boardinghouse and what was not.(3)

A report in May 1940 highlighting the proposed arrival of 800 children aged between 10 to 14 years in St Ives quotes the Town Clerk who, it seems, is utterly beside himself: 'I am at my wit's end to know what to do about it. As far as I can see there is no other town in the county faced with such difficulty in this matter as St Ives. If St Ives is forced to take this number of children it means that the activity of the town will be completely stopped.'(4) And while all this hand-wringing went on; just across the bay, Hayle was expected to take 1,000 children; and did so with no fuss. The Town Clerk continues: 'We have considered the question of putting up huts for their accommodation but the problem of water, sanitation and drainage seem to raise such technical and financial difficulties as to make the suggestion impracticable.'(5)

A month later in June 1940, the *Cornishman* was reporting on the probable drastic intervention by higher authority, as St Ives Town Council discussed the threatened imposition of compulsory billeting of the children. The steadier-nerved members of the council considered this a drastic step, but accepted that: 'The children will be coming and have to be accommodated.'(6) As usual, the good, decent majority of St Ives people rose to the occasion and accepted the children into their homes and families, and thereby ending the procrastination down at the Guildhall.

At Penzance with the arrival of the evacuation trains the situation was very nearly getting out of hand. The over 1,000 children having endured a twelve hour journey from London were made to sit for a further hour and twenty-five minutes in their train, with chaos seemingly reigning at the collection centre at St John's Hall, with more children having arrived than had been prepared for. All went smoothly until it was reported that: 'Then for some unknown reason "red tape" stepped in and took a hand. Believe it or not, it was approaching midnight before some of those children found a resting-place for the night. Outside St John's Hall there were crowds of people only too anxious to take the children home if only for the night . . . the people clamoured to be allowed to take them – and they were prevented. Finally exasperation at the unnecessary "red tape" got the better of those waiting, and almost by main force, they besieged the officials, and took the children away bodily.'(7)

Mr H. Hartley Thomas the forthright and splendid managing director of *The Cornishman*, in a condemnatory full-page report, described how he spent an hour and three-quarters in his car with 5 children but got no answers. (It seems that many of the residents of the more affluent parts of Penzance had conveniently left their houses for the day). Mr Thomas wrote: 'Finally a Treneere resident offered to take the children, and they at last found rest. A man said he would not give evacuees the same food as he ate himself; why should they live in luxury.' Mr Thomas is scathing; 'Yes my readers that statement was made. I have my opinion of that man. Let him visit the poorer districts of our town and the way those grand women are feeding the children.' Mr Thomas concludes: 'To people of the east ward mainly Treneere Estate, Adelaide Street, Alverne Buildings etc belongs the greatest credit. But for these it might well be that the children would have spent even longer in St John's Hall.'(8)

A year later and how very different it all was. Plymouth had been heavily bombed on the 14th May 1941 and the prestigious private educational establishment Devonport High School was to be evacuated to Penzance. Again the *Cornishman* was present to observe proceedings: 'Another contingent of evacuees from Plymouth came to Penzance early on Wednesday afternoon. They were three hundred and sixty-seven boys from Devonport High School. After their arrival in Penzance the lads were welcomed by the Mayor (Alderman Robert Thomas). The Mayor expressed the hope that they would be happy in their new surroundings and said the people of the borough would do all they could to make their stay pleasant. Mr Thomas told a reporter that: "pupils of this school were a splendid type who looked smart and clean." The boys were taken to the Regent, Queens, Western and Union Hotels.'(9)

The reason for this highly divisive accommodation procedure did not rest with the Penzance Council Welfare and Evacuation Committee. They were merely, to use the Nuremburg defence, 'carrying out orders'. The policy of billeting boarding schools and private day-schools in luxury hotels (officially described simply as 'hostels') was devised by the senior civil servants in London. One can accept their reasoning when dealing with boarding schools where most pupils lived in parts of the country far from the school, many with parents overseas, the school acting truly *in loco parentis*. The anomaly in the regulations, and Devonport High School is a prime example, was the inclusion in the scheme of private day-schools where the pupils were living at home and in every respect except funding, were identical with council financed schools. The effect of this action by the 'Mandarins' of Whitehall was, as the Headmaster recalled some time later, to transform Devonport High overnight from a day school into an opulent boarding school.(10)

At Camborne-Redruth Council a mischievous question was asked by Mr F.J. Benbow who, 'enquired the number of children billeted with clergymen and ministers and also asked to be furnished with the names of members of that council who had accepted evacuee children. Feelings ran very high in the district.' A Mr Tossel said that question was the 'biggest piece of cheek that has ever come from any human being, and not the business of the council.'(11) In West Cornwall some older people can still remember a local vicar who gave his reason for not taking children into his spacious house because it was 'haunted'.

The newcomers at Hayle were mainly from two London County Council schools, Dockhead in south-east London, and St Mary's Paddington, both in less affluent areas of the city. Classroom accommodation was, at first shared with the two Hayle schools, Penpol and Bodriggy, each school using the premises on a half-day basis. Later the evacuated schools were permanently settled, each in its own premises in the schoolrooms of Copperhouse and Foundry chapels. It is interesting to note that both these London schools were Roman Catholic establishments; but settled quietly in what at the time was a staunchly Methodist Hayle, even to the extent of using the Methodist church's premises, with little or no friction. This might have been due to Hayle's close contact with Roman Catholicism through the benign presence of the nuns at St Michael's Hospital.

In April 1942 it was announced that the allowance to keep an evacuee would be:

Age	Allowance	(if more than 1)
5 years old and under 10:	10/6d per week	(8/6d " ")
10 " " " " 12:	11/- " "	(10/6d " ")
12 " " " " 14:	12/- " "	(10/6d " ")
14 " " " " 16:	13/- " "	(12/6d " ")
16 " " " " 17:	15/6d " "	(15/- " ")
17+ " " " " ——	16/6d " "	(15/- " ")

(12)

In Sept 1942 it was reported that Penzance Town Council had paid £2,684-11s-6d to Mr Cox owner of the Royale Hotel for the furniture.(13) (The Royale was at the time the home to eighty boys of Devonport High School).

By November 1943 *The Cornishman* reported that there was a total of 1300 evacuated children in the Borough of Penzance. 900 of these would have been billeted with ordinary families, while the 400 boys of DHS were still being accommodated in the town's luxury hotels.(14) How the Welfare and Evacuation Committee (Chairman, the Mayor; Chief Clerk Mr T.F. Retallack) managed this on the allowances given above, even to the extent of supplying strawberries and cream for the boy's Sunday teas in Summer, is a mystery so far unexplained.

By 1942 a number of Penzance councillors including Alderman JM Hitchens and Mrs K Meek, were in a rebellious mood, quoting what were described as 'amazing sums' being spent by the Welfare and Evacuation Committee on Devonport High School. They claimed that they were being 'extravagantly treated' as against other evacuees in private homes. Costs were averaging £15 per week per boy as against £2-12s per child in billets. Fruit and vegetables alone were costing £3,500 per year (2005 value = £105,000).

In the face of growing awareness and public unease at the obvious difference of treatment between ordinary evacuees and those of Devonport High School, Penzance Council prepared a carefully worded statement that even today stands as a perfect example of local government double-speak and sophistry that would make a 21st century PR man gasp in admiration.

The Cornishman report reads:

'The Town Clerk said he was surprised to hear that there was differentiation. He could assure the council that there was not the slightest intention to differentiate. The reason why Devonport High School had better accommodation was because the council had had twelve months experience of hostels before that school arrived and secondly, the accommodation was provided under a scheme of the Board of Education whereby Devonport High School was kept as a unit. The only premises were of the hotel class, and had better sanitary arrangements and so on. Rather than lowering the standard of DHS's accommodation he would rather see the accommodation of the other hostels brought up to that level. Any alterations should be definitely upwards instead of downwards . . . He was surprised to hear that there was a difference in diets. They must remember that mere quantity of food was not sufficient to compare the menus. It depended on the person who cooked the food.' (15)

In Hayle by middle-to-late 1942, with the practical cessation of heavy air raids on Britain by the Luftwaffe, many of the evacuee children had drifted back to their London homes in the belief that the days of air attack were over – a sense of security that would be rudely shattered with the arrival of the V1 and V2 terror weapons in 1944.

With the reduction of numbers of children the two evacuated schools were merged into one at Foundry Chapel, and eventually that school closed and the remaining evacuee children were taken onto the registers of Bodriggy and Penpol schools under the care and guidance of Cornwall County Council Education Committee.

So over the evacuation period the children had mostly settled down, the majority of them quite happily with their surrogate families, contrary to the legendary post-war stories of hordes of rebellious, foul-mouthed ,diseased and verminous children, clad in rags with no under-garments to speak of, who descended on the good ladies of the countryside in their sensible tweeds who undertook to put things smartly in order with hot baths, carbolic soap, scrubbing brushes and Lysol disinfectant.

Such shameful tales propagated and published nationwide, even by such august bodies as the Women's Institutes and the BBC have done a grave disservice to these poor waifs and the kind decent people who accepted them into their homes and families. Obviously, in the nature of human life there were without question cases of bad behaviour and physical neglect in some of the evacuated children, just as there were host families found wanting, but the myths that have grown so mightily by repetition since that period unfortunately tend to outweigh the usually benign experience of the evacuees and the kindly surrogate families that nurtured them. Even fifty years after the events scurrilous statements were still being spread via hearsay and the media.

The official instructions indicate a different aspect. Parents were told to send the children to their schools on departure day with the following articles: Hand luggage containing, gas mask – change of underclothes – night clothes – shoes – spare socks or stockings – toothbrush – comb – towel – soap – facecloth – handkerchief – and if possible, a warm coat or mackintosh.(16)

In July 1944 the German secret weapons, the V1 flying bomb and the V2 rocket, were unleashed on London and Southern Britain; and another evacuation scheme was hastily put into operation with trainloads of children dispatched to the west country. *The Cornishman* in July 1944 reported the arrival of 250 evacuees of whom Penzance while keeping 100, dumped 150 on poor little St Just, where the authorities complained bitterly that they now had 1,000 extra wartime visitors. At Penzance the Town Council billeting committee quite brazenly and without compunction, reverted to the bad old habits they had so unctuously renounced in August 1941 when explaining away the luxury accommodation of Devonport High School; and unashamedly adopted the billeting on individual households system again, for these children from Middlesex and London fleeing the terror weapons. Once again no luxury hotels for council schoolchildren.(17)

In Hayle the defunct British Restaurant was re-opened to provide meals for the 'large numbers of evacuees who had arrived in the town.'(18)

In sharp contrast to the derogatory scare stories about evacuees mentioned above, are the moving scenes described by the various reporters covering the eventual departure of the evacuees. With the end of the war in Europe the time came for the inevitable return of the children to their own homes and families. In the very nature of things, over a period of up to five years a strong personal bond had formed between these young children and their surrogate parents; and the sad scenes recorded by the anonymous reporters give lie to the myths perpetrated since, regarding the behaviour of both the host families and the children concerned.

The Cornishman reported the Hayle departure under the headline '"Evacuees Farewell" – As the little children assembled at the Parochial Hall, Hayle, with their foster parents at 8am on Wednesday of last week (20th June) to start on their homeward journey to London, there were touching scenes. As each arrived with their little bundles of treasures and dolls and reported to the billeting officer they were conducted to waiting buses for transfer to Penzance to join the special train leaving there for London. These little ones will be missed in Hayle, in the homes, Sunday and day schools where they had endeared themselves to all. Hayle wishes them happy re-unions at their homes.'(19)

A description of the departure of a typical evacuee train from Penzance, where the Mayor attended in person to say goodbye, highlights the poignancy of such partings with even household pets, some to go home with the evacuees and some brought down to say farewell to the children: '. . . there were dogs and cats of all sizes. Many tears and goodbyes. Tears mingled with smiles.'(19)

Under the headline "Even the Skies Wept a Bit," *The Cornishman* reported the departure of a returning evacuee train twelve coaches long when: '. . . the rain fell a little, symbolic of the tears that were shed later as the long train drew out of the station to waving of handkerchiefs and the cries of "goodbye".'(20)

At Praze-an-Beeble the local reporter is noticeably moved by the situation: 'A number of sad hearts were left behind at Praze on Monday evening (28 May). The children assembled at the Praze Institute where a large gathering assembled to give them a good send-off. As the time came for their departure the children and foster parents broke down, a rather touching sight which will be remembered in Praze for a long time . . . the children will be sadly missed by everyone for the love they brought not only in the homes, but also the church and chapels which they attended regularly. The Central Methodist Church presented each child who attended with a gift of 2/-.'(21) There was also the same sad sight at Camborne Station where the children from Praze were joined by children from other villages, '. . . here the men as well as the children openly broke down.'(22) The twelve coach train mentioned above that left Penzance carried 472 evacuees from Penzance and Hayle, 107 joined from St Ives, 130 at Camborne and 132 at Redruth – a total of 841 passengers.(23)

Back at Penzance, of course, the due time also came for the departure of Devonport High School back to Plymouth. *The Cornishman* carried a report on the Final Assembly of the school held in Richmond Methodist Church. This it appears was a formal well-ordered affair in the best tradition. The lack of emotion seemingly involved in contrast to the other departures owed much perhaps, to their almost total isolation and social distance from the local population during their stay, except for a few inter-school events with the local grammar and high schools; and as many of the boys, over the years had been going home to join their parents in Plymouth on a regular weekend basis. A privilege not available geographically or financially to the London children.

The occasion was considered sufficiently distinguished and grand, however, for the worthies of Penzance Council to turn out in considerable force. Led by the Mayor (Alderman Robert Thomas) the delegation included the Town Clerk (Mr D.J. Beattie), the Borough Treasurer (Mr C.R. McCleod) and the District Education Clerk (Mr W.F. Jackson). After proudly listing the schools academic achievements, the Headmaster Mr W.H. Buckley thanked the town for its hospitality, and presented a cheque from the parents to the West Cornwall Hospital of £94-10s-6d.[25] In August 1945 it was reported that the Hotel Royale (now emptied of its DHS schoolboys) had been, 'sold for £10,500.'[26]

Chapter Eleven:

THE *ROSSMORE* & THE *MARENA*
The Battle of the North Coast

IN APRIL 1941 at a meeting of Hayle Parish Council sympathy was expressed to the relatives of the 'Hayle merchant seamen reported missing from enemy action.'[1] Because of official censorship this passing comment was the only public reference at the time to an incident that brought the full horror of war home to Hayle.

The sinking of the SS *Rossmore* which had operated out of Hayle for many years and was crewed by Hayle seamen affected many people who until then the war had seemed rather remote from their daily lives. Before this tragic incident only some individual families had been affected in the form of a dreaded telegram announcing the death in action of a loved son or husband, in some cases in the poorer sections of the community, the poignant fact was that this might be the only telegram they would ever receive in all their lifetime.

So war came to Hayle in a very personal sense on the 25th March 1941 when two of the best known ships that traded from the port; the SS *Rossmore,* 627 tons, owned by the County of Cornwall Shipping Co. of Portreath, and the SS *Marena,* 300 tons, both crewed by Hayle seamen, departed the harbour on the tide, in ballast for Barry

---

The SS *Rossmore*, bombed and sunk by a Condor off St Agnes Head, 25th March 1941. Capt. Roberts and five crew from Hayle were killed in the action.
Photograph via: William 'Bing' Hosking

Dock, South Wales. Travelling light and sailing together for mutual protection, they were hurrying at their top speed to catch up with the clockwise coastal convoy some distance ahead of them proceeding up the coast. At 5.45pm that evening, when the two ships were approximately twelve miles north-east of Godrevy Light at 50.24.30N. 05.14W they were attacked by a German aircraft.(2)

The raider was a Focke-Wulf 200C-1 Condor, a four-engined reconnaissance bomber, almost certainly of 1/KG40 based at Bordeaux-Merignac.(3) This aircraft was probably on the routine surveillance flight from Bordeaux to Stavanger in Norway. This flight flew around SW Cornwall and Ireland to observe and report the movements of the great convoys in and out of Liverpool and the Scottish ports, and also to record advance weather conditions for the German meteorological service.

Thus in the fading light of the late March day the Condor swooped down to attack the two Hayle coasters, raking them with cannon and machine-gun fire. The ships replied, as best they could with the small calibre machine-guns that were their only defence at that stage of the war. The Condor crew concentrated their main attack on the *Rossmore*, at 627 tons much the larger vessel, and using high-explosive bombs soon blew her apart, despite the valiant efforts of William 'Bucksie' Bray of Hayle aboard the *Marena* who was hammering away with the ship's Lewis Gun at the raider, conducting his own private and personal war.(4)

Joseph Richards of Portreath. Joseph was a survivor of the *Rossmore*. He hid under some wood when the German plane machine-gunned the survivors in the water.

Photograph and Information: Mr and Mrs Desmond Philp

So approximately four miles off St Agnes Head the *Rossmore* went down taking with her Captain Roberts of Hayle, and six of her crew of ten. One of the survivors, Dai Trewartha of Hayle had come up from below to see what the commotion was all about, and was standing beside Capt. Roberts when a bomb went down into the engine room and exploded. Capt. Roberts was struck in the back by a piece of the concrete cladding from the bridge. As the ship began to sink, Dai Trewartha a very strong man and a powerful swimmer, physically threw the captain and another crew member over the side and then dived into the sea himself. He and other survivors had to shelter under a raft when the Condor machine-gunned them in the water.(5)

With the appearance of RAF fighters in the far distance approaching fast, probably Spitfire Vs from 263 Squadron at RAF Portreath, newly opened, the Condor with her maximum speed of over 200mph, made off to the west and safety.(6) It has been asserted in some quarters that Focke-Wulf Condors which were usually deployed far out in the Atlantic shadowing allied convoys, would not have been operating near the coast of Britain, despite the positive identification by a survivor.(7) In the comprehensive book *Warplanes of the Luftwaffe* edited by David Donald it is stated that: '. . . from July 1940 the Condors. . . added weight to the Luftwaffe's assault on the UK, usually flying a wide sweep, west of Cornwall and normally west of Ireland, dropping four bombs and heading for Norway, making the return trip a day or two later.(8)

After the attack the little rust-streaked *Marena* turned back to St Ives Bay having picked up the *Rossmore* survivors, who were landed at St Ives on the morning of the 26th, and two injured crew members were conveyed to Redruth Hospital. Later she came back into Hayle where she tied up at South Quay, her tall funnel riddled with bullet holes.(9) The grimy little old ship, long the butt of many good-natured jokes in the town because of her many strandings and groundings on Hayle Bar over the years resulting in large amounts of cement being placed in her bottom had been given the nick-name of 'the concrete submarine.'(10) She had justly earned her battle honours and with her scars from the 'Battle of the North Coast' the venerable old lady was never to be laughed at again in the port of Hayle.

In the early years of WWII the coastal waters of Britain were a very dangerous place for a merchant seaman to follow his trade. During the months of March, April and May 1941 a total of 500,000 tons of British and allied shipping was sunk by German aircraft.(11) This, of course, includes the unfortunate *Rossmore*.

The SS *Marena*, one of the many merchant vessels crewed by Hayle men. On March 25th 1941, the *Marena* came under attack in the same engagement which saw the SS *Rossmore* sunk by a German aircraft *(as described in Chap. Eleven)*.

Chapter Twelve:

THE RED DUSTER
Merchant Shipping in Hayle

THE PORT OF Hayle, although restricted to small coasting vessels, played a vital part in the second world war. Coal was the principal cargo landed, mainly for the power station and for industrial and domestic use. Coastal oil tankers brought in bulk petrol and oil for the storage and distribution depot on North Quay. The ICI bromine extraction works received cargoes of chemicals. Regular shipments of potatoes were unloaded and general goods were transported by Coast Lines Ltd. Thomas W. Ward Ltd despatched scrap metal out of Hayle to the iron foundries and war industries. On Lelant Quay (Norwayman's Wharf) a large lightly-framed corrugated iron building was constructed to store the black powder for the Bickford Smith fuse factory and dynamite for the mines etc. These ships from Nobel's Ardeer explosives factory in Scotland, flew the red danger flag at their masthead and were not allowed to berth any closer in Hayle Harbour. Overseeing this activity, and controlling all movements in the harbour were the sole owners of the facilities, quays and waterways, the famous former engineering business, Messrs Harvey and Company Ltd. They were also Lloyds Agents, builders' merchants and property landlords. From their main office under the clock in Foundry Square and the Harbour Office on North Quay, they master-minded every aspect of shipping interest in the port, subject only to wartime regulations and Admiralty instructions.

Many ships became regular visitors during the wartime years, plying the west coast route from the South Wales area to the North Cornish coast, under the protection of the clockwise and anti-clockwise coastal convoys conducted by the Royal Navy. Unable to carry their anti-dive bomber balloons into Hayle because of the high-tension cables that crossed the mouth of the estuary they would be serviced by the RAF balloon tender that operated from St Ives. The Hayle ships would have to be out in the bay on the previous high tide, and race to join the convoys which did not stop when picking up joining ships or dropping off others, as the formation passed the bay.

The ships' names and the crews' faces became familiar to the people of Hayle, and many of the vessels are remembered today. The largest bringing coal for the power station included the *Rossmore* sadly to be lost through enemy action; the *Dunleary* and the *Avonville*. A regular visitor was the Free-French tanker the *Port Lyauty* proudly flying the French *tricolour* at her stern. She was later lost in the Bristol Channel. Also to be seen were the sister ships the *Eastcoaster* and the *Westcoaster* and not forgetting the dear old Hayle-crewed coal-burning *Marena* together with an occasional Bridgwater sailing vessel. In addition to the MN crew members would be the Royal Artillery and Royal Navy DEMS (Defensively Equipped Merchant Ships) gunners who sailed in the coasters and manned the Lewis guns and later Oerlikon cannons as defence against enemy air attack. These seamen could be seen on the streets of Hayle or leaning over their ship's rail, but mostly in the evenings frequenting the town's pubs.

Among the ships using Hayle regularly in the war, and very popular were the Dutch *schuyts'* (pronounced 'skoots'). They were flat-bottomed little coasters designed to work the shallow waterways of Holland in the days before the German armies swept across that country. Smart and modern in comparison with the rusty old coal-burning British coasters, they were mostly family owned and crewed, and seemed always freshly painted outside, and spotlessly clean inside even when carrying cargoes of coal. Some even sported embroidered curtains at the portholes of the living quarters. Unknown to the people of Hayle at the time, but recorded more recently is that after their escape from Holland over forty of these little ships, under the temporary command of junior Royal Navy officers and flying the White Ensign performed a great service in the evacuation of the British Army from Dunkirk. Over the years from 1940 to 1945 the names of these vessels were to become familiar along the Hayle waterside scene, their flat-bottomed design being ideal for the shallow north Cornish tidal harbours. Some of the names can still be recalled by older residents of Hayle, and a few are listed below with, in brackets, the number of soldiers rescued at Dunkirk.

The MV *Oranje*	231 tons	(605 men)
The MV *Reiger*	232 tons	(592 men) – *five crossings*
The MV *Rian*	232 tons	(257 men) – *on last trip was firing on two cylinders only*
The MV *Rike*	197 tons	(300 men)
The MV *Ruja*	175 tons	(300 men)
The MV *Twente*	239 tons	(1,139 men)

(1)

On the 2nd of December 1943 the *Reiger* carrying a cargo of coal had to be beached at Carbis Bay after she suffered damage to her hull causing a severe leak. This was stated to be 'not due to enemy action.'(2)

It is interesting to note that the *Rian* was experiencing engine trouble at Dunkirk. This was to plague her throughout the war, her engines needing attention constantly. Her last long stay in Hayle occurred in 1945 when she was stranded in the port for many months, tied up at South Quay with technical problems. Her Captain Nenderikus Meertens even buying a motorbike to tour the local countryside; and on which he had a nasty accident near Long Rock involving himself and a crew member Cornelius De Bruin, both suffering severe head injuries.(3)

Norwayman's Wharf, Lelant, showing the explosives quay and frangible dynamite and black powder storage shed.

Photograph: M.M. Sullivan

When in port the Dutch crew members, always well-behaved and well-liked by the people of Hayle would have their favourite pubs that they would frequent. A popular venue was the former Globe Inn opposite the present library. My father, a personal friend of the landlord Leslie Streete, was a talented natural pianist; and at Leslie's invitation, he would play for the customers any tune that they would request for a singalong. In the desperate winter of 1941/2 when everything seemed to be going wrong for Britain, the *schuyt* crew members that happened to be in port, would ask him if he could play a Dutch tune. Holland not being a great source of popular music, there was only one song that he could remember from pre-war days.

So in that small room, with blacked-out windows and full of cigarette smoke, packed with soldiers and civilians, warmed by the big central enclosed stove, my father an ex-soldier wounded and gassed in the First World War, himself a slowly dying man in the last year of his short life, would play over and over again *Down by the Zuider Zee*; and standing around the piano the young Dutch seamen, their eyes moist with tears, would be transported for a while in nostalgia and spirit to their Nazi-occupied homeland and their unreachable families.(4)

Apart from the normal arrivals and departures, unusual vessels would call, either in transit or weather-bound, such as a flotilla of RAF air-sea rescue launches; and when the barge-building was in progress, the big ocean-going US tugs would call, looking strange with their large superstructures almost appearing too top-heavy to stay upright.

All the merchant ships would be brought in and out of Hayle by the Trinity House pilots based at St Ives. Men whose faces were familiar at the office of Harvey & Company, where they would call to sign their dockets. They were fine seamen, former master mariners such as Capt. Paynter, Capt. Ninnes and Capt. Treloar.(5) They would be picked up and dropped at their ships by the St Ives pilot boat which sometimes brought the pilots into Hayle if necessary.

Very occasionally at busy times, use would be made of Mr Hughie Love, the well-known Hayle general-duty boatman, fisherman and town 'character.' A life-long non-swimmer, his many hair-raising adventures and mishaps were told about for years around the Hayle waterside, especially when in his younger days, the *Taycraig* let go her anchor down through Hughie's boat and he had to scramble up the fast-descending anchor chain in a desperate race to avoid being drowned.

Small boat activities, in and out of Hayle, were strictly controlled in wartime, but Hughie because he acted as a semi-professional waterman was the proud possessor of what he called his 'Admiralty pass, but this restricted him to daylight-only movement. During the earlier days of the war, when invasion was thought to be imminent, vessels fishing or having business in the bay were required to have an Admiralty Pass, and if needing to enter Hayle or St Ives harbours after dark they had to have a signal lamp to flash the code letter which the naval authorities changed daily.(6)

On one famous occasion Hughie had been delayed out in St Ives Bay where his boat sprung a leak (a not unusual occurrence for Hughie), after baling furiously to little effect and with darkness rapidly descending, he decided to run for Hayle, crossing the bar on a falling tide. By this time, however, unknown to him a lookout had reported an unidentified vessel approaching Hayle, and by the time he had cleared the bar and was entering the harbour, he was confronted on the Lelant side of the ferry by a heavily armed contingent of the St Ives & Carbis Bay Home Guard ready to blast him out of the water, and on the Hayle side by a full force of Hayle policemen, regulars and war-reserve under the leadership of Sgt Woolcock. When challenged to identify himself; or to surrender if he was the spearhead of a German invasion force, Hughie's response was, as he told us in his own words years later by the fire of the old Phillack pub: 'I was standing in my boat, up to my neck in water, waving my Admiralty pass, and shouting "Can't you see I'm sinking you silly buggers – let me through." He never did explain how he could be standing up to his neck in water in a boat that was still afloat. We all assumed that it was a use of dramatic licence!(7)

Hughie's life was never without incident for long, and the *Cornishman* in 1942 recorded an escapade that was typical of Hughie. It reported that Mr Hugh Love and a friend: 'went out in St Ives Bay on Thursday evening and when returning with their catch they hit a sandbank on the bar and were stuck. Mr Leonard Gilbert saw them and went to their assistance, but the current was too strong. A motor launch from St Ives was called. The two seamen were rescued and sailed triumphantly into Hayle with their catch – one mackerel!'(8)

The port of Hayle was privately owned by Harvey & Company. Traditionally the Chairman was appointed the Consular Agent for the Scandinavian countries, because of the large timber imports that the company handled and the ships and crews from the Baltic ports.

Chart issued by the Naval authorities early in 1941 warning Breton fishermen to stay clear of the convoy routes around Land's End and Mount's Bay.

Via the late Clive Carter

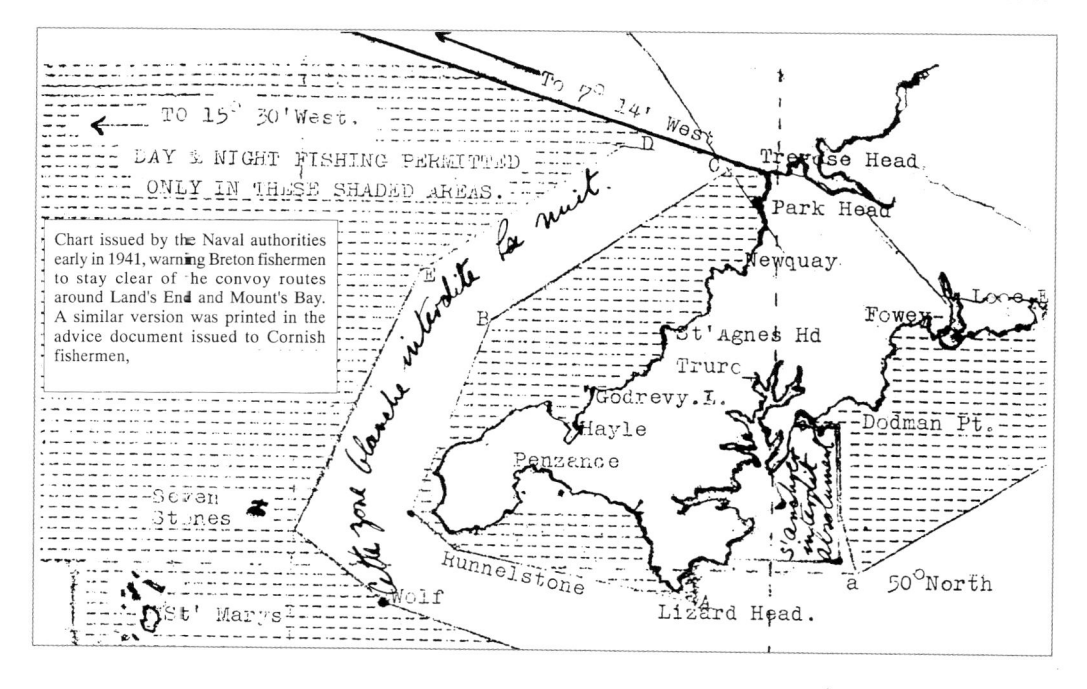

Chapter Thirteen:

THE MYSTERY OF THE FRENCH CRABBER

MANY OF THE happenings and occurrences in wartime Hayle, while unexplained at the time because of the necessary restrictions of censorship for reasons of security, have since been explained or uncovered in recent times as the war receded into distant history. One incident, however, remains shrouded in the murky mystery of possible wartime clandestine activity; the wreck of the French fishing boat on the sands of the Cot Pool between Hayle and Lelant.

Hayle Harbour was, in those days, a scene of intense activity. At any one time as many as fifteen or more ships could be seen tied up awaiting the tides to join their relative coastal convoys. Overseeing all this activity was the time-honoured firm of Harvey and Co. where everything that moved in the harbour was meticulously recorded in copperplate handwriting in the huge ledgers and day books by elderly clerks who stood all day at their high desks in the Foundry Square Head Office – truly still at that time a Victorian counting house.

Early one morning during this period the clerk in charge of the Harbour Office on North Quay, a man who never missed any occurrence, however small, was doing his rounds of the quays and waterways when he noticed a foreign registered fishing vessel, lying on its side and stranded on the sandbanks of the Cot Pool. It was French, and was apparently abandoned. Hastening back to the Harbour Office, he duly informed his superiors on the extension phone and the corporate wheels were set in motion. Due umbrage having been taken at this incident having occurred in their harbour without their being notified, and the persons involved having departed without paying their respects, or more pertinently any financial dues that might well have arisen, Harvey & Co. it seems, at once contacted all the relevant authorities to enquire what exactly had happened.

It is said that they were extremely miffed and quite affronted when they were informed that the matter did not concern them and to forget all about the boat and its occupants, in effect to mind their own business.

Of course, as was quite normal in wartime Britain, the rumours ran around Hayle like a forest fire. The most logical and certainly the one held by those who worked on or frequented the quays and harbourside pubs, and seemed to be more 'in the know' than many others was that the vessel had come across from occupied France on a clandestine mission carrying British agents, and being unfamiliar with Hayle had taken the wrong channel and grounded on the sandbanks. The hulk of the fishing boat forever after known as the 'French Crabber' lay on its side, providing a useful diving platform for the Hayle children until it gradually rotted down to just a single rusty iron keel late in the century, its mystery mission, if such it was, being long-forgotten.[1] The above account, because of wartime security and secrecy is, as stated, based mainly on local supposition and hearsay.

Recently an alternative explanation has been offered by the St Ives Archive Study Centre. Their information is that the vessel was simply one of three sailing tuna boats that escaped from Concarneau to the UK. The article containing this version does not explain why this vessel separated itself from the other two, which went into Newlyn, and it then came around to Hayle; and why it is that to this day it has remained unidentified by name or number unlike the others, and why it was simply left, unclaimed, to rot away.(2) One recent explanation is that she was a tunny boat which after the crossing was found to be badly damaged, so was being brought into Hayle to be laid up and repaired at Lelant. Piloted in by a St Ives fisherman she became stranded on the sandbanks of the Cot Pool, and after inspection was considered beyond repair and so left abandoned.(3)

The hulk of the mystery 'French Crabber', c1949.

Photograph: the author

Chapter Fourteen:

SOCIAL LIFE
The Light in the Darkness

IT IS DIFFICULT to convey the atmosphere in wartime Hayle to the two generations that have been born since the times that are written about in this book. Many people, even some in their early sixties, will have no recollections of the town in the war years. Imagine the entire district in total darkness all the night hours, with not a glimmer of light from any window; and street lights dormant and unused. In the evenings the families in their blacked-out houses would sit around the fire listening to their 'wireless' sets, with mother, perhaps, weaving camouflage nets that hung from hooks by the fireplace, or knitting heavy vests from balls of parcel string with large wooden needles, for the seamen on the convoys to Russia. The streets would be dark unless illuminated by moonlight, or on cloudless nights by the faint eerie starlight. There were no signposts to guide you – all had been removed in order not to assist an invading German army. A few people used hand torches suitably dimmed with tissue paper, but batteries were always in very short supply.

In contrast, however, the church halls, cinemas and the pubs were warm and welcoming and very much used. It should not, therefore, be inferred from the grim accounts of 'black-out' conditions, food rationing, empty shops, cessation of most local sports activities and the departure of the younger men from the town, that a miserable atmosphere of doom and gloom descended on Hayle during the wartime years. Quite the contrary, in fact, was the case. The population responded in a spate of activities for entertainment for all ages on a scale not seen before the war or since; even in the hedonist youth culture of the latter years of the twentieth century. Committees were formed for organised events such as the savings weeks described in other chapters. Local musicians formed themselves into dance bands to play at the regular dances held at the Drill Hall or the popular Masonic Hall. Sewing groups made comforts for soldiers, and cadet units were formed for the pre-service age youngsters.

The Palace Cinema at Copperhouse flourished throughout the war years. With a programme change three times a week, it would be full every evening with many people often turned away. The films were usually American or British 'flag wavers' depicting heroic deeds by 'our boys' interspersed with lighter fare such as comedies and star-studded musicals. If the air raid siren had sounded – it was inaudible in the cinema – a hastily scratched overlay stated that: 'Patrons may leave to take shelter if they wish, but the programme will continue.'

Best loved of all, however, was the 'Hayle Merrymakers' concert party. They endeared themselves in the hearts of the people of Hayle and the surrounding towns and villages. Their concerts were eagerly awaited and invariably packed out. Started by and featuring mainly the Quinn-Moon families the success of their shows and the slickness of the performances were excellent by any standards. Under their motto: 'For Others' they usually comprised the Producer/Director, MC and comedian Mr Norman 'Norrie' Quinn: his nieces Iseult, Stella and Vera Moon; main musician Desmond Philp; and other performers when available. Norrie was the usual link-man, comedian and raconteur. He regularly brought the house down with locally-referenced anecdotes and his famous rendition of *The Little Pudden Basin that belonged to Auntie Flo*. The piano accompanist was Miss Iseult Moon (later Mrs I. Tonkin) and her sister Stella was a solo singer. Mr Des Philp was a regular with virtuoso performances on the 'banjolele' and guitar. Miss P. Hayes played the piano-accordian. At a concert on 25th September 1941 the *Cornishman* reported that in addition to the regular performers noted above, a Cornish tale recited by Mr Blight of Lelant, the 'well-known raconteur' was the high spot of the evening and 'greatly appreciated.' The compere on this occasion was Mr Clifford Harris. The concert ran to a second night and raised £24.(1)

Over the year 1943, the *Hayle Merrymakers* raised over £1,000 for charity, and from January to December 1944 the concert party gave 72 shows raising approx £700. The *Cornishman* recorded that 'no member received any remuneration for services given.'(2) With most of them now long dead, and largely forgotten, Hayle should be very proud of its 'Merrymakers' – they brought great credit to the town, brightened its image and enhanced its reputation in the wartime days and after.

For the younger children, at their parties and tea-treats and other festive occasions the entertainment invariably included a demonstration of 'magic' by 'Professor Edgar' the 'Hayle Wizard,' a conjurer and ventriloquist. By the time of the war years, he was getting close to old age and was naturally beginning to lose the manual dexterity that had been perfected over many years. The result was, sadly, that a large part of his act would be interrupted by the children shouting: 'It's up your sleeve' or 'It's in your pocket' correctly denoting the location of a hidden card or other object. In fact, quite inadvertently, in his latter days the conjurer was performing a Tommy Cooper style act thirty years earlier than the star.

On the more slightly serious side, the Hayle Drama Class were giving concerts with music supplied by Phillack Orchestra under the direction of Miss Monique Pool

---

The Hayle Merrymakers Concert Party, photographed post-war.
Back row, left to right: Norman 'Norrie' Quinn; Howard Cowlin and Syd Bennett.
Front row, left to right: Des Philp; Ivy Jose; Iseult Tonkin and Norma Quinn.

Photograph via: Mrs Philp

The St Erth Operatic Society is reported to have performed 'an excellent production of *The Rajah of Rajapore* for the Prisoners-of-War Fund,' which was 'well received.'(3) Later the same group presented *Pedro the Fisherman*, J & F. Pool Ltd had a Works Entertainment Committee. The officers were: Chairman Mr E.S. Turner; Secretary Mr E.G. Peek; Treasurer Mr J. Lawry. In December 1942 a dance was organised by 'B' shift of J & F Pool.(4)

Of all the social events of the war years in Hayle, the most popular, especially with the younger age group were the dances held every Saturday, and very often midweek too. With the town full of young unattached servicemen, there were partners in abundance for the young ladies of Hayle – and even the not-so-young. Also prominent among the younger girls would be the members of the Women's Land Army (WLA) dancing in their distinctive uniforms and with their hats slung on their backs Mexican-style. The music for the larger dances was supplied by the numerous dance bands both civilian and military from the army units stationed locally. On other occasions up-to-date recorded dance music would be supplied by a young Mr Gerald Berry with his portable turntable, amplifier and loudspeaker.

A sample list of the dance bands that played at Hayle over this period would include:
- The Arcadians (under Francis Andrews)
- The Climax Light Orchestra
- The Corona Dance Band
- The Crewenna Dance Band
- The Cremona Dance Band
- The Elite Dance Band
- The Hayle Pre-Service Dance Band
- The King's Own Regimental Dance Band
- The Martlets Dance Orchestra
- The RAF Nighthawks Dance Band
- The Riff-Raff Dance Band (RAF Portreath)

There was also the Hayle Variety Orchestra under its leader Mr Roy Polkinghorne, the Hayle Post Office counter clerk, who also played occasionally as a guest in some of the above bands.

Under the control and supervision of a lively and urbane MC these dances were real community and social occasions. The usual standard 'pair' dances such as the 'quickstep,' 'waltz,' 'foxtrot' and for some expert couples the 'tango' would be interspersed with the very democratic 'general excuse me' waltz where part way through the dance a man or girl could tap a couple on the shoulder and ask that the partner dance with him or her. The 'general excuse me' would be followed later in the programme by a 'ladies invitation' where social practice was reversed and girls were free to invite any man to dance the next number with them. The protocol was that despite, perhaps, being asked by the least attractive 'wallflower' the man was honour-bound to dance that dance with her; a gentle courtesy quite alien to and unthinkable in the cruel attitudes of today.

Another popular method of mixing the dancers was the 'Paul Jones' where the men would form a large outer circle, holding hands and facing inwards and the young ladies would form an inner circle facing outwards. To the tune of *Here we go round the Mulberry Bush* the two circles would rotate, one clockwise and the other anti-clockwise, until when the music suddenly stopped the couple who happened to be facing each other were partners for the next dance. It is hard to imagine such dances being possible in the surly, selfish, possessive days of the 21st century – they simply would not work.

Much hilarity and almost 100% participation took place in the non-partner communal dance numbers such as the *Palais Glide*, the *Hokey-Cokey* and the newest of all, the American-imported *Conga* where to the well-known rhythm of a South-American tune, a line of dancers would form, one behind the other hands on the hips of the person in front and following a flamboyant leader at the head, snake-like they would twist and turn around the hall in convoluted bends and circles, often bursting out through the front door and around the building with the front of the 'snake' re-entering the door as the tail end was leaving – and all to the repeated chorus of *Ay! Ay! Conga* matching the beat of the music and with hips swaying and legs kicking out to the side in unison. Perhaps these popular group dance items were symptomatic of those dangerous days, and the unconscious need to join as one in a socially cohesive manner to reinforce a sense of togetherness that external circumstances do not require today.

More restrained entertainment in the traditional Cornish style was provided by the Ventonleague Prize Male Voice Choir under their conductor Mr Cyril Williams. A Christmas concert in December 1941 included the soloists: Mr H. Biggleston, Mr Pellow and Mr M. Jane; together with the contralto Miss M. James, and the soprano Miss Emily Murphy.(5)

Fund-raising for medical charities in those pre-NHS days continued with even greater vigour, but sadly St Michael's Hospital was not able to hold its annual fete for the duration of the war, but the organising secretary Mr S.S. Spray announced that a

The ICI Bromine extraction plant at North Quay, Hayle.
The factory produced anti-knock additive for aviation fuels,
the UK's only source during WWII, and did a sideline of ladies cosmetics.

Photograph: the authors collection

flag day would be held instead.(6) In December 1942 Mr J. Daniel of Hayle had raised £1-13s for St Michael's Hospital X-ray Fund by selling a coconut (an extremely rare item at this period).(7)

The *Cornishman* of 16th December 1942 published the annual statistics for 1941 relating to St Michael's. The hospital had 60+ beds and recorded 723 admissions, 336 medical and 387 surgical. There were 210 major operations and 279 minor. 1,500 X-ray examinations were carried out and there were 4,504 massage and electro-therapy treatments. The hospital was classed as 1A in the Emergency Medical Service.(8)

To prepare for their medical and surgical needs the people of Hayle and St Ives etc. could join the St Michael's Hospital Contributory Scheme which had started in 1930 with 30 members, and by 1942 had expanded to a membership of 2,200. The Chairman of the Fund was Dr W.H. Palmer, and the Hon. Treasurer was Mr B. Gilbert. In 1941 they collected £1,303-11s and paid for 94 in-patients and 94 out-patients.(9)

The author's mother's wartime ID card which allowed access to North Quay and the Hayle Power Station where she was employed.
Authors collection

Young children's interests were looked after by the Hayle Infant Welfare Committee – a formidable body of dedicated ladies. The Chairman was Mrs V. Wills; the Secretary was Mrs Kessel; the County Assistant Superintendent Miss Bath; and the Committee: Mrs S. Peek, Mrs Sandercock, Mrs Michel and Miss Carvolth.(10)

In 1942 Cornwall County Council advertised for a 'Ward maid and helper at the Emergency Maternity Home, Hayle. Apply Miss G.I. Ellis, Bodriggy House, Hayle.'(11)

Social activities for women included the Copperhouse Bible Class under Miss Runnals, and the Copperhouse Sisterhood with Mrs Roberts. Foundry Methodist Church had the Foundry Women's Bright Hour with Mrs J.M. Naisbit, piano player Miss P. Richards; and the Foundry Methodist Guild was conducted by Miss A.M. Rodda.

To make up for the lack of adult labour it was the practice in WWII to employ schoolchildren extensively, both in voluntary work and in paid employment. mostly in support of their often very poor families.

The voluntary tasks, such as collecting waste paper and tin cans for recycling, would be conducted via the various youth organisations such as the Boy Scouts and the cadet units. Paid work usually consisted of newspaper delivery and shop assistant work or as a grocer's errand boy; and, of course, various work on the neighbouring farms. In August 1942 an advertisement was published by Cornwall War Agricultural Executive Committee regarding 'Employment of Schoolchildren in Agriculture, Redruth and Helston District.' It goes on to state that: 'Arrangements have been made for the following schools to close for the periods indicated for the special convenience of farmers urgently needing additional labour. Children must be over 12 years old.'

    31st July to 28th August 1942
    Basset Road Council School
    Bodriggy Council School
    Penpol Council School
    Hayle Foundry LCC School. LCC = London County Council (evacuee) School
    Hayle Copperhouse LCC School.(12)

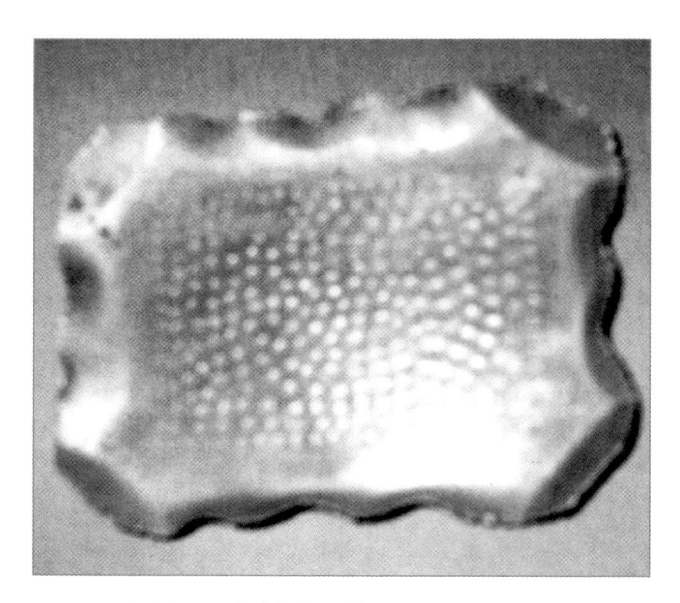

Ashtray / Trinket Tray.
Tray's like this were made, unofficially, by workers at J & F Pool's Factory.
Photograph: the author

Twenty-seven other schools were listed from Leedstown and Connor Downs to St Agnes and Mount Hawke. All of them were elementary schools which were providing the basic minimal level of education to enable the pupils eventually to work in their pre-destined occupations as shop assistants or factory hands and agricultural labourers. Even this meagre scale of education was to be temporarily curtailed and replaced by manual labour.

These little serfs were paid 4d per hour (13s-4d per 40 hour week) – lower than the wages of mid-Victorian agricultural workers. It is of note that the pupils attending the County and Grammar schools did not have their already enhanced education reduced in this arbitrary manner – it was simply the poorer and most socially-deprived children who were accorded this privilege by Cornwall County Council.

Hayle at this period had a small number of private schools ranging from the well-known and highly regarded Hayle Grammar School (known locally as *Wagner's*) on Station Hill, down to a number of minor prep schools usually owned and run by ladies of uncertain age. Among these were the Hayle Kindergarten and Preparatory School, Principal Miss I.G. West, NFU, MRST. Miss West's school mostly averaged 14 pupils. There was also the Riverside School, 54 Commercial Road, Principal Mrs L.S. Tredinnick.

In April 1943 there was a firm indication of the approach of final victory and the lightening of life in the fact that in future church bells, the former dread warning that a German invasion of Britain had commenced, could now be rung freely.(13) Reminiscences of pre-war rural pastimes were stirred by the announcement that a Horse and Pony Show in aid of the Red Cross Local Prisoner-of-War Fund would take place on Saturday 28th August 1943 at Treloweth Manor St Erth, organised by the St Erth Horse and Pony Society, President W.A. Eddy, Chairman R. Warren Esq.(14)

Most people in Hayle possessed a radio or 'wireless' as it was then known, and the programmes were very popular in the long dark winter evenings. They included serious war reports and discussion groups and the light entertainment and comedy programmes. The 'listening in' as it was termed reached a peak of popularity particularly in the younger generation during the lead up to D-Day, when a combined service was started called, 'The Allied Expeditionary Forces Programme.' This included many pre-recorded American radio productions, especially comedy shows with leading Hollywood stars; and big band performances, the best-known being Glenn Miller with his 'American Band of the AEF' which was based in the UK and broadcast live using the BBC studios. At the time a number of houses in Hayle still had no electricity supply, relying on town gas for lighting, cooking and heating. These people had to have battery powered radio sets, with high-tension and grid-bias batteries, and the well-remembered low tension lead-acid accumulators which had to be recharged every week at Mr Berry's or Blewett's radio shops; or if one was lucky to have a relative who worked at the power station the accumulator could be charged free in the charging room.

Christmas in wartime Hayle was by modern concepts of that festival a very unusual occasion. Whether anyone at the time speculated if the Christ-child favoured one side or other in the conflict is not clear, and we cannot know. Certainly British public opinion was utterly convinced that God supported the Allied cause. Not a glimmer of realisation was ever given to the fact that the people of Germany were simultaneously celebrating their *Weinachten* despite the atheistic principles and philosophy of the Nazi hierarchy.

In blacked-out Hayle no church bells could ring out, no carol singing groups strolled the streets. However, behind their blacked-out windows in the chapels of Foundry, Copperhouse, Ventonleague, Mount Pleasant and Angarrack the beautifully blended voices would harmonize on the rendering of such well-loved Cornish carols as *Lo the Eastern Sages Rise* and *Lo He Comes an Infant Stranger*; while at Phillack Church and at Father Faithfull's High Anglican St Elwyns, classical renderings of *Hark the Herald Angels*, with the choirboys descant soaring to the uppermost height of J.D. Sedding's magnificent building.

For the duration of the war, Midnight Mass at the Roman Catholic Church of the Holy Ghost at St Michael's Hospital was out of the question for all sorts of reasons. A tradition had grown up in Hayle, that for many years a large proportion of the congregation for Midnight Mass was made up of worshippers from other denominations in the town, both Methodist and CofE., despite the fact that the service was entirely in Latin, and the great Christmas hymn *Adeste Fideles* (*O' Come All Ye Faithful*) was also sung in that language. A short carol service was held just prior to midnight when familiar traditional carols in English were sung for the benefit of the guests. So during the war mass was held on Christmas morning when the main body of the nuns, whose chapel it was,

---

On the right is J & F Pool's No. 1 Works with Pool's office on the left.

Photograph: the authors collection

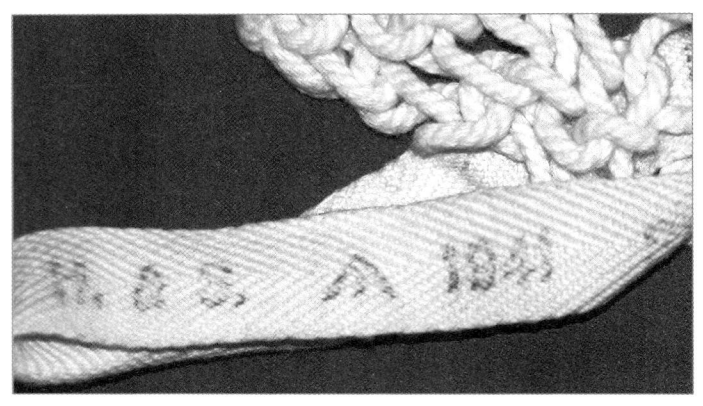

This is a genuine World War II Artic Convoy string vest as issued to Royal Navy personnel. The vests were knitted by housewives in Hayle, St Ives, Penzance, Newlyn and Mousehole who also made camouflage netting at home.

The Items were taken to Hamptons factory in St Ives for inspection and processing.

Photograph: M.M. Sullivan - authors collection.

---

would gather together with the local Roman Catholics who used it as their parish church. The numbers would be swelled by the inoffensive Italian soldiers, in their uniforms marked with prisoner-of-war patches, marched over from St Erth.

On Christmas morning the young children of Hayle would wake to find toys, mostly of a military nature such as model tanks and ships, made locally from wood; and for the girls second-hand dolls dressed in home-made uniforms as Red Cross nurses etc. There were no oranges or Brazil nuts to fill their stockings and very few sweets. Things would improve vastly for children with the arrival of the American soldiers who would organise lavish tea parties for them with sweets and presents generously given and paid for by the GIs. Mothers and teenage girls presents were a problem that could be solved helpfully by buying the limited 'home-made' range of clandestine cosmetics and lipsticks produced in the laboratories at the large ICI chemical complex on North Quay. The make-up was supplied in all sorts of odd shapes of recycled pots etc. with crude typewritten labels. These products helped to sustain the needs of Hayle women throughout the war. Likewise fathers could be presented with ashtrays fabricated from aluminium and produced unofficially during night shifts at J & F Pool's factory.

For Christmas dinner mothers would roast a plump chicken or 'fowl' as they were invariably called in those days, always locally killed, picked and cleaned. Christmas puddings were made to the wartime recipes with grated carrot serving as a substitute for the unobtainable dried fruit. The traditional Cornish Christmas saffron cake and buns had to be made using the highly coloured 'saffron' flour.

Through Christmas Eve and night, silent watchers would be positioned around the town and the surrounding hills. Not shepherds tending sheep but duty AA gunners in steel helmets, and with greatcoat collars turned up, leaning on their gunpit walls, watching the night sky, binoculars ready, looking not for Santa and his sleigh but for possibly much more deadly manifestations in aerial transit. Along the coastline of the bay, on the cliffs gunners and Home Guards shivering in the chill of the early hours alert not for approaching 'Magi' and their guiding star, but the possible sighting of an enemy vessel, and a brilliant star-shell heralding the arrival of an invasion fleet. So the quiet wartime Christmas night would pass over the darkened town. A truly 'silent night' lit only by moonlight or starlight awaiting the dawning glow in the east to announce another wartime Christmas Day.

Chapter Fifteen:

AIR CRASHES
Hayle Area

FROM TIME TO time a great excitement would spread among the youngsters in Hayle with the news that an aircraft had crashed or crash-landed in the vicinity. The first of these occurred fairly early in the war when at 20.40 hrs on the 7th November 1940 a Lockheed Hudson No. P3124 of 220 Squadron based at RAF St Eval made an emergency landing between Black Cliff and Strap Rock, on the beach near Gwithian. The aircraft was extensively damaged, but the pilot P. Travell and his crew of three survived the crash.(1) In July 1989 Mr Travell returned to the scene and later signed the Phillack Church visitors' book.(2)

On the 2nd February 1941 a most intriguing incident occurred in St Ives Bay when a Consolidated Catalina Mk1 flying boat No. W8405 at 16.45hrs, '. . . landed (sic) in the sea off St Ives. Crew of four and two civilians (Canadians) safe. Aircraft was making for Pembroke Dock when told by radio to proceed to Plymouth, but on arrival it was fired on by AA guns, there was slight damage to the wings, and aircraft flew off to land at St Ives. Important papers were being carried and these were taken to London. Safe arrival confirmed and plane departed for Pembroke Dock.'(3)

On the 24th March 1942 a much more serious and tragic incident occurred over St Erth when at 22.00hrs two fighter aircraft from RAF Portreath collided in mid-air. Spitfire Vc No. AE462 flown by 35128 Squadron Leader D.E. Cremin DFC c/o of No. 66 Squadron RAF Portreath crashed at Frythens Farm and was burnt out; the pilot was killed. He was buried in the RC plot at Wardour, Wiltshire, presumably his home town. The second aircraft Spitfire Vc No AB496 piloted by 404315 Sgt W.D. Norman, Royal Australian Air Force of No. 130 Squadron crashed in a field at Trevessa Farm and was burnt out. Sgt Norman was killed.(4) He is buried in the Military Cemetery section of Illogan Churchyard, a beautifully kept but poignant place where are buried officers and other ranks who died when serving at RAF Portreath in WWII. Many were overseas servicemen; Australians, Canadians, New Zealanders and Polish – British casualties could be buried in their home parishes if their family so wished, and a few sad gravestones denoting 'unknown RAF flyer of WWII.' Sgt Norman's stone carries the family inscription; *Tell England he died for her and here he lies content*.

On the 25th March, 1941 it is recorded that at approx. 15.30 hrs Handley Page Hampden No AT118 of 50 Squadron crashed at Rosevidney Farm, St Erth, the four crew having baled-out safely after engine failure when heading for its home base at RAF Swinderby, Lincolnshire. The aircraft was burnt out.(5)

On the 3rd of August 1942 an Armstrong Whitworth Whitley bomber No. Z9190, YG-J of No. 502 Squadron based at RAF St Eval was on patrol off south-west Cornwall when an engine fire broke out. Coming in over St Just trailing smoke an attempt to reach RAF Predannack was unsuccessful, and the aircraft was forced to crash-land on the beach at Hayle.(6) Coming in from the sea, low over the waves, the aircraft, by some miracle, managed to avoid the people on the busy beach and finally came to rest at 15.20 just touching the barbed wire surrounding the minefield that stretched from The Bluff Hotel to the river mouth – a lucky escape indeed, a few feet further in and the Whitley would have been blown to pieces.

Of the crew of six two were seriously injured and one was slightly hurt.(7) The crew were assisted through the minefield area by troops of the Green Howards who were stationed on Hayle Towans, and taken to the Towans Stores & Cafe where they were given a meal by Mrs Williams, the proprietor.(8) The nose-art of the aircraft was of the famous *Daily Mirror* wartime cartoon character 'Jane' in her negligee diving down cradling a large bomb in her arms.(9) Although the intrepid Hayle youngsters – including the author – managed to sneak aboard and into the Whitley, they were soon chased off by the RAF guards. The aircraft was then dismantled into its assembly sections, and removed from the scene most carefully on 'Queen Mary' transporters.(10)

On the 20th October 1942 a Miles Master No. T8512 training aircraft from RAF Portreath landed in a field at North Cliffs, two miles north-west of Camborne. The crew of two were both injured. The accident occurred at 16.45hrs.(11)

Another incident concerning a Lockheed Hudson, this time from RAF Davidstow, occurred on the 29th of March 1943 at 18.40hrs when the aircraft came down in the sea, one mile east of St Ives. Of the five crew one was confirmed dead and four were missing.(12)

The next crash on Hayle Beach was that of the B-17F Flying Fortress on the 5th April 1943. This incident is described in detail in a separate chapter.

On the 10th October 1943 at 11.45 a Spitfire No. P8260 A-FE from RAF St Eval crashed at Roseworthy Farm, three miles east of Hayle Police Station. The pilot was uninjured.(13)

Of all the interests in wartime Hayle the most widespread was the identification of aircraft. This is natural as the skies over Britain were beginning to fill with aircraft of all types, friendly and hostile, and it, indeed, could be a matter of life or death if the aircraft overhead was wrongly identified. Many industrial workers were allocated duties as factory rooftop aircraft spotters ready to give a final 'raiders overhead' alarm to close down production, and for the employees to seek shelter. Groups of these spotters together with interested civilians began to form clubs meeting to discuss and test their prowess at 'aircraft recognition'. A magazine titled *The Aeroplane Spotter* was the highly popular official organ of what became the National Association of Spotters' Clubs. In June 1944 an official spotters' club was organised in Hayle (N.A.S.C. Club No. 760) by Mr I. Millett who lived at that time on Hayle Terrace.(14)

Chapter Sixteen:

THE B-17 THAT DIDN'T QUITE GET TO THE WAR

IN MID-1942 the first bomber groups of the United States Army Air Force began to arrive at their designated bases in East Anglia, to form the pioneer units of what was to become the 'Mighty 8th' Air Force in England. The B-17 'Flying Fortress' and the B-24 'Liberator' bombers were flown across the Atlantic using two main routes. The normal and shortest passage was the northern one staging through Greenland, Iceland and Scotland during the summer months; but the severe conditions of the northern winter, however, made the South Atlantic option a more safe and reliable, but much longer route to the UK.

So it was that in early 1943 Boeing B-17F-20-DL Flying Fortress No. 42-3062 pristine-new from the Douglas Aircraft factory at Long Beach California, where 600 of the B-17F model were built under sub-contract, lifted off from a base in southern Florida, almost certainly Morrison Field in Palm Beach, and headed due south far away from the northern hemisphere and the European war zone.

A description of a typical South Atlantic journey a year later by members of the 467 Bomber Group setting out to join the 8th Air Force in Britain notes: 'Morrison Field, West Palm Beach, Florida was the shoving-off base . . . After crossing the Equator, right on the banks of the Amazon River, the next stop was Belim, Brazil – From Belim part of the planes flew to Forteleza and others to Natal.' Later describing the last leg, Marrakesh to the UK, they write: 'Crews kept a very sharp watch for German planes as they skirted Portugal and Spain and passed by the Brest Peninsula . . . Take-off was at 23.45 hrs. At altitude it soon became colder as we neared the northern climes, so out came our woollies. The navigator had to make sure he stayed on his meridian. Too far east and Jerry might come up and give us a good going over. Too far west and we are liable to run out of fuel.'[1]

The usual south Atlantic route was given in another publication as:
- Morrison Field to Borinquen Field, Puerto Rico
- Borinquen to Atkinson Field, British Guiana Atkinson to Belem, Brazil
- Belem to Natal, Brazil
- Natal to Dakar
- Dakar to Marrakesh, Morocco
- Marrakesh to St Eval, Cornwall UK[2]

In the early months of 1943 the Bay of Biscay was an extremely dangerous area for allied aircraft, but one that had to be crossed in both directions for operational reasons. The long-range Ju88C-6 fighters of KG40 had a tactical radius of 1,600 – 1,800 Km (994 – 1,119 miles). In May, the month that 42-3062 made its lone journey northbound to the UK, records show that the Luftwaffe shot down thirteen British aircraft, and in June another eight including the tragic DC-3 G-AGBB of KLM/BOAC which carried the famous actor Leslie Howard. This civil airliner on flight No. 777 from Lisbon to Whitchurch Airport, Bristol was ambushed and shot down at 9 degrees 40 West. On one occasion the Ju88s had intercepted and destroyed an RAF Whitley as far out as 14 West.

When B-17 23062 took-off on the ten to twelve hour final stage from Marrakesh to RAF St Eval, for the crew everything now changed; no longer the lazy sunny cruise through balmy tropical skies. Now the Southern Cross was falling away behind them and they were navigating by the Northern Hemisphere stars, and entering the unforgiving war zone of Northern Europe. As they swung out past Spain in order to avoid the marauding Ju88s, it should be noted that 23062 was not part of an operational bomber squadron positioning, well armed and manned by a fully-trained action-ready crew. This B-17 was a replacement aircraft flying alone with just a five-man Ferry Command crew. Although fully equipped with the necessary turrets and guns, there were no air gunners to operate them. A normal B-17 would carry up to thirteen crew members including trained gunners to man and operate the turrets. In this case 23062 was virtually no more protected than the unfortunate DC-3, throughout the ten plus hour night flight. With the dawn of a day which promised to be sunny and clear, as the bomber swung in to the welcome sight of the rugged coastline of the Penwith peninsula, the crew were just relaxing with their tensions relieved when their tranquillity was shattered by, perhaps, the most heart-stopping incident that could happen on a flight-deck – an in-air engine fire warning.

It was fortunate, if that is the expression to use in such desperate circumstances, that the fire occurred just as the aircraft had reached the west coast of Cornwall. It was just possible that they might have been able to hold out long enough to have reached the cliff-top runways of RAF Portreath only five minutes flying time away; but what a relief it must have been after passing over the unforgiving cliffs and awesome rock-strewn high country, south west of St Ives to suddenly have opened up to them, the great sandy arc of St Ives Bay, as good an area as a pilot, faced with

A photo-simulation of the USAAF Boeing B-17F, 42-3062, which crashed on Mexico Beach, Hayle on 5th April 1943.

Photograph: the author & M.M. Sullivan

an emergency landing situation could desire. There was, however, still one problem. In 1940 to deter German aircraft landing on the long, wide Hayle Beach in the event of an invasion, hundreds of large tree trunks had been set up vertically in a criss-cross pattern. 23062 had to be set down in a narrow strip between the obstructions and the sandbanks and cliffs.

Given the dire circumstances it was a second stroke of good fortune for the crew that the man with a firm grip on the control column that morning was no neophyte boy-pilot with 100 hours, but a very experienced aviator with 3300 flying hours under his belt, a man aged 42 who had flown in all weather conditions on a wide variety of aircraft. For the last two years, before joining the USAAF Ferry Command he had been an American pilot officer in the British Air Transport Auxiliary (ATA), an organisation of men and women civilian pilots who delivered the many aircraft types to RAF stations throughout the United Kingdom in all kinds of weather conditions.(3) Nathan Kohn had been one of the ATA pilots who in April 1942 had ferried the fleet of Spitfire fighters destined for Malta, up to Scotland to be carried aboard the United States aircraft carrier the USS *Wasp*, to be flown-off later in the Mediterranean by RAF pilots in 'Operation Calendar' to reinforce the beleaguered island's air defences.(4)

Given this wealth of experience, what better hands to have your life in under the circumstances than those of Capt. Nathan Stoltzer Kohn, and without question he dealt calmly and coolly with the situation. Skilfully he weaved between the poles and the cliffs, and made a perfect touch-down on the firm sand. Realising that the cliffs and sand hills were coming up fast he took the only option left open to him and retracted the landing gear and slammed the aircraft down on its belly – an action which suddenly brought it to a safe but sandy and salty stop at 10.30hrs on the 5th April 1943.

Life-raft paddle from USAAF Boeing B-17F, 42-3062.

Photograph: the author collection

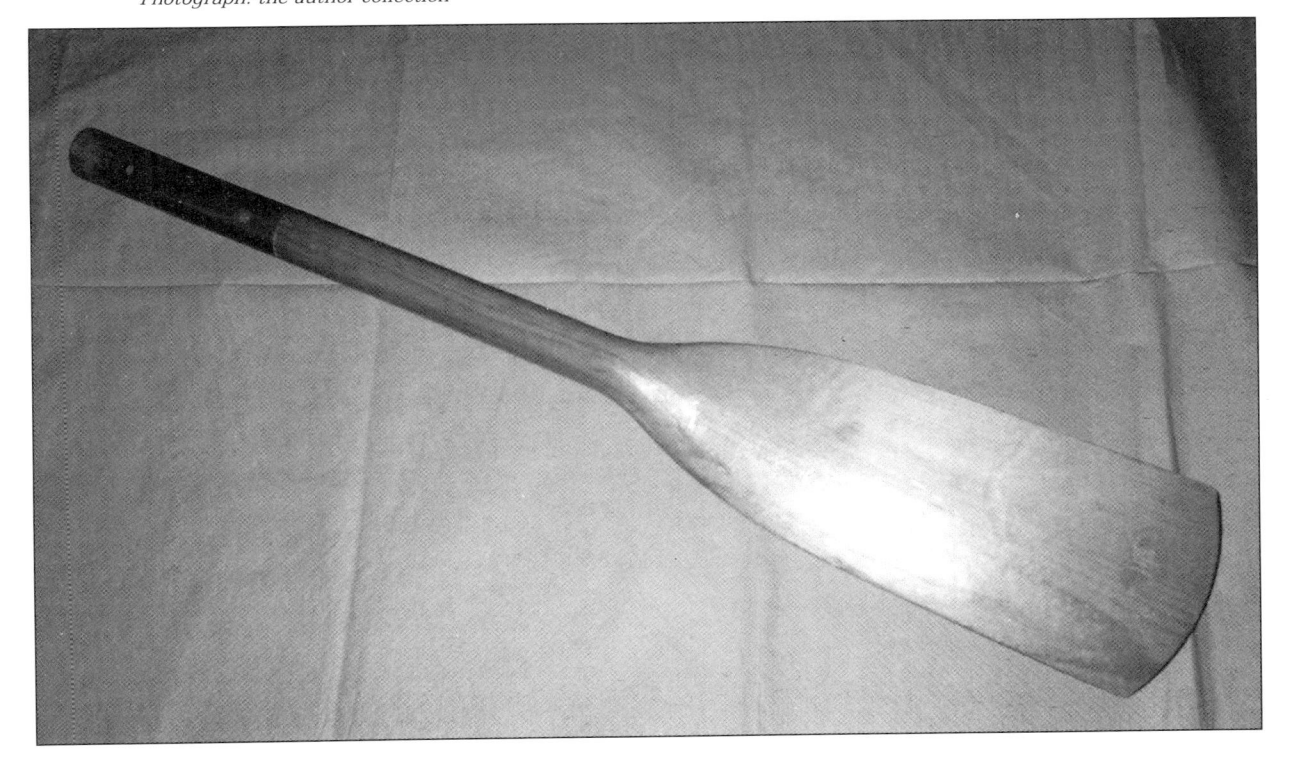

The official USAAF crash enquiry report in its summary states:

> 'On 5 April 1943, Capt. Nathan S. Kohn and his crew took off in B-17F 42-3062, to fly a ferry mission from Marrakesh to the United Kingdom. At about 10.15, there was a fire in flight necessitating an immediate forced landing or bail out. They jettisoned the bomb bay tanks and positioned the aircraft for landing into the wind, on the beach at Hayle near St Ives, Cornwall UK. The elevator control burned away before they could land, but the landing was accomplished using various flap positions to control aircraft pitch attitude. The ship touched down on the wheels, but the crew retracted the landing gear to stop the aircraft in the short distance remaining before reaching the hill. British personnel assisted, and the crew evacuated the aircraft uninjured. The entire aircraft was damaged by fire, salt water, and sand.'(5)

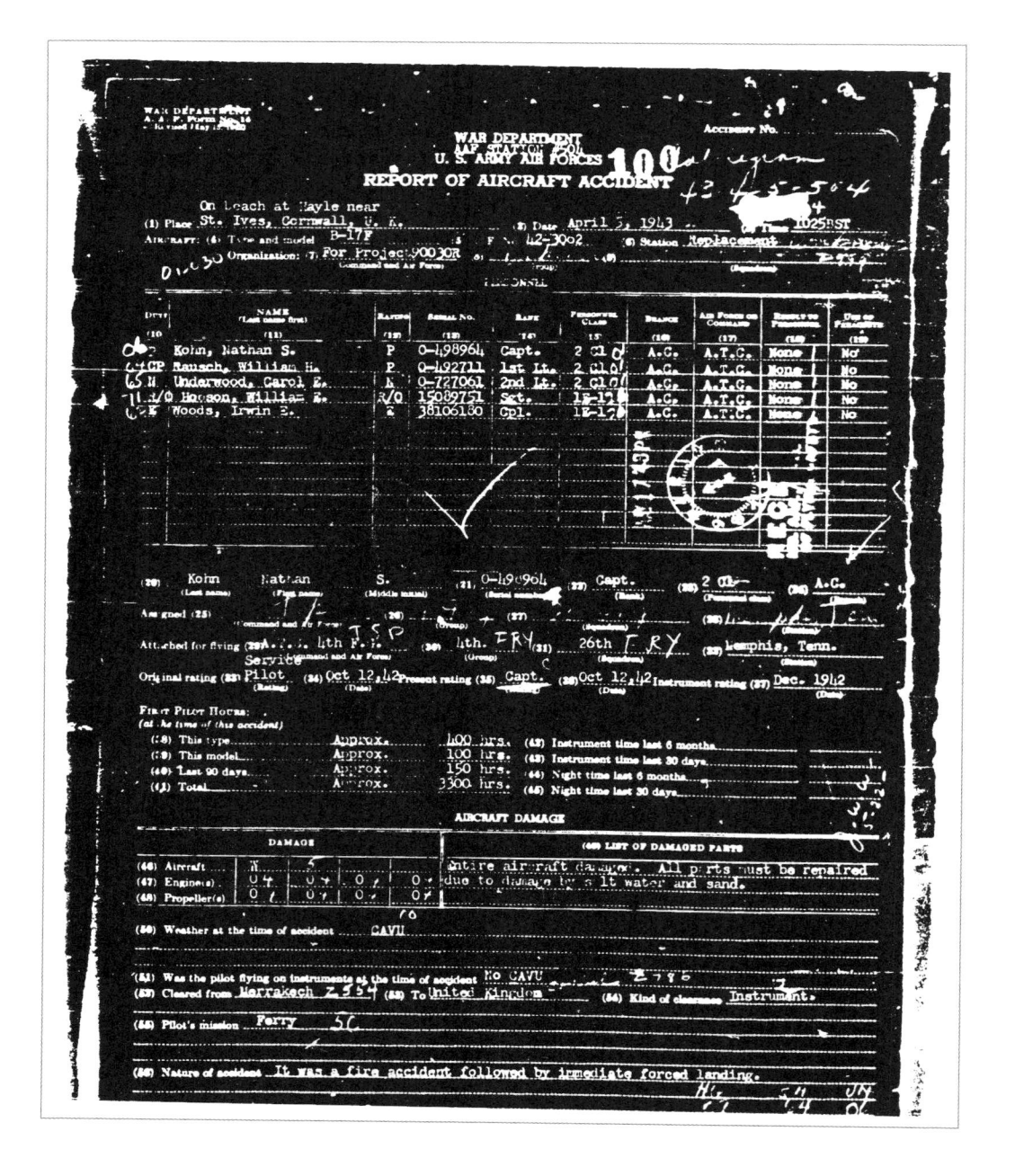

The crew members were:

1st Pilot	Capt.	Nathan S. Kohn
2nd Pilot	1st Lt	William H. Rausch
Navigator	2nd Lt	Carol E. Underwood
Radio Op	Sgt	William E. Hooson
Engineer	Cpl	Irwin E. Woods[6]

Word spread like wildfire amongst the youngsters of Hayle, and by teatime that day the aircraft was surrounded by dozens of kids. Like most of these delivery flights 23062 had been stuffed full of goodies before leaving the USA for delivery to the American airmen in the UK. These items were quite generously distributed to the delighted children who could be seen eating ring donuts for the first time, and other confectionary items unobtainable in strictly-rationed Britain. When the incoming tide had surrounded the stranded aircraft, and the American engineers could do no more work and had departed for the night, the more agile boys would jump up and swing onto the wing-tip, run down the wing and into the fuselage, and avail themselves of any souvenirs that they were capable of removing.

Subsequently with all military equipment removed, the bomber was quite brutally torn apart by the wrecking crew, but a number of pieces were left to be buried by the shifting sands of Mexico Beach. Every once in a while a holiday child digging with his spade will uncover a piece of elevator or a section of corroded aluminium. The Police will be informed and make a note of it; Radio Cornwall producers will get all excited and send a reporter down to interview ageing locals who can remember the incident; and then in a day or two interest will fade once more, and the timeless sands of Hayle Beach will blow across and cover again the few remains of 42-3062 – the B-17 that didn't quite get to the war.

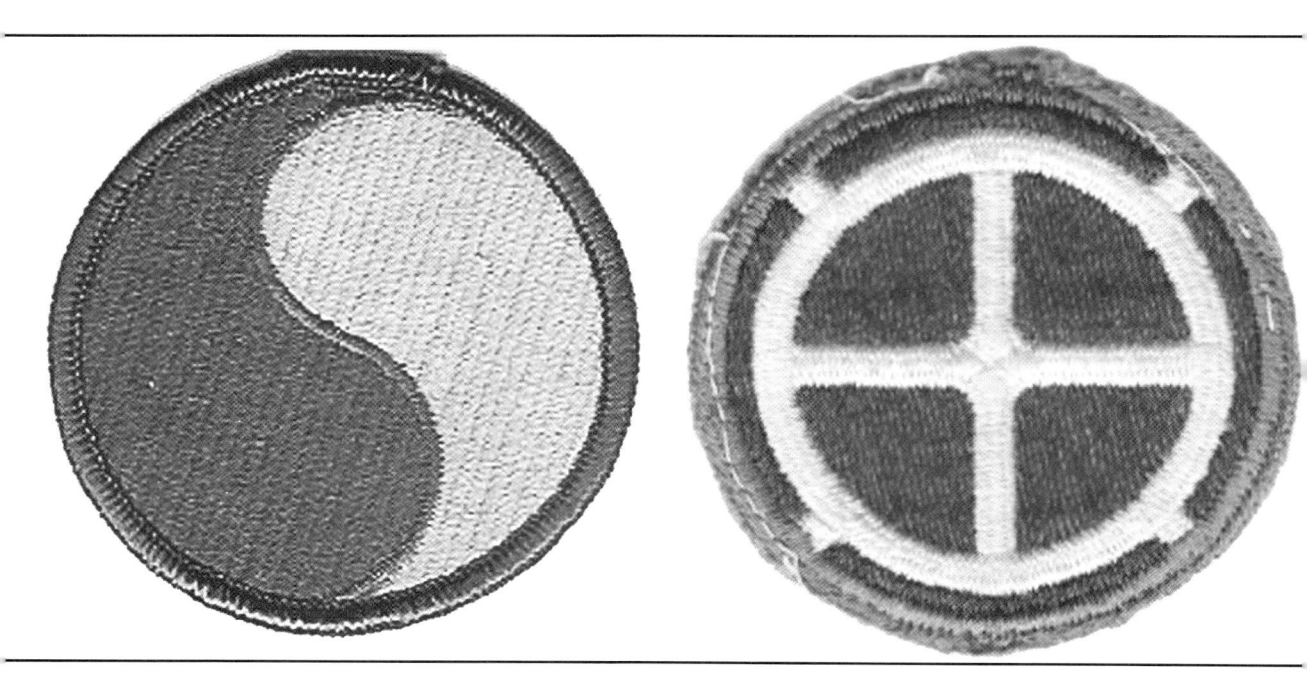

The arm patch of the US 29th Infantry Division (left) who were stationed in Hayle during the run-up to D-Day.

Right is the Arm patch of the US 35th Infantry Division from Kansas, Missouri and Nabraska who where stationed in Hayle during May, June and July of 1944.

The badge is the 'Santa Fe Trail' marker showing a white cross in a wagon wheel on blue.

Chapter Seventeen:

'THEY'RE JUST LIKE US'
The US Army in Hayle

IN ANY COUNTRY at the outbreak of a war after the bringing to readiness of the regular armed forces, and the calling-in of the reserves, the next formations to be mobilised are the civil militias or territorial units. So it was that one of the first reserve formations of the United States Army to be called to the colours after the Japanese attack on Pearl Harbor was the 29th Infantry Division. The 29th Division was a typical National Guard (UK – Territorial Army) outfit raised and based mainly in the States of Virginia and Maryland. It was distinguished by its arm patch of blue and silver not unlike the Chinese Yin-Yang symbol. The Division sailed from New York in September and October 1942 in the *Queen Mary* and the *Queen Elizabeth*, and after several stays at various locations in the south and west of England, they arrived at their final bases throughout Cornwall and Devon in early August 1943. The 29th spent so long in this country that they called themselves 'England's Own'.

In the UK in 1943/44 the Headquarters of the 29th Division was at Tavistock. The troops based in the Hayle – St Ives – Camborne – Penzance and Helston areas belonged to the 175th Combat Infantry Regiment with its HQ at Pendarves, Camborne. Known as the 'Dandy Fifth' the regiment was first raised in 1774 in Maryland. The WWII 175th Regt were mostly from Baltimore. The troops stationed at Hayle and St Ives were the 1st Battalion. The US soldiers were accommodated all across Hayle, mainly in Riviere House and the Penmare Hotel, The Bluff, Taylor's Tea Rooms and numerous bungalows and chalets on Hayle Towans.(1)

During their long stay the GIs endeared themselves to the people of Hayle, especially the children, who suffering under the severe rationing particularly of sweets, were delighted when the Americans were always ready to hand out chewing-gum, Hershey chocolate bars, and other goodies from what seemed an inexhaustible supply of candies. It may be due to having a common language, and the sharing of a mutual heritage via the Common Law, but more likely through the enormous influence of the cinema that the Americans in Britain or ordinary average British visiting America seem to be perfectly at home, blending in seamlessly. Thus it was that the 'Yanks,' as they were universally called in the Second World War, felt at home in Hayle, as one US soldier, based in East Anglia, in a letter home after visiting a local family as a guest, wrote: 'Why, they're just like us, Mom.'

The American soldiers involved themselves in every aspect of social life. The Roman Catholic Chaplains celebrated Mass in the local RC churches and their Methodist Chaplains preached in the Cornish chapels The preacher at Foundry Methodist Church at their Choir Sunday on the 30th April 1944 was the Rev. W.C. Francis, BD of the USA.(2) A number of concerts were given at Methodist churches in Hayle by a group of US soldiers known in the vernacular of the time as *The American Coloured Singers*. Their concert at Angarrack Chapel on Wednesday 26th April 1944 was reported as: 'The first appearance in the West Country.' An address was given by Chaplain Floyd Merrill. The singers 'delighted the audience with songs and spirituals so inimitable to that race.'

Private First Class 'Mike' Foley of the 175th Regt, 29th Infantry Division, US Army.

PFC Foley was stationed at the Penmare Hotel, Hayle between 1943-44. He lost an eye in the Division's attack on St Lo and was awarded the Purple Heart decoration.

Photograph: M. Foley

On the 19th May Ventonleague Chapel hosted the *American Coloured Singers*, Chaplain Floyd Merril, preacher.(3) A newspaper report of the 1st June 1944 noted that at Mount Pleasant Church . . . 'The American Coloured Singers were unable to appear'(5) The date is significant in its proximity to the D-Day operations on the 6th June. Presumably the soldiers were confined to their quarters for security reasons, or too fully engaged in the invasion. However, later in the month the newspapers were able to report that the Mount Pleasant Anniversary Service was conducted by Chaplain Floyd Merrill US Army with a musical programme by the *American Coloured Singers*.(6) Given their appearances at various Hayle chapels, it is probable that the singers came from the black contingent of US Army engineers based at the time in the town, although given the time lapse this cannot be confirmed.

The GIs organised Christmas parties at the soldiers' own expense for the Cornish children, who soon had their favourites among the 'doughboys.' A great character, highly popular with the Hayle youngsters, was a GI of obviously Mexican or South American extraction who was known to all by the nickname of 'Cisco.' He, in fact, looked very like the 'Cisco Kid' of 'B' movie fame, with a tanned face and slim moustache. He would saunter into the little Palace Cinema, his GI hat down over one eye at a jaunty tilt, smoking his cigar at a rakish angle, and with his latest girlfriend proudly on his arm. At his appearance a great shout of 'Cisco!' would arise from the younger members of the audience way down in the cheapest seats; whereupon with a huge grin on his face he would wave to everyone and shower the youngsters with a seemingly endless quantity of chewing gum, Lifesavers candy, and chocolate bars from his well-filled pockets. 'Cisco' was also famous for his ability at the bareback riding of St Michael's Hospital resident donkey on charitable occasions.(7)

So the GIs settled down in Hayle that autumn, winter, spring and early summer, happily mixing with the local population, falling in and out of love with the young girls, or drinking in their favourite pubs from the White Hart to the Angarrack Inn, hopelessly taking on the regulars at darts matches. A very popular pub with the Americans and convenient for those living in Riviere House was the New Inn (now re-named The Bucket of Blood) at Phillack Churchtown. When the landlady Mrs M.G. Taylor, who was well-liked and respected by the GIs, died in early 1944 the report on her funeral on the 12th March stated: 'She was of a genial disposition, and will be greatly missed by all, especially many members of the US Army.' Listed among the mourners is 'a contingent of the US Army.' Among the wreaths was one from 'The boys of the US Army.'(8)

As part of their training for the invasion, in December 1943, the 175th Regt combat troops left West Cornwall and undertook a successful practice attack on Slapton Sands, Devon from landing craft of Task Force 126.4 from Falmouth.

In June 1944 the 175th sailed for France in Convoy B3 (Lt Cdr TW Greene USN) which consisted of twenty-four LSTs from Falmouth, four LSTs from Fowey and three from Helford. The escort was three destroyers, two corvettes, three AIS trawlers and two US Coastguard cutters. All the vessels loaded between 31st May and 3rd June 1944. They sailed at six minute intervals starting at 05.00 on the 5th June. Most of the LSTs towed pontoons (almost certainly Hayle-built 'Rhino Ferries'). The 175th Infantry were ordered to land from the LSTs at 09.30 on the 7th June, on Omaha Beach.(9) The 1st Battalion 175th Regt, C/O Lt Col. R.S. Whiteford embarked at Trebah in LSTs *27, 28, 266* after deploying in a holding area 'sausage' at Long Downs/Helston as Follow-up Force 'B'. The 1st Battalion were to land on Dog Green sector of Omaha Beach on the 7th June. LSTs *27* and *28* left on the third tide plus 2hrs and LST *266* on the 3rd tide plus 4hrs, approx 09.30 and 11.30am.

With the 29th Division now in France fighting their way out from Omaha Beach to the bloody battles for and the capture of St Lo the troops that replaced them in Hayle were the 35th Infantry Division whose arm patch was the same as the route markers for the famous 'Santa Fe Trail' of early Western history and fame. The 35th Division soldiers who arrived on the 8th June 1944 occupied the same accommodation that the 29th had left, but they did not stay very long. They departed for France after only one month, landing there on the 11th July 1944.(10) They later took part in many major actions in central France (and Germany) including the attack on St Lo, and later the infamous Battle of the Bulge.

Another large group of US Army personnel stationed at Hayle at this time were the soldiers of the Engineering Corps engaged on the barge building operations at Carnsew (see Chapter 18 entitled *Rhinos' on the Weir*). They were mostly living in a tented camp set up on the Recreation Ground at Copperhouse. A large proportion of these were black GIs employed mainly on driving the military trucks that carried the pre-fabricated sections of the barges from the railheads at Memorial Walk and St Erth Station.(11)

US Army ID tag of one Sheridan Thompson discovered by Paul Frost when metal detecting in Phillack/Hayle Towans area c.2000.

Photograph: the author

A serious social problem arose in Hayle and Camborne because of these troops colour. It was not with the local Cornish people, who welcomed them just as they did the other white Americans, the problem was with their fellow Americans. The US Division resident in Cornwall at the time was a National Guard formation, locally raised in the Southern states where at that time a colour bar still existed with racial attitudes strongly held. Friction arose for instance at dances in the Masonic Hall and other venues, when white soldiers would intervene if local girls were dancing with black GIs, and tell them to stop. This led to serious disturbances and outbreaks of fighting, sometimes with weapons, and quite beyond the ability of the Hayle contingent of Cornwall Constabulary's regulars and 'war specials' to cope with. The outbreaks would only be quelled with the arrival in Jeeps of the fearsome US Military Police (the 'Snow Drops') in their white painted helmets and carrying and using the long heavy 'nightsticks' and with their 45cal automatic pistols ready in their holsters. An affray at Camborne between black and white American troops resulted in one death.(12) The situation was resolved by applying the rule of allowing soldiers of one race out in the evening, while the others were confined to their billets; and the reverse on alternate nights.

And then they were all gone. The 29th and the 35th from Riviere House and the Penmare, and eventually the Engineers from Carnsew, and Hayle was very strangely quiet and seemed unusually empty. A few survivors of the 29th later came back down from their hospital near Gloucester, some with scarred faces and, perhaps an eye gone, some with only one leg or arm to visit girlfriends or other acquaintances in Hayle but they were few in number and they eventually returned to their own homes and country. Some came back to Cornwall after fifty years to honour the anniversary of D-Day and the memory of their long-dead comrades. In September 1944 Dr Alfred M. Tucker, Captain US Army Medical Corps, thanked the people of Cornwall, especially Penzance.(13)

An hitherto unknown aspect of the US Army's involvement in the D-Day operation and a well-hidden scandal at the highest level was revealed at the retirement of a Penzance GWR guard, Mr Stan Hendra. Retiring after forty-five years on the railway Mr Hendra recalled an incident that happened about three months before D-Day.

Between St Austell and Truro, after leaving Plymouth on a Penzance-bound train, Mr Hendra commenced a routine check on the recently vacated compartments. When checking a 1st class compartment he found a large unsealed envelope marked 'Secret' and with the name of a US General written on it. On arrival at Penzance he contacted the Stationmaster who informed the local Penzance Police, who not wanting to become involved, suggested he contact his superiors. The GWR Superintendent was telephoned and he advised contacting Mr Matthews, Chief Superintendent at Paddington, who duly informed the War Office. They ordered that the plans must stay at Penzance. The envelope was placed in the Stationmaster's office concealed among other papers. A member of the Home Guard was posted outside the door all night until the envelope was collected. When the contents of the envelope had been examined earlier by Mr Hendra and the Stationmaster there were charts of the French coastline and the names of regiments and units to take part in the landings. After the D-Day landings were announced they saw that it was the same stretch of coast and the same troop units landing on the correct designated Normandy beaches.

At the time the Stationmaster had warned Mr Hendra that if any details leaked out: 'We could be shot or put in prison.' Advice that was totally unnecessary as Mr Hendra had served on the Somme in the First World War and realised that the slaughter he had witnessed there could be repeated in Normandy if the secrets passed into enemy hands. In an editorial on the occasion of Mr Hendra's retirement in 1957, *The Cornishman* newspaper castigated the authorities for his not receiving any direct expression of appreciation, although at the time thanks did filter down through various levels from the GWR officials.(14)

Chapter Eighteen:

'RHINOS' ON THE WEIR

AS THE DETAILED planning got under way for the proposed invasion of Europe (D-Day), it was soon realised that for practical reasons many of the smaller vessels and landing craft to be used would need to be built on this side of the Atlantic. So it was that a US Army Engineering Corps Unit selected, among a number of other sites in Cornwall, the Carnsew area of Hayle, known locally as 'The Weir' as an ideal place to construct a large number of pre-fabricated barges. These vessels officially termed 'Rhino Ferries' were built to a US Navy design. Rear Admiral John Wilkes (US Navy) was put in charge of securing and building landing craft for the invasion.(1)

Rhino Ferries were flat-bottomed barge-type vessels rectangular in shape and weighing approx. 500 tons, measuring 200ft in length and 70ft in beam. They could couple to the large LSTs in deep water and load tanks, trucks and guns straight onto the Rhino's unobstructed deck. They were able to completely unload all the vehicles off one LST. Drawing only 2ft of water and powered by two 60hp Chrysler marine outboard motors they were able to ply back and forth to the beaches at a steady 2 to 3 knots. Extremely flexible in use they could be linked together in twos (possibly fours) to make a vessel of up to 1400 tons for greater carrying capacity and at times would carry up to 40 assorted vehicles. They were also used as static support pontoons for the Mulberry Harbour roadways. On 'Operation Overlord' (D-Day) at 'Omaha' and 'Utah' beaches they were operated by the Plymouth-based 111th Naval Construction Battalion (111th NCB) US Navy (The Fighting Seabees) under the command of the 25th US Naval Construction Regiment (25th NCR).

The barges were described in action as '. . . those queer sectional pontoons, like a bunch of oil drums strung together to ferry army transport ashore, driven by a monstrous outboard motor which can be lowered or raised.'(2) Rhinos were operated at the British beaches by the maritime units of the Royal Engineers. This little-known vessel provided an invaluable contribution to the success of the landings, but is rarely recorded in either the many British or US books or official histories. Heavily laden with a massive load of tanks, trucks and troops, and ploughing steadily towards the beaches but presenting an ideal target, inevitably a number of Rhinos and their crews were lost to enemy fire especially at Omaha Beach.

The newsletter of the CEC/Seabee Historical Foundation states: 'They are very useful inventions by the Seabees that made an irreplaceable contribution to the amphibious landings of Army and Marine forces in World War II. The ferries themselves were deceptively simple. It was only a matter of joining a number of the pontoons to form the desired length and width for the floating barge, and then attaching one or more of the specially built outboard propulsion units to the rear of the barge and it was done! But that was the only easy part. The hard part came when it was time to pilot a large slow moving target, totally unprotected, and loaded with critical cargo of men, tanks, artillery and ammunition, towards the landing beach through the churning waters of a hotly contested combat zone. Many brave Seabees died or were horribly injured undertaking this hazardous mission. Many more were lost overboard and never seen again.'

The US Navy operated the Rhinos in three main forms; the standard Rhino in its single, double or quadruple combination (RHF), the Rhino Tug (RHT) and the Rhino Warping Tug (RWT).

The US Army Engineering Corps unit that built Rhino Ferries at Hayle was mainly from Michigan, particularly the Detroit area, and was a mixed race formation. Under the command of Capt. (later Major) Marquette they took over the derelict former shipyards of Harvey & Company, and the Carnsew Spit leading down to the ferry. Local labour was engaged, many coming from towns such as St Ives, Penzance and Camborne although, of course, the largest component of this labour force was composed of men and boys from Hayle.(3)

The civilian labour was engaged, paid and administered by the Totnes-based firm of Frank Curtis Ltd, who also had similar contracts at Malpas, Truro and in the Fowey area. In addition to their American contracts to build Rhinos, Frank Curtis Ltd also undertook to build two Boom Defence Vessels (BDV) for the British Admiralty using traditional methods on the old Harvey & Co. shipyard where fifty years before, the great 4,000 ton steamships such as the *Ramleh* and *Tongshan* had been built. At the height of the maximum production of Rhino Ferries, there were twenty-one slipways in use on the Carnsew Spit launching the barges into the Cockle Bank area of Hayle Harbour or the Cot or Cock Pool across. the Spit. Seven of these slipways were manned and operated by personnel of the US Army Engineering Corps and fourteen were British operated with the workers under the control of Frank Curtis Ltd. It was thought that this arrangement would engender an element of competition into the undertaking, but subsequent checks showed that given the same equipment and power tools there was no difference in output between the American soldiers and the British labour force.(5)

Royal Navy Boom Defence vessels under construction in Hayle.

Photograph: Adrian Southcott, via Mrs Maureen Southcott

The manager at Hayle for Frank Curtis Ltd was a Mr Saunders, although from time to time Mr Curtis himself would come down on routine inspection or to settle disputes should they arise. On one notable occasion when the workforce downed tools because the company had apparently defaulted on a promise and was not paying them the correct bonus, Mr Curtis addressed the men personally near the 'Black Houses' sluice tunnels. Not satisfied with his uncooperative attitude and totally negative response, a large number of the workmen bodily hoisted up the huge American limousine in which he travelled the country, up over their heads, and threatened to throw it into Hayle Harbour if he did not give them what was due to them.(6)

In addition to the local labour force which included a number of key workers brought down from Totnes, some of the labouring work was done by German and Italian prisoners-of-war, closely guarded by GIs armed with Thompson sub-machine guns.(7) The American soldiers were accommodated in such diverse places as Foundry Methodist Chapel schoolroom and even the disused Mellanear Smelting Works of Williams, Harvey & Co. Many others, particularly the black GIs, were in a large tented camp on the Recreation Ground.(8) Conditions at the Recreation Ground were primitive, with washing and bathing facilities being provided by using the river running in front of Beatrice Terrace.

The barges were assembled from pre-fabricated sections shipped over from the United States, some of which were unloaded and stacked at St Erth railway station and many at the spur-line siding laid down from the Hayle Wharves branch along part of King George V Memorial Walk, alongside where the Hayle Swimming Pool is now located. The sections were then loaded on to US Army trucks and carried to the slipways. At Tolroy Garage a petrol pump was allocated to the US Army and manned by a flamboyant GI known to one and all only as 'Michigan' who refilled the procession of trucks all day long.(9)

In May 1944 an inquest was held on Mr William Thomas Cock aged 64 of Angarrack who died after a collision between a bicycle and a US Army 2½ ton 6x6 truck. There were twenty-five men in the truck. Sgt Melvin D. Anspach said they were going to work from the Recreation Ground. The driver was a soldier of the US

Royal Navy Boom Defence vessels under construction in Hayle.
Photograph: Adrian Southcott, via Mrs Maureen Southcott

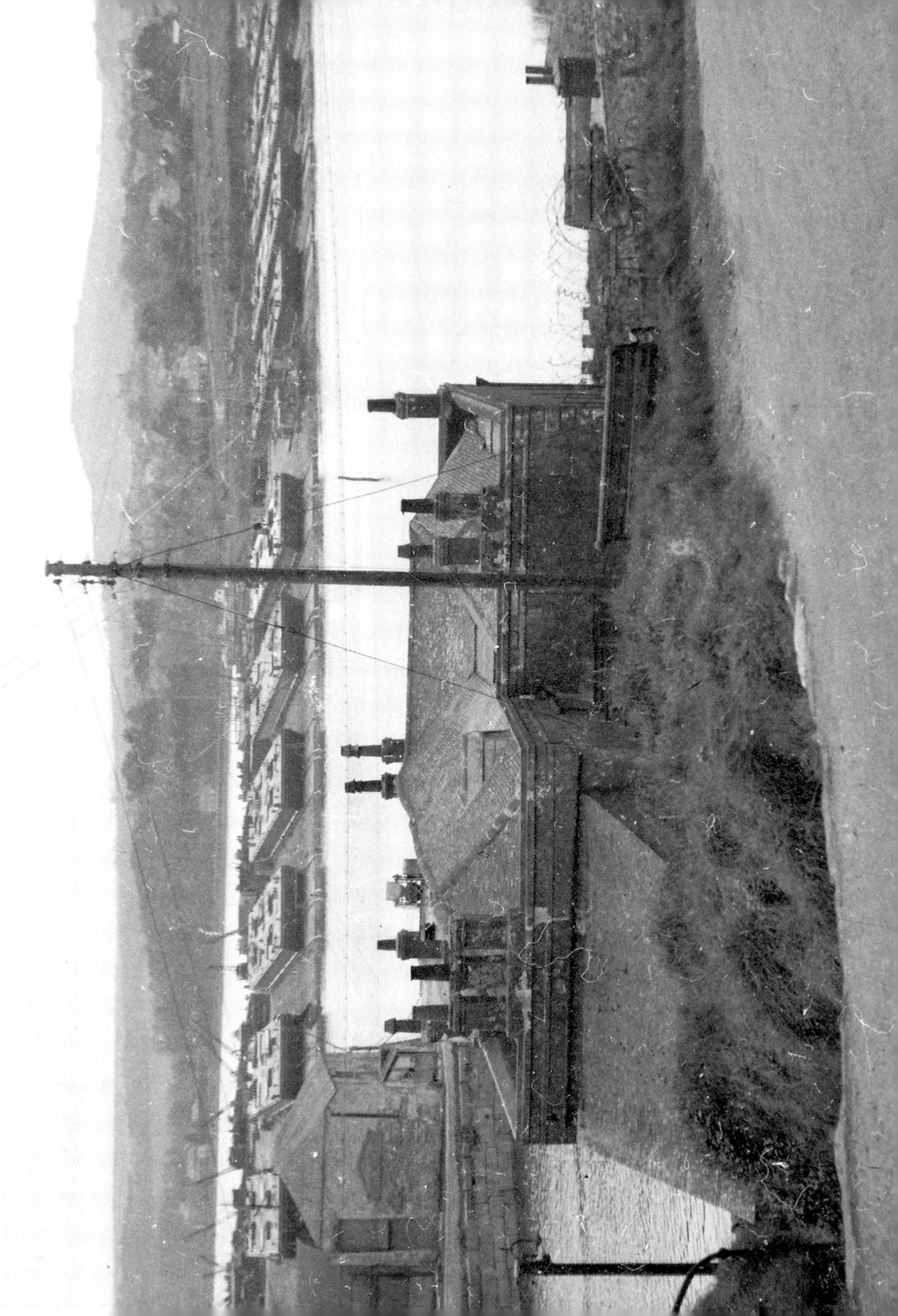

Army, Corporal Sinclair Millar. He had been driving in Hayle for two months.(10) Another serious accident involved the US Army trucks carrying the pre-fabricated barge sections from the temporary siding laid along King George V Memorial Walk. For the journey to the Carnsew slipways the sections were carried on flat-bed trucks and were not tethered. As the trucks swung right, off from the swing bridge onto the main road, the heavy sections would often slide off the trucks. A news report in June 1944 stated: 'Mr John Roberts of Hayle met with a nasty accident which might have had even more unpleasant consequences on Tuesday morning. He was walking on the footpath at the side of the road when an approaching lorry came round a corner. The motion of the vehicle caused two large plates which it was carrying to overbalance and they fell on Mr Roberts, badly injuring his foot. Dr Stephens was called and the Hayle ambulance took Mr Roberts to St Michaels's Hospital.'(11)

The technology introduced by the Americans was awesome by the local standards of the time. Twenty-one Caterpillar cranes, obviously one allocated to each slipway and large numbers of the nippy Hyster cranes painted olive grey drab, which could manoeuvre at high speed with quite respectable loads, and could be seen bouncing through the streets of Hayle all day. A tug named *Seahorse* was stationed at Hayle to tow the completed 'Rhinos' two by two, out to St Ives Bay where they would be collected by US ocean-going tugs waiting to take them away four at a time to the US Navy CB bases such as Plymouth etc.(12)

Unfortunately, but not unexpectedly given wartime shortages, quite a large amount of equipment, tools etc had a habit of disappearing from the site. Many of the pumps and outboard motors simply vanished, and a number of court appearances ensued.

With the success of the D-Day landing the need for barges ceased abruptly, and the age-old problem returned to Cornwall and Hayle in particular, unemployment. The two boom defence vessels under construction, were sold to Thos. W. Ward for scrapping, the ships now being surplus to Admiralty requirements. The name of Frank Curtis Ltd being relegated to join the many others in the history of Hayle.

A curious little incident marked the departure of Frank Curtis Ltd from Hayle, when in July 1945 the company was fined £50 for permitting a quantity of cheese to be wasted, namely fifteen cheeses weighing 431lbs (195.5kg) which was equal to a week's ration for 3,448 persons. On the 14th December 1944 the Food Enforcement Officer, Mr H.W. Turner had agreed that surplus food stocks could be got rid of; six weeks later the cheeses were still there. The Company stated that there had been less demand for cheese as the employees had suddenly been reduced from 800 to 400. Frank Curtis Ltd had nine canteens and had provided for as many as 3,000 men and had never had a conviction before.(13) They had obviously never dealt with Mr Harry Turner, Hayle's ex-police sergeant before.

The local press reported at the end of June 1944 that 250 men became redundant at Hayle where wages had been pretty high at £10 per week. Fifty of these men were directed to work at Devonport for a wage structure of £4 per week plus a lodging allowance of £1-4s-6d plus a 5/- transfer allowance, but with no guarantee of overtime. Many men refused to work for these rates of pay, claiming they could not keep two homes going on this level of income. Four of them were charged and taken before the Bench at West Penwith Sessions.(14)

Facing page:
Rhinos on their slipways along Hayle estuary.

Photograph: Adrian Southcott via Mrs Maureen Southcott

Late in the life of the Hayle shipyard a tragic accident occurred when a man was killed by a metal plate which slipped from a crane.(15) At about the same time a concert was staged at St Ives Guildhall by workers of Frank Curtis Ltd which was attended by Mr Frank Curtis (Chairman of the firm) who thanked everyone. The proceeds of the concert, ominously, went to the 'Employees Benevolent Fund.'(16)

By May 1945 the situation had become extremely serious with *The Cornishman* of the 24th reporting under the headline 'Hayle Fights for Shipyard' that Hayle shipyard had closed and described the efforts of the men's committees to get the yard reopened for commercial shipbuilding and boatbuilding. Meeting in the canteen on Friday the 18th May about 200 men, in the ratio of sixty-five married men to thirty-five single men, decided to finish work at the end of the day; a suggestion that they might continue until the following Tuesday being turned down. The Admiralty had decided that the work on the two Boom Defence Vessels, now so tragically abandoned on the stocks, one three parts finished and the other its bare ribs showing, should cease. It was fifty years since a ship was launched at Hayle: another week or two would have seen another ceremony, but the vessels under construction became redundant with the progress of the war.

A deputation, Mr A. Style (Secretary of the Yard Committee), Mr L. Strongman (representing the shipwrights), and Mr F.G. Cargeege (AEU) went first to Falmouth to see the Port Admiral, and then went to London to see an official of the Contracts and Labour Department of the Admiralty, but received no satisfaction. They then lobbied Capt. Alec Beechman (MP St Ives) and Commander Peter Agnew (MP Camborne) who said that they would use their best endeavours. They next visited Bristol to meet the Board of Trade and the Regional Employment Exchange. They were reassured that everything would be done to help. On their return to Hayle they learned that the Admiralty had definitely decided that work on the two boom defence vessels should cease.

Lt Col. E.H.W Bolitho, Lord Lieutenant paid a visit to the shipyard and promised to do what he could to get new work for the shipbuilders. In the House of Commons on Thursday 17th May Cdr P.G. Agnew (Con. Camborne) asked the First Lord of the Admiralty what work he would allocate to Hayle Shipyard in the immediate future, such as that in connection with the reconditioning and conversion to peacetime requirements of trawlers and other small craft. Capt. Pilkington, who obviously was in total ignorance of the area and its history, replied, in writing. That 'He presumed the establishment he referred to was that at Hayle used for shipbreaking prior to the war, but adapted during the war for the construction and assembly of certain special craft required for war purposes.'(17)

This typically misguided parliamentary gentleman, it seems, had no idea that Harvey & Co's shipyard had been designed for and had built 4,000ton steamships in the 1890s, and was confusing the traditional real shipyard with the temporary American barge-building slipways further down the weir. He continued: 'The Admiralty had carefully considered the possibility of using this establishment for the purpose Cdr Agnew had in mind but had decided it was not suitable.(18) The Civil Service 'Mandarins' at the Admiralty, true to form, were completely out of touch with reality – Hayle Shipyard would have been most suitable for this type of work.

Later discussing the closure of the Carnsew shipyard, Hayle Parish Council was told that about 250 men would be 'thrown out.'(19) On the 2nd August 1945 it was reported that West Penwith RDC had received a letter from the Ministry stating that it was 'Not considered appropriate to maintain the shipyard at Hayle for permanent employment.'(20)

Chapter Nineteen:

CADETS
Teenage Life

THERE CAN BE no question that all interest and activity in WWII Britain was focused on and conducted by the adult population. The unfortunate ones in the scheme of things at the time were the young children of school age. The interests of government, both national and local, were directed almost exclusively, as it had to be, to the conduct of the war and the hoped for eventual victory. Education, except at the higher levels was relegated to a low priority in the struggle for survival. The children at the bottom end of the education system were disadvantaged to a degree that would affect many of them for the rest of their lives. For what we would later come to call the 'teenagers,' however, the story was much different. It may have been that they were being groomed to fight in the armed forces when old enough, but for whatever the reason, large sums were allocated to the formation of cadet units in every town. In Hayle, apart from the Scouts, who had been well established in the town for many years, the main organisations set up were the Army Cadet Force, the Air Training Corps, the Girls Training Corps and the St John Ambulance Brigade Cadets.

The Army Cadets, at first for a short time were known in the town as the 'Home Guard Cadets.' A newspaper report in March 1942 reported the first meeting (in Hayle) of the 'Junior Home Guard,' one of the first in the area. The Officer-in-Charge was the Rev. R.G. Faithfull, and the enlistment was thirty-five boys.(1) They were later given their correct title; Army Cadet Force, Hayle Platoon, D Company, 1st Cadet Battalion, 12 Battalion Home Guard DCLI.(2) The cadets under the command of Lt The Rev. Faithfull, and Sgt (later CSM) 'Bob' Doe met for instruction and drill at the Drill Hall. Sgt Doe, an ex-regular with long military experience, was a superb drill and field-craft instructor and was held in great awe by other cadet units when he was put in charge of the massed parades and drill sessions at annual camp.

The Hayle cadets had the use of the small-bore rifle range at the Drill Hall under the expert tuition of Henry Luke, and also were able to use the full-bore range that he owned on Hayle Towans for their .303 Lee-Enfield firing. The cadets cooperated with the Home Guard during anti-invasion exercises acting as 'runners' (messengers), sleeping overnight on the floor of the Drill Hall, and going out in the morning with the individual sections to take back messages and information to the HQ at Hayle. They also acted as 'casualties' for the purpose of Civil Defence exercises, being bandaged, splinted and carried to St Michael's Hospital in ambulances, from diverse locations in and around Hayle.

The other main cadet unit in Hayle was the Air Training Corps (ATC) formed in November 1941. It was designated No 1834 Flight with the Commanding Officer named as Acting Flying Officer Kenneth Uren (Mr K. Uren was the Hayle Dental Surgeon). The committee appointed was given as: President Lt Col. Norman; Chairman Mr C. Rosewarne, JP, CC; Vice-Chairman Mr T.K. Blackmore; Hon. Sec. Mr H. Bond; Hon. Treasurer Mr H. Michell. There then followed a recruiting drive.(3) On Wednesday 26th November a foundation meeting was held and following volunteer instructors were appointed: Messrs Renowden, Oaks and Nicholls (Morse); Webb (Navigation); Mitchel and Josephs (Mathematics); Penberthy and Morris (Radio);

Jane (Engineering); Mills (Physical Training) and Sgt Major Holland (Drill).(4) On 27th June 1942 the Hayle ATC held their first sports day. The Warrant Officer (WO) for Hayle ATC is given as WO C.L. Mills.(5)

On the 5th July 1942 the Hayle Flight ATC now seventy-two strong held a church parade for 'ATC Sunday' at Foundry Methodist Church. The parade was under the command of FO K. Uren, and the service was conducted by the Rev. J.W. Naisbitt. Afterwards the parade in Foundry Square was inspected by Col. John Ellis, Flt Lt N.A.J. Spencer (the Liaison Officer between the RAF and ATC), and the Commanding Officer FO K. Uren.(6) In 1943 the instructors for Hayle ATC are given as Capt. Reardon, Lt Nicholls and Mr Oaks. The Adjutant is named as PO H.F. Bond.(7) Although not stated at the time Capt. Reardon was an officer in the Royal Signals working at the top secret radio station located at St Erth Praze. He instructed the cadets in Morse Code and Air Navigation. Mr Harry Bond was the manager of the bulk petrol depot on North Quay and had represented Cornwall at cricket and rugby in the 1930s. He subsequently became the Commanding Officer of the Hayle Flight on the retirement of Mr Kenneth Uren.

In January 1943 it was reported that the 'Aircrew section of 1834 Flight ATC held a social evening at St Elwyns Hall.'(8) The ATC at this time was divided into two categories: the 'aircrew' section which studied navigation, the theory of flight and morse code; while the ground trades section which mainly comprised engineering

---

Members of the Hayle Army Cadet Force on August 29th 1942.
Back row: Kenneth Toye; John Casey; DCLI Corporal; Peter Downing;
Nick Berryman; Ivor Ellis and James Uren.
Middle row: Tommy Baumbach; unknown; Stanley Jenkin;
Major Wynne-Harley, Hayle Home Guard; Lt Col. C. Norman, O/C 12th (Land's End)
Battalion Home Guard; Rev. Faithfull; Alex Pybus; 'Skip' Wills;
Brian Sullivan; Charles Pedler.
Front row: Leonard Rowe; 'Plug' Thomas; Cyril Roberts; CSM 'Bob' Doe;
Jack Baumbach; Donald Kemp and ? Stephens.

Photograph: authors collection

apprentices concentrated on aero-engines and rigging. They could work on the BA Swallow aeroplane kept at Loggans Mill. This aircraft was the former G-AESL which had been impressed into the RAF, and taken on charge as 3412M.(9) The BA Swallow 2 was a pre-war two seat light monoplane, wingspan 42ft 8in, length 26ft with a 90hp engine giving a top speed of 112mph.

The Cornishman reported a sad occasion when on the 15th April 1943 the Hayle Flight was called upon to act as bearers and burial party for the funeral of Sgt J.W. (Jacky) Burrows. Wireless Operator/Air Gunner.(10) Only one RAF representative, a sergeant colleague, was present. The RAF may not have been aware of the funeral taking place and a military funeral was not organised although there were thousands of personnel on the seven RAF stations in Cornwall at the time. Sgt Burrows had died in a brave attempt to save a Sunderland flying-boat that capsized in a gale at the RAF No4 (Coastal) OTU at Alness in Scotland.

In June 1943 the annual ATC Sports were held at the Trevassack Cricket Ground (now the home of Hayle Soccer Club) with the Home Guard Battalion Band in attendance.(11) Later a shooting match was arranged between the Hayle Home Guard and Hayle ATC, which was won by the Home Guard. The ATC team is listed as Sgt Dowrick, Cpl Thomas, Cadets Boase, Berry, Stephens, Berriman, Semmens and Pedlar.(12) In February 1944 it is noted that Mr Jack Reynolds the Warrant Officer of Hayle Flight had been promoted to Pilot Officer.(13)

In June 1944 Flight Sergeant P. Bridger of the unit won a University Scholarship in the teaching profession.

In August 1944 Hayle ATC spent a week at camp on the Royal Naval Air Station at St Merryn (HMS *Vulture*, the School of Naval Air Warfare) where they enjoyed flights in an RAF DH Dominie (Dragon Rapide) and a Percival Proctor; and also

---

1834 (Hayle) Flight ATC, 29th August 1942.
In the centre of the middle row are: Kenneth Uren, Commanding Office and Warrant Officer, C.L. Mills.
Holding the cup in the front row is Robert 'Bobby' Peller.

Photograph: via Mrs Marion Peller

underwent the unusual experience (for the cadets) of sleeping in hammocks in Nissen huts.(14)

The Cornishman of 15th February 1945 records an ATC aircraft recognition and rifle contest between the Penzance squadron and the St Ives and Hayle Flights. On the 28th of the same month the Penzance and Devonport High School squadrons paid a return visit for competitions. In aircraft recognition Hayle swept the board with 499 points (Pz 470, DHS 464). A pasty supper was provided and prizes awarded to the top three cadets in each competition.(15) In March 1945 Hayle ATC visited the Devonport High School cadets at their luxury hotel, the Royale, Penzance, for an aircraft recognition contest, thereby awarding the author his only justly earned mention in the text of this book as he is named as receiving a prize for the highest score in the contest.(16)

With the end of the war in Europe changes were announced in the structure of the ATC. Hayle was to lose its independent status as No. 1834 Flight, and together with St Ives become part of No. 24F Squadron, Penzance.(17)

The Hayle cadets enjoyed a day out on Saturday the 15th September 1945 the first 'Battle of Britain Day,' when RAF Predannack was opened to the public.(18) Among a number of fighter pilots, was the famous French 'ace' Sqdn Ldr 'Maurice'.(19) In late 1945 with the lessening of wartime activities on the Cornish airfields opportunities arose for extending the facilities for cadets. On the now redundant fighter station RAF Perranporth, No. 95 Elementary Gliding School was established to teach cadets the rudiments of non-powered flight. The equipment included an ex-Barrage Balloon winch, powered by a Ford 8 engine, along with two Beaverette armoured cars to retrieve the gliders. Apart from the early, very primitive, Dagling gliders which, thankfully, were soon lost when they were blown over the cliff in a gale, the main craft for solo flights were the three Kirby Cadet basic gliders. No. 95 Elementary Gliding

---

1834 (Hayle) Flight ATC mustered in Foundry Square on 5th July 1942 for Church Parade Service in the Foundry Chapel.
Front row: Warrant Officer C.L. Mills; Rev. J.W. Naisbitt;
Flying Officer K. Uren CO Hayle ATC; Flt Lt N.A.J. Spencer, RAF Liaison Officer and Colonel John Ellis.

Photograph: via Mrs Rozanne Ellis

School was staffed by two officers and several civilian instructors. Each Sunday twelve cadets attended and were allotted three launches each per day, per cadet.

In December 1945 at the annual supper of the Hayle ATC the Commanding Officer, Flying Officer Jack Reynolds gave an up-to-date summary of the wartime membership of the unit. Over two hundred cadets had passed through the register. Thirty-two to the RAF; nine to the RN; eleven to the Army and two to the FAA.(20) With the end of the war the ATC continued its excellent service to the youth of the town, as indeed, it does to this very day. It is a fine organisation with very much to its credit.

It may seem that all these organisations for the teenagers of the town were concentrated on activities for the boys and young men as, indeed, it mostly was, but the young girls were not neglected by the pre-service units. A national cadet force for young ladies was formed under the name of the Girls Training Corps, usually shortened to 'GTC.' The local press noted that it was proposed to form a GTC unit in Hayle, and the first meeting was held on the 21st January 1943 at 7.30pm.(21)

In February 1943 it was reported that the Hayle GTC meets twice weekly at Penpol

The Peller family of Hayle, July 1942.
Back row: Margaret Peller (aged 16); Fred Peller (aged 26); Bob Peller (aged 19) ATC; Bill Easterbrook, RAF pilot and friend of Ken Peller; Kenneth Peller (aged 21).
Front row: Alfred Peller, manager of the Hayle Power Station and Elizabeth Peller.
Photograph: via Mrs Marion Peller

School 7.00 – 9.00pm. Mrs J.R. Rogers was appointed Commandant; Miss Wickens, Company Adjutant, gives art lessons; Miss Jones of Hayle Grammar School is to give French lessons and Mrs Piper will give some lessons in Shorthand. In the 'Handyman's Course' Mr I.G. Reynolds will instruct on 'Electricity in the Home': Mrs Rogers takes PT, and Mr Mills of the ATC takes Drill. The Basic Course is: First Aid, Hygiene, Dispatch Carrying, Handyman's Course, Fire Fighting, Gas and Company Drill and Physical Training. The report goes on to say that, 'The girls are extremely keen but are hampered in getting equipped by lack of funds, and coupons for their uniforms. There are already 38 members, but many more are needed.'(22) (Note for feminists: No funds or clothing coupons were required for the ATC or Army Cadet uniforms.)

The GTC took an enthusiastic part in the Hayle 'Wings for Victory' savings week, June 19-26 1943. The 'Wings for Victory Queen' was GTC member Miss Betty Williams, (now Mrs Betty Reed), one of the Williams twins of Hayle. On the opening day, Saturday 19th June, after the crowning ceremony at 8.00pm, in keeping with the occasion, instead of the usual carriage she was taken through Hayle seated in the ATC BA Swallow aircraft mentioned above, and towed by the ATC cadets themselves, to the Masonic Hall where she held Court at the Official 'Wings for Victory' Ball. The

Robert Desmond Peller of Hayle, October 1940. 'Bobby' is wearing the uniform of the Air Defence Cadet Corps (ADCC). He would have been on the rolls of 24 (Penzance) Squadron. The uniform was simplified when the ADCC was absorbed into the Air Training Corps (ATC) in 1941.

Photograph: via Mrs Marion Peller

music for the evening was supplied by the famous 'Riff-Raff' Dance Band From RAF Portreath.

The social activity of the unit is highlighted also in a report of a GTC dance at the Masonic Hall where the MC was Lt A.S. Nicholls of the Royal Signals.(23) Lt Nicholls was presumably from the St Erth Radio Station. Six months later the annual social of the Hayle GTC was held in the Drill hall on Saturday 5th February 1944. The arrangements were made by the Commandant, Betty Eddy OC Hayle GTC, and consisted of dancing and games. The MC for the evening was PO J. Reynolds of the ATC.(24) Unfortunately without the military resources available to the two cadet units for young men, and the reduction of the women's sections of the armed forces the GTC did not survive for long following the cessation of hostilities.

An indication of the 'swords into ploughshares' atmosphere prevailing after the war can be seen in a report announcing the initial meeting of the 'Hayle Horseshoe Club' at St Elwyn's Hall. One hundred youngsters aged 15 to 22 enjoyed dancing and games. Mr L. Bolitho, the President, was MC, the Vice-President was Sheila Pedler. The music was supplied by Mr Gerald Berry.(25)

In conclusion it must not be forgotten that alongside the military cadet units, civilian organisations for youngsters still flourished and, indeed, expanded under wartime conditions. Notably, of course, the Boy Scout movement which although semi-militaristic in its uniforms and training, was not directly affiliated to any of the fighting services, but provided valuable support and back-up duties in aid of the civil defence organisations.

Likewise, the cadet sections of the St John Ambulance Brigade were very strong in Hayle, both in the Ambulance and Nursing departments. The Lady Cadet Officer is recorded as Mrs S.F.J. Petters, and the Lady Divisional Superintendent as Mrs H. Turner.(26) The SJAB cadets included both boys and girls and provided valuable candidates for future adult membership.

Lesser-known youth organisations existed during the war, mainly attached to religious bodies in the town. In 1943 there was in being the Hayle Salvation Army Scouts, with R. Toye as Scoutmaster.

Earlier, in late 1941 it was reported that, 'On Sat 14th December at Hayle Salvation Army 21 girls were inaugurated into the Life Saving Guard Troop, which is affiliated to the Girl Guides. This troop is the first of its kind in Cornwall.'(27) At Highlanes Chapel schoolroom in October 1943 the 1st Hayle Company, Girls Life Brigade met under Capt. Mrs E.M. Webster and Lt Mrs I. Tonkin.(28) In January 1946 the 1st Hayle Company held its New Year Party in the schoolroom of the Baptist Chapel (now the Roman Catholic Church Hall).(29)

Chapter Twenty:

NATIONAL SAVINGS
The Weeks

WITH INDUSTRY ALMOST totally converted to the production of materials for war there soon arose an extreme shortage of what were termed 'luxury' items; things that were not strictly necessary for sustaining everyday life. This situation was compounded by the almost complete cutting off of the importation of non-essential goods. At the same time the incomes of the millions of civilians engaged in the war industries, began to rise far faster than had been the norm, and so a classical inflation problem faced the government; that of too much money chasing too few goods. Various compulsory systems were introduced to cool down the situation including the Post War Credit deductions and the introduction of the socially divisive and grossly unfair P.A.Y.E. tax regime that has persisted to this day; it being so attractive to all succeeding governments, perhaps, because it is so inequitable to the wage-earning and salaried employees as compared to those on other tax schedules.

Despite these severe measures, people still had a fair amount of disposable income that it was considered desirable to take out of circulation. The method preferred and adopted was to greatly expand the National Savings movement through a huge advertising campaign, and the organising of factory, street and school savings groups. In May 1940 came the announcement that Mr W. Bew (Headmaster, St Erth School) had been appointed as the Hon. Secretary to the Hayle Savings Committee.[1]

Every year from 1941 onwards a 'Savings Week' was organised throughout the country with a theme of supporting one of the armed forces, and bringing together a combined effort by all the savings groups in a geographical area. The first 'week' in April 1941 had the general title of 'War Weapons Week,' and was followed in 1942 by 'Warships Week.' In 1943 it was 'Wings for Victory' week and in 1944 'Salute the Soldier.'

In West Cornwall, the 'weeks' were run by the combined authorities of Penzance Council, West Penwith RDC, St Just and St Ives councils. Hayle, although nominally under West Penwith RDC, operated semi-independently, and had its own targets for the town, always indicated by a huge painted thermometer erected on the facade of the Passmore Edwards Institute to the right of the main door. As is invariably the case, all did not run smoothly from the Hayle point of view. The major events that were organised by the joint committees, always seemed to be centred on, and to take place in, Penzance (as ever before and ever since). This caused resentment to build up among those struggling so assiduously in the surrounding areas.

Hayle Parish Council meeting to receive a report on the 'War Weapons Week' (19th – 26th April 1941) was scathing about the treatment Hayle had received. The entertainment at Hayle, in general, had been 'a washout.' On the Tuesday a military detachment scheduled to do a display had driven straight through the town. On another day a cinema van which arrived at 12.45pm to give a show had to be in St Just by 2.00pm.[2] The only thing that was on schedule was a captured enemy warplane. The aircraft was a Messerschmitt Bf 109E fighter shot down over the UK in the Battle of Britain. Carried with its wings detached and folded, on a RAF transport it was displayed beside the Hayle War Memorial.[3] The Council pointed out that Hayle had contributed a total of over £42,000, an average of over £10 per head of the population.[4]

For the next yearly effort, dedicated this time to the Royal Navy and entitled 'Warship Week,' the Hayle sub-committee Chairman was Mr A.T.S. Sampson and the Hon. Secretary was Mrs M.L. Coles. The committee consisted of Rev. H.J. Moysey, Rev. R.G. Faithful, Rev. C.A. Amey, Mr J.B. James, Mr W.L. Barnes, Mr J. Tripp, Mr J. McCabe, Mr R.L. Sandercock (Manager, Lloyds Bank), Mr M. Mitchell (Manager, Barclays Bank) and Mr C.W. Jaco (Postmaster).(5) In August 1941 it was reported that Hayle Parish Council had set up a 'Hayle Spitfire Fund.'(6)

The Cornishman of the 12th November 1941 reported that the Warship Week target for Penzance, West Penwith RDC and St Just was £210,000 to pay for the hull of a destroyer, HMS *Witch*. If £700,000 could be raised the whole ship could be paid for.(7) This would seem to indicate the progressive financing of a new warship; but the contribution to the construction costs seems rather odd and a little belated when one considers that HMS *Witch* (D89 Modified 'W' Class) was a very old WWI destroyer, all bought and paid for, and certainly not a new vessel. She was launched in 1916 and eventually survived WWII intact. She famously took part in the defence of Convoy ON115 against 6 U-boats of Group 'Wolf' in August 1942 . . . until the convoy reached safety in the fog banks off Newfoundland.(8)

In July 1942 a different ship was adopted. This was the 'F' class Flotilla Leader Destroyer HMS *Foresight* (H68), built in 1935. This adoption was tragically short-lived, HMS *Foresight* being torpedoed by Italian aircraft off Sicily on the 12th August 1942. She was part of the tragic 'Operation Pedestal' convoy that attempted to supply Malta. Fourteen merchant ships left Gibraltar, escorted by two battleships, four aircraft carriers, seven cruisers and twenty-six destroyers. HMS *Foresight* was lost along with one aircraft carrier, two cruisers, and nine of the merchant ships. Only five battered but vital merchantmen reached the beleaguered island to resupply the desperate armed forces there.(9) An attempt was made to tow HMS *Foresight*, but the vessel had to be scuttled the following day. In the event four crew were lost and one hundred and forty saved. A dance organised at the Winter Gardens, Penzance with the band of the 'King's Own' Regiment, to raise money for comforts for the crew of HMS *Foresight*, sadly, had to be changed into a benefit for the dependents. The sum raised was £25.(10) Some of the fund-raising activities for Warship Week in Hayle involved a number of items that were in short supply in wartime. Onions were very scarce in 1941–2. At J & F Pool's factory the sale of an onion raised the sum of £2 for the savings week. Likewise at Primrose Dairy, an 'onion weighing' competition realised £4 for the same cause.(11)

For the 1943 campaign, 'Wings for Victory' taking place June 19th – 26th, the Hayle target was £35,000, and the town was 'confident of passing it.' This was said at the time to cover the cost of seven Spitfires.(12) In fact the Hayle effort raised £88,000 which would have covered the nominal cost of nearly eighteen Spitfires.

Events for the week in Hayle included the selection of a 'Wings for Victory Queen' to be crowned by no less a person than the famous pre-war woman aviator and record-breaker, Miss Jean Batten.(13) Jean Gardner Batten CBE, 1909 – 1982 was born in New Zealand. She came to the UK in 1929 and at 21 took her pilot's licences. She broke Amy Johnson's UK – Australia solo record in 1934 and completed the return journey. She flew other solo flights including UK – Argentina 1935; UK – Brazil 1936; and UK – New Zealand 1936 among others.(14)

A poster to be displayed in shops etc prior to and during the 'Week' was designed by Mr R.W. Wakeford, a Hayle pharmacist and noted local comedian and raconteur. The text incorporated many names of then current RAF aircraft in capital letters in case some might be overlooked. Reading it still causes one to wince as it did in its day. It went:

'Hayle Beware! It is coming quick as a LIGHTNING, with the speed of a TYPHOON and the blast of a THUNDERBOLT, in fact a regular HURRICANE that will SPITFIRE, and you will be caught up in its WHIRLWIND. It will be of no avail to hide in your FORTRESS and be DEFIANT, muttering "Go to HALIFAX," for like WELLINGTON, they will conquer you – they are after you with a TOMAHAWK, and will sting you harder than a MOSQUITO. So LIBERAT(OR) your cash and show your STIRLING qualities, because 'Wings for Victory Week' is coming.' (15)

The 'Week' in Hayle began on Saturday 19th June with the election and crowning of the 'Queen' Miss Betty Williams, who then processed through the town to the Masonic Hall where a grand dance was organised. On Sunday 20th there was a Mass Parade of HM Forces and local organisations to the Recreation Ground where a March-Past and Drumhead Service was

'Week Queen' Miss Betty Williams (centre) with attendants.
Photograph: via Jack and Betty Reed

held. On Monday 21st the revue 'Over to You' was performed by personnel from RAF Predannack at the Drill Hall. On Tuesday 22nd there was a children's film show at the Palace Cinema and a concert by Ventonleague Prize Male Voice Choir plus RAF films at the Drill Hall. Wednesday followed with another concert this time by Mousehole Male Voice Choir together with a demonstration by the RAF on Air-Sea Rescue. The Thursday 24th events included a Garden Party & Baby Show at Glanmor (now Paradise Park) with music by the DCLI Regimental Band. Friday 25th presented

Hayle GTC girls spell out 'Wings for Victory' during the Wings for Victory Week.
Photograph: via Jack and Betty Reed

108 Hayle in World War II

Hayle ATC 'Wings for Victory' promotional leaflets.

Photograph: via Jack and Betty Reed

a military occasion when the Home Guard marched through the town led by the Home Guard Band. At the Recreation Ground they gave demonstrations of battle drill, signalling, foot drill, arms and gas drill. There were exhibitions of weapons etc. Saturday 26th was a Sports Day at Trevassack. Later at the Drill Hall there was a programme of plays arranged by Miss Andrew and members of the Hayle Dramatic Society and music by the Elite Dance Band. The day and the 'Week' concluded with a dance at the Masonic Hall organised by the NFS with music by the Arcadians.(16)

At the end of the Hayle 'Wings for Victory' week a surplus over expenses raised from concerts etc amounted to £227-13s. It was decided to loan the amount to the government free of interest until after the war. The trustees appointed were Mr R.J. Hammil and Mr R.A. Vague (manager, Barclays Bank). Mr Vague suggested that the money be earmarked as nucleus for the building of a Public Hall as the need of such a hall during the 'Wings' week had been 'very acute.' It was decided to form a Memorial Hall Committee to build a hall as a tribute to the Hayle servicemen.(17) This was confirmed at a meeting of Hayle Parish Council on the 4th October 1943, and again in January 1944.(18)

A public meeting was held on Thursday 6th April 1944 at the Ambulance Hall to further discuss Hayle's War Memorial Hall, Mr R.J. Hammil presided. A committee was formed: Mrs Kevern; Mrs Peek; Mr F. Hollow; Mr J. Chinn; Mr R.J. Harvey, with the Chairman, Vice-Chairman and the Clerk to the Council. Mr C. Blewett, pharmacist, suggested a building in line with Station Villas, to be surrounded with lawns and gardens.(19) (This site would have been the meadow now occupied by the bungalows opposite Hayle Station). Early in 1945 at Hayle Parish Council the subject of the Memorial Hall came up again. Suggestions were made that it be sited at St Elwyns Place or at the Recreation Ground.(20) A letter was later received from Mr F.W. Rolfe, County Planning Officer saying that the proposed site at St Elwyn Place was not suitable. The other suggested site, Mount Pleasant Chapel was better but might be delayed by housing programmes.(21)

Back in 1943, still on an aviation theme, it was reported that the pupils of the Hayle Kindergarten and Preparatory Schools (Principal, Miss I.G. West, NFU, MRST) had raised £3-4s in National Savings towards the cost of a rubber dinghy.(22)

Between the major savings drives it was the endeavour of small to medium towns to save a sufficient amount to cover the cost of a fighter aircraft, the Spitfire being the popular choice. Larger cities and town could finance a bomber. These were termed 'dedicated' aircraft and the name of the town was painted on the side. At Hayle the savings 'thermometer' on the Passmore Edwards Institute indicated target of £5,000 to cover the cost of a Spitfire. It appears that although the sum was achieved, a Spitfire was not dedicated to Hayle. It seems the money was just absorbed into the West Penwith general savings funds. Among a number of other Cornish town Spitfires was a Mark V BL709 named *St Ives, Cornwall*. (23) So at least their efforts were justly rewarded and acknowledged.

The 1944 savings drive 'Salute the Soldier Week' was announced to take place July 15th to the 22nd inclusive.(24) In May at a meeting of the Hayle Branch, National Savings Committee, Mr P. Felderman of Frank Curtis Ltd was appointed to the committee and Major Venn of the Home Guard was put in charge of publicity for 'Salute the Soldier Week.'(25) In the event the amount saved in the week in Hayle amounted to £70,000.

In conclusion it must be noted that by any standard of comparison the scale of personal saving in the district was immense. Over the period from 1940 to 1944, in

WINGS FOR VICTORY

Sunday, 20th June — Air Training Corps Day.

10.30 Tour of Hayle by the R A F Publicity Van
2.30 Grand Parade of H M Forces and Local Organisations, with the Home Guard Battalion and Camborne Town Bands in attendance. The Parade will assemble at Carnsew, and march through the main streets to the Saluting Base at the Recreation Ground, where the Salute will be taken by Group Captain D. M. Somerville.
3.15 Drum Head Service at the Recreation Ground conducted by Sqdn. Ldr. the Rev. J. L. Stradling, Chaplain to the R A F Station, Portreath, supported by the Rev. Moysey, Chaplain to the Hayle A T C, and other Ministers of Religion. Singing to be led by Massed Choir, conducted by Mr. W. C. Harris. Music by the Bands
4.30 Speeches by Group Captain Somerville, The Lord Lieutenant of Cornwall (Lt.-Col. E. H. W. Bolitho), Commander P. G. Agnew, R N, M P and Mr A. Beechman, M P. Speakers to be introduced by Mr. J. Woolcock, Chairman Hayle "Wings for Victory" Committee
8.0 Copperhouse Methodist Chapel (by kind permission of the Trustees) Concert by the Climax Light Orchestra. Conductor: Mr. B. F. Thomas, Pianist: Cecil Whear, L R A M assisted by Miss Peggy Henbow, Soprano (B B C) Mr. Jesse George, Baritone (B B C)
Programmes 1s- Proceeds of concert for R A F Benevolent Fund

Monday, 21st June — Army Cadet Force Day

7.30 p.m. Drill Hall, R.A.F. Revue, "OVER TO YOU" Presented by R.A.F. personnel from Predannack
An R.A.F. Fighter Pilot will relate some recent experiences
An Entertainment you cannot afford to miss !
Tickets 2/- Reserved, and 1/- obtainable from members of the Army Cadet Force

Tuesday, 22nd June — Civil Defence Day

3.0 Film Matinee at the Palace Cinema, Hayle, for the School-children, by kind permission of the Management. Admission 6d. and one 6d. Savings Stamp will be handed to all children attending this show
7.30 Drill Hall, Film Programme presented by R.A.F. Station, Portreath, including "Venture Adventure," "Pilot is Safe," "In the Drink," "R.A.F. in Action." etc.
Musical items by Ventonleague Prize Male Voice Choir
Conductor: Mr. C. Williams
Tickets 1/6 and 1/- from members of the various Civil Defence Organisations.

Wednesday, 23rd June — Ambulance Day

7.30 Drill Hall — Concert by the Mousehole Male Voice Choir. Conductor: Mr. W. Potter
Air Sea Rescue display by D F C Pilot
Tickets 1/6 & 1/- from members of the Hayle Ambulance

Thursday, 24th June — Ladies' Day

3.0 Garden Party and Baby Show at "Glanmor" by kind permission of F. S. Harvey, Esq. Organised by the W.V.S. and the Infant Welfare Clinic
Admission 6d Refreshments extra
Side Shows, Competitions, Hoop-la, etc.
Music by the D.C.L.I. Regimental Band
7.30 Mammoth Whist Drive at the Drill Hall
Tickets 1/- from members of the Hayle Company of Girl Guides

---

the area covered by Penzance, St Just, Hayle and West Penwith the amount invested in National Savings totalled over £5,000,000.(26) To compare it with current figures this amount would have to be multiplied by a factor of 25 to 30.

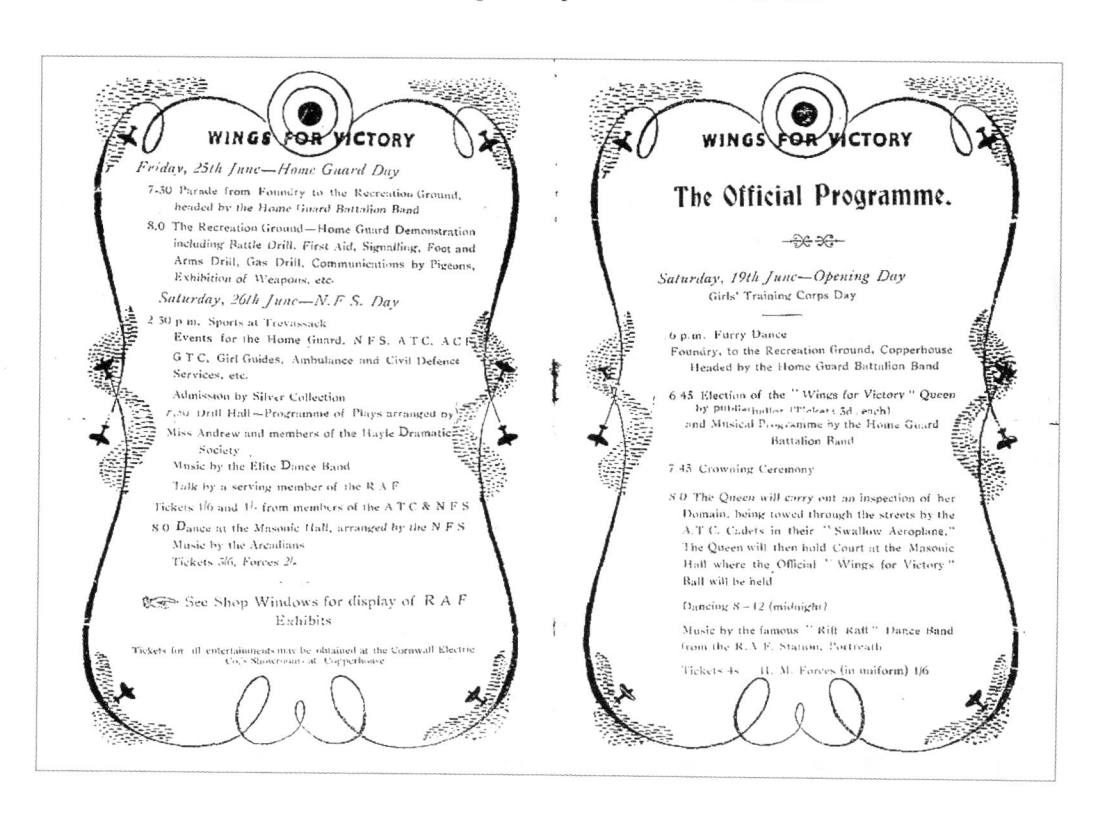

WINGS FOR VICTORY

Friday, 25th June — Home Guard Day

7.30 Parade from Foundry to the Recreation Ground, headed by the Home Guard Battalion Band
8.0 The Recreation Ground — Home Guard Demonstration including Battle Drill, First Aid, Signalling, Foot and Arms Drill, Gas Drill, Communications by Pigeons, Exhibition of Weapons, etc.

Saturday, 26th June — N.F.S. Day

2.30 p.m. Sports at Trevassack
Events for the Home Guard, N F S, A T C, A C F, G T C, Girl Guides, Ambulance and Civil Defence Services, etc.
Admission by Silver Collection
7.30 Drill Hall — Programme of Plays arranged by Miss Andrew and members of the Hayle Dramatic Society
Music by the Elite Dance Band
Talk by a serving member of the R A F
Tickets 1/6 and 1/- from members of the A T C & N F S
8.0 Dance at the Masonic Hall, arranged by the N F S
Music by the Arcadians
Tickets 3/6, Forces 2/-.

☞ See Shop Windows for display of R A F Exhibits

Tickets for all entertainments may be obtained at the Cornwall Electric Co.'s Showrooms at Copperhouse

---

WINGS FOR VICTORY

The Official Programme.

Saturday, 19th June — Opening Day
Girls' Training Corps Day

6 p.m. Furry Dance
Foundry, to the Recreation Ground, Copperhouse
Headed by the Home Guard Battalion Band

6.45 Election of the "Wings for Victory" Queen by public ballot (Tickets 3d. each)
and Musical Programme by the Home Guard Battalion Band

7.45 Crowning Ceremony

8.0 The Queen will carry out an inspection of her Domain, being towed through the streets by the A.T.C. Cadets in their "Swallow Aeroplane."
The Queen will then hold Court at the Masonic Hall where the Official "Wings for Victory" Ball will be held

Dancing 8 – 12 (midnight)

Music by the famous "Riff Raff" Dance Band from the R.A.F. Station, Portreath

Tickets 4s- H. M. Forces (in uniform) 1/6

Chapter Twenty-One:

THE SHORT & UNHAPPY LIFE OF A BRITISH RESTAURANT

IN THE EARLY days of the war very few of the industrial concerns operated canteen units for their employees. Contingency plans had to be formulated by central government to introduce dining facilities in town centres to feed the working population, and the general public with at least one substantial meal per day at an affordable price. These establishments were named 'British Restaurants' and served their customers plain but nourishing meals to supplement their basic food rations. The Hayle British Restaurant, which was designed by the West Penwith RDC surveyor, Mr J.H.M. Craze, was situated on what is now the Commercial Road car park, approximately where the Age Concern Centre now stands. When proposed it was a very necessary addition to life in Hayle. No employers at the time provided any facilities for their workers, and there were no restaurants or cafes of sufficient size in the town, just a couple of little tea rooms that did not provide full hot meals. The workforces simply had to eat their pasties or fish and chips beside their machines, or in summer sitting out on the roadside kerbstones.

It would appear that the proposals for a British Restaurant at Hayle had been made in early 1943 for in July of that year it was reported that although the equipment had been there for six weeks, the foundations for the building were not yet ready.[1] Steady progress seems to have been made after that hiatus, for by the 11th August 1943 West Penwith RDC were able to advertise for the appointment of a 'Cook-Supervisor.'[2]

The formal opening of the restaurant took place on Friday 15th October 1943 by Mr E.G. Shovel, Chairman of West Penwith RDC. It was described as the first in West Penwith, and had a capacity of 200 persons. The Supervisor was Mrs E. Barnes. It would be open Monday to Friday inclusive, from noon to 2.00pm. The meals would cost 1s 2d for adults and 7d for children, and would consist of a main dish, sweet and tea. Mr A.T. Sampson (Chairman, Hayle British Restaurant Committee) said that 'several pessimists were going around wondering if it would last a week or two or three days.'[3]

After its initial success in 1943, by March 1944 it was obvious that things were not going very smoothly. A report by West Penwith RDC recorded a deficit. It stated that the restaurant needed to supply 180 meals per day to break even, and 200 to make a small profit. The number of meals served on average over the eleven weeks to 31st December 1943 was 120 with daily takings amounting to £7-3s. By January 1944 the numbers were down to 88 meals taking £5-2s. The Ministry had announced that it would not make up the deficit.[4] By May 1944 the restaurant was in serious trouble and its future was in jeopardy. The West Penwith Council Clerk reported that by Monday May 1st the number of meals served had fallen to 36 per day.[5]

How did this grave situation develop? The town obviously needed this facility, yet its failure and closure were almost a forgone conclusion. The fault was, as it almost always is in Britain, bungling at the highest level. The catering was fine, the food wholesome and good, the staff were efficient, the customers happy. Where then must we look for the failure?

The original concept was to provide a restaurant for the hundreds of workers in Hayle, including the many travelling daily from outside the town. So once the Hayle British Restaurant was up and going what did the Civil Service 'Mandarins' at central government do? Within weeks they funded the setting-up of factory canteens in two of the largest workplaces in Hayle; thereby depriving the British Restaurant of its main customer base, and effectively destroying this worthwhile, beneficial undertaking. These two factory canteens, it appears, were heavily subsidised by the government, and as the Hayle councillors suspected and claimed, were receiving far better allocations of supplies per head from the local food offices and were thus able to provide much better meals. The councillors complained bitterly that they had been pressurised by the Ministry of Health to initiate the Hayle British Restaurant. Had they known at the time that the two works canteens were planned they would never have undertaken the operation.(6) To add to their anger and frustration, they then discovered that the two other canteens were rated at only a quarter of the gross figure.

By late May 1944 the situation was critical; West Penwith RDC served notice on Hayle British Restaurant that it had a fortnight's grace from the 24th May.(7) This sanction must have resulted in closure, for we see no further reference to the Hayle British Restaurant until its temporary re-opening to feed the large number of 'Flying Bomb' evacuees who arrived in Hayle in August 1944.(8) The works canteens, naturally, flourished also providing venues for concerts, and BBC 'Workers' Playtime' broadcasts until the end of hostilities. With the end of the war the former British Restaurant building was used for a short while as the Labour Exchange for Hayle, but was demolished later to increase the car parking area.

After a number of years the J & F Pool's canteen building in Copperhouse was sold off to become a frozen food centre and supermarket warehouse and in the 21st century, greatly refurbished, it became the headquarters of a national pet care charity, The Cinnamon Trust.

Chapter Twenty-Two:

FLIGHT LIEUTENANT MEYER D.F.C.

IT IS NOT often that one can connect a local individual with one of the more important major strategic events of World War II. In this case it can be done in relation to the birth of high-altitude precision bombing. In the years immediately prior to the outbreak of war in Europe, the US Army Air Corps was developing an advanced long-range high-altitude bomber, mainly to serve across the Pacific to cover the vast distances separating its island bases. The preferred option was the new Boeing B-17, known as the 'Flying Fortress.'

Britain in 1940 was desperately short of four-engine heavy bombers. Later that year the British Purchasing Mission in the USA was able, with the agreement of the American Government, to acquire twenty B-17Cs, the latest model of the Boeing Flying Fortress. In the Summer of 1941, at a critical stage of the war for Britain, these aircraft were delivered to the RAF in the UK where they were designated 'Fortress 1s.' The aircraft were taken on the strength of No.90 Squadron at RAF Polebrook, Northamptonshire, where specially selected crews were trained for high-altitude operations.

The squadron operated twenty-six daylight raids against such targets as Emden, Kiel, Brest, Bremen, Rotterdam, Borkum and Wilhelmshaven, losing eight aircraft. The reliability proved to be poor, with twenty-six out of fifty-one sorties aborted. The Norden bombsights did not live up to expectations. The defensive armament proved to be inadequate and the guns froze up. The aircraft suffered from severe icing problems and there were failures of the crews oxygen systems.[1] The enemy anti-aircraft guns were able to engage them and the German fighters, especially the Bf109s, proved against expectations to be able, climb to the same height and shoot the bombers down. Things were all so very different in the awful climatic conditions of Northern Europe from those in the United States. With the Fortresses struggling to maintain an altitude above 30000ft with combat loads, their projected original advantage was negated, and so after forty-eight bombing sorties by September 1941, Bomber Command withdrew them from operations. In mid-October 1941 they were despatched via RAF Portreath to the warmer climes of Egypt where, after a number of raids over the desert and further losses the remaining Fortresses were returned to the UK to serve out their time with No. 220 Squadron, Coastal Command at RAF Nutts Corner, Northern Ireland.[2]

The first inkling that a local person was involved in these early experimental operations came in a news item in November 1941 which stated that a Hayle airman had been on the Flying Fortress raid on Brest on the 24th July 1941. No other details were given.[3] Two weeks later, however, the newspaper was able to announce the award of the Distinguished Flying Cross to Flt Lt Kenneth Meyer of Hayle. He was a former pupil of Penpol School who had joined the RAF in 1934, aged 16. Before serving in the RAF he worked with Mr W.H. Green in the carpentry trade.[4]

Following this item we hear no more about the career of Flt Lt Meyer for over three years until a report appears in January 1945. 'Over three years ago *The Cornishman* described a Hayle boy, ex-Penpol School, who was a member of the crew of a Flying Fortress which dropped the first bomb on Germany (sic). He is Flt Lt Kenneth Meyer

DFC, the grandson of the late Mr John Lloyd of Foundry Hill, Hayle. After leaving school he was apprenticed to Mr W.H. Green, a builder of Penzance. On February 13th 1944 he was reported killed in action, but to the great relief of his parents, it is now known that he is safe and a prisoner-of-war.'(5)

When the United States entered the war in December 1941, the USAAF built on the pioneering experience of the RAF in daylight raids in the early Fortresses, and corrected many of the drawbacks and failings of the B-17C model. They developed the magnificent B-17E, F and G Flying Fortresses, producing them in thousands to become the mainstay of the 'Mighty 8th' USAAF in Europe.

Chapter Twenty-Three:

EVERYDAY LIFE IN WARTIME HAYLE

THE NUMBER OF occasions when the major dangerous effects of the war impinged on the life of people in Hayle were, fortunately, few in total but it is worth recording the way in which wartime activities, and especially regulations affected the population in their everyday lives. This was faithfully recorded in the local press. Some aspects of pre-war social life lingered on. A 'Daily Maid' was wanted at a bungalow in St George's Road; and Dr T. Mudge was in need of a 'Cook-General.'[1] In the dark days of the winter of 1940/41 Mr Kennedy suggested to Hayle Parish Council that onions and cabbages be planted in King George V Memorial Walk. This suggestion does not appear to have been acted upon.[2] Poverty was still prevalent and, rather surprisingly, the workhouse system still flourished. A fight was reported in Redruth Workhouse (Barncoose) involving Hayle men.[3]

Older Methodist people in the town were shocked to read that a former minister of Copperhouse Chapel (c1920/21), Mr Thomas Hamilton Groves, aged 67, had been shot after failing to respond to a challenge by a sentry, in Framlingham, Suffolk. Mr Grove who was said to have been very deaf, was leaving a service in the village, and was shot and wounded in his car. He died later. At about the same time the closure of the Cornish Shovel Company at Roseworthy Hammer Mill, which had opened in 1805, was announced.[4]

Methodists were again slightly taken aback by the news that the Rev. C. Garret Udey, a native of Hayle, who after thirty-four years as a Methodist minister, had been received into the Church of England.[5]

Public alarm was raised in early December 1941 when a serious meat shortage was reported in Hayle, Gwinear and Gwithian because of a suggested Ministry of Food blunder. Concern was expressed that there was a possibility of serious disturbances in Hayle. People in the area could only get a third of their rations.[6]

In December 1941 the Cornwall Electric Power Company was taken to court for blackout contravention offences at Hayle Power Station. Given the vital importance of the power station this was a far more serious matter than the usual domestic infringement. Co-accused with the company was an employee, Harry Williams. In its defence the company resorted to the time-honoured practice of British senior management, and tried to divert all of the blame on to the person least able to defend himself; in this case the lowly employee also charged. The company's legal representative put it to the Court that a 'chain was only as strong as its weakest link.' At this even the senior Police Officer presenting the case, Superintendent Rowland, appeared to have been taken aback by the craven behaviour and avoidance of responsibility by a large and prosperous company (Edmunsons Electric); and quite exceptionally, he felt he should speak up for Mr Williams. He asked the Bench to 'show him every consideration seeing the conditions under which he worked.' The Company was fined £50, and Mr Williams 5/-.[7]

In February 1942 it was announced that, 'Artificer (Class 1E) Arthur Biggleston of HM Submarine *Triumph* had been awarded the Distinguished Service Medal (DSM). He was the son of the late Mr and Mrs Biggleston of 10 Mount Pleasant ,Hayle.'[8]

In March 1942 as the result of a salvage drive a week earlier, Hayle Parish Council noted that there were 100 tons of scrap metal at Hayle. By April the council was complaining that the scrap metal was still at Hayle and West Penwith RDC would not collect it. The Ministry was being contacted about the matter.(9)

In June 1942, Mrs Kate Trestraill, the owner of the little Copperhouse sweetshop 'The Kabin,' received the sad news that her brother Mr R.H. Ellis of the Merchant Navy had been killed at sea.(10)

Later, in June 1942, it was reported that Capt. Richard Thomas, Merchant Navy of 16 Penpol Terrace had been commended for gallantry, and for his work at the evacuation from Dunkirk. The *London Gazette* stated that he was awarded the OBE: 'For brave conduct when his ship was attacked by submarines, aircraft, ships and mines.'(11)

In its issue of 8th July 1942 while the brave men of the Merchant Navy were battling through the Atlantic storms, and facing U-Boat torpedoes to bring urgently needed, highly-dangerous cargoes of petroleum spirit for the aircraft and tanks of our armed forces, the local press noted, without comment, that council officers in Leicester, and presumably elsewhere, had been allocated 30 gallons (166 litres) of petrol each per month.(12)

At this time Mr Harry Turner, the Food Enforcement Officer, was complaining that the West Penwith RDC Food Committee did not proceed with prosecutions of traders for not taking coupons, and overcharging. Only one case out of many sent down by the Divisional Food Office at Bristol was proceeded with. He stated that there was an avoidable delay in reporting cases of excessive charges and investigations. It must have been very frustrating for Mr Turner, an upright dedicated retired police sergeant at Hayle, to have his cast-iron cases not undertaken by West Penwith RDC.(13)

In October 1942 it was announced that Lt Col. C.J.A. Hockin of The Anchorage, Hayle Towans had been awarded the Efficiency Decoration for 'Services to the Territorial Army.' He was the only son of a former vicar of Phillack. In the Great War he had served in the Royal Naval Air Service. He and his wife were largely responsible for the revival of the rifle shoots on the Hayle Range. They were both excellent shots, always appearing in the top of the County List. In the Second World War he had received rapid promotion to the rank of Lt Col. and the award mentioned above.(14)

As 1942 moved into its final quarter with General Montgomery's massive build-up for the Eighth Army's attack at El Alamein in ten days time reaching its final stage, the 3/- (15p) per day private soldiers digging their foxholes in the heat and sand flies of the desert, would have been cheered up immensely and greatly inspired to face Rommel's Panzer Divisions were they able to read the announcement that the Chief Officers of Penzance Council had negotiated themselves rises averaging 15 to 20% in their already substantial salaries.(15) This patriotic gesture by the senior administrators of the community occurred at the very time the Government was desperately trying to curb wage inflation, and was attempting to withdraw currency from circulation by every means possible from National Savings campaigns to the notorious Post-War Credits system.

In early February 1943 Mrs A. Peerless of Fore Street, Hayle received a decoration awarded to her husband, the late A/Chief Petty Officer William D. Peerless by Queen Wilhelmina of the Netherlands. The Silver Medal of the Order of Orange-Nassau was 'Merited in valuable services given to Me, my House, and my Country.'(16)

Shortly after this Hayle heard the sad news that Mr Emmanuel Ellis, described as a 'well-known Hayle character,' and his son William, both merchant seamen, were missing off Falmouth. The son's body was later washed ashore at Penryn. They were missing for three weeks. They had capsized in a small boat going out to join a ship. They were buried at a double funeral service at Hayle.(17)

In March the press reported that Mrs K.M.A. La Touche conveyed to Hayle Parish Council the piece of ground known as Clifton Terrace Slope down to King George V Memorial Walk. The Council resolved to incorporate the Slope into the Walk and fence the path.(18) In the same month Special Constable R. Galloway of The Cott, Loggans Mill received head injuries and severe concussion on the afternoon of Thursday 18th when he was knocked down by a train working on the quay. He was taken to St Michael's Hospital.(19)

Also in March 1943 an Angarrack man was highly indignant when he was brought up before the Bench for having only one light on his trap. He protested at the injustice of it all: 'If I have too much light you get me for that; if I have not enough you have me for that.' When charged he said: 'You can go ahead, I shall fight the case.' A second man who was accused of a similar offence said that he had lent one of his lights to the first man. They were each fined 10/-(50p).(20)

An item in *The Cornishman* of March 31st 1943 brings us right up to the 11th September 2001 tragedy with a report that: 'In the dock opposite Penpol Terrace this week, some children were playing along the water's edge, and, without any of them noticing it, one youngster, Cyril Roscorla (sic),fell in. Ronnie Williams was the first to notice the boy floating in the water, and ran to the spot and succeeded in pulling Cyril out.'(21) The boy, of course, grew up to be 'Rick' Rescorla, the hero of the Twin Towers outrage.

Once again Mr R.A. Kevern, the Hayle butcher and stalwart fighter for and defender of the town, was ordered out of a West Penwith RDC meeting after police were sent for when he was said to have made an offensive remark.(22)

The local newspaper in May 1943 concerned itself with matters military. It noted that Samuel James Philp, aged 25 of Hayle, had received his Commission in the Army; and that Private Adrian Southcott, also of Hayle, had had the unusual experience of being captured by the Germans, and then being re-captured by our own forces.(23) What the report did not mention was that Mr Southcott was badly injured having been hit by two bullets.

Following the outstanding success of the 'Wings for Victory' weeks in 1943, it was announced that after the RAF week there would be a 'RAT' week, devoted to decimating the rat population which was said to be: 'Succeeding where Hitler failed' as 'The rat is actively assisting the Nazi in the foul ambition to overturn and subjugate European countries.'(24) There appears to have been no follow-up or progress report as to the success or otherwise of the 'Rat Week' in West Cornwall.

On a more sombre note, a surprisingly early indication of the growing awareness even here in the far west, of what was later to be called 'The Holocaust' was reflected in an advertisement for a meeting to be held on Saturday evening at 6pm in the Centenary Hall, Chapel Street, Penzance, 'To form a committee in connection with the ghastly massacre of the Jews by the Nazis.'(25)

Congratulations were offered to Capt. L.C. Marcus Spray MBE, Royal Marines, of Hayle on his promotion to the rank of Major. For the last three years Major Spray had been serving with the Middle East Forces but was recently transferred to India.(26) Also noted was the fact that: 'Another honour has been conferred on Mr Gordon L. Bastian (son of Capt. N. Bastian), Second Engineer who has been awarded the Albert Medal for gallantry in saving life at sea. This was in recognition of his bravery in saving the life of two of the crew of a ship which was attacked by the enemy. He was awarded the MBE in the New Year's Honours List for "Meritorious Sea Service".'(27)

To a background of ceaseless U-boat warfare and the unimaginable consequences for the crews of torpedoed petrol tankers, a major oil company calmly announced record net profits of £7,790,282 for 1942, against only £3,202,315 for 1941; an increase of 143 per cent.(28) It is not widely known that for the first two years of the war, until the Essential Works Order of May 1941 came into force, that when a British ship was sunk by enemy action the owners stopped the survivors pay from that moment, as the crew were no longer gainfully employed on a company ship.(29) When between voyages and awaiting their next ship in the UK they were retained on just half-pay.

In August 1943 it was reported that Mr R.W. Wakeford of the Hayle Ambulance Brigade gave a lecture to the Salvation Army Scouts at the request of Scoutmaster R. Toye.(30) At the September 1943 funeral of Miss Edith Rawlings, aged 87, of Pencliff, Hayle, it was stated that her half-brother, Vice-Admiral Bernard Rawlings could not attend as he was on active service.(30) Miss Rawlings was the daughter of the late Mr W.J. Rawlings of The Downes, Hayle, and the sister-in-law of Henry Jenner.

A tiny glimmer of a perhaps, brighter, more normal future, yet still a long way off, is given in a report of a dance held for 'Hayle Demobilised Serviceman's Fund.'(31) Also in September 1943 a vote was recorded at Hayle Parish Council indicating a total lack of confidence in West Penwith RDC. The vote was proposed by Mr J.H. Woolcock who said that: 'Hayle is being treated by WPRDC officers as a "second class village" Hayle's resolutions were always referred back or turned down . . . officials override members in all matters, and it was time to put Hayle's foot down.'(32)

An echo of the great Battle of El Alamein was contained in a tribute by the Mayor of Hastings to Private Francis Roskilly, Royal Sussex Regt for 'Bravery under Fire at El Alamein'. He laid a signal wire after his sergeant had been shot. He then went out three more times to repair the wire after it had been broken by mortar fire. He was an old pupil of Penpol School, and the son of Mr and Mrs Willie Roskilly of West Terrace, Hayle.(33) The Hayle Xmas Gift Fund for the Services decided to send a 5/- parcel to every serving man (34) – and presumably every service woman.

A further hint that the people were looking forward to peacetime conditions even at that early stage was contained in the report that Hayle Parish Council were entering into discussions with the Cornwall Electric Power Company regarding the overhaul of the Hayle street lighting, in preparation for the eventual ending of the 'blackout.'(35) War, however, was still to be coped with. It was announced that Mr J. Nicholas, the manager of the International Stores, Hayle, had been appointed employee member of West Penwith Food Control committee.(36)

By January 1944 indirect hints regarding the build-up to the invasion of France (D-Day) and its priorities, still six months in the future, were appearing in the press. An advertisement by ICI said: 'A serious situation may arise at anytime in which railway companies would be unable for an indefinite period to accept certain traffic, including fertilizers. Order Sulphate of Ammonia now.'(37) No one, big or small escaped the regulations. Farm Industries (the successors to HTP) were fined for manufacturing 10 tons of pig and poultry feed, instead of the two tons permitted, at Hayle and St Austell.(38)

Also in January *The Cornishman* carried the news that Capt. Frederick Martin of St Erth had been awarded the OBE for meritorious service to the Merchant Navy.(39)

In the same month Hayle Parish Council was still pursuing the subject of street light restoration when conditions permitted.(40) The fact that the stringent wartime conditions still applied was highlighted by the news that a tailor's shop in Penzance had been fined £3 for supplying trousers with turn-ups.(41) The esteem in which Soviet Russia was held at that time, and the sympathy that was felt for its people was indicated by an advertisement announcing the first public meeting of the Hayle Communist Party at 7pm Sunday 30th January in the Ambulance Hall, Hayle.(42)

During February 1944 alarm was being raised in the district because of the acute shortage of 'Aspro' tablets (a patent form of Aspirin) due to the 'recent flu epidemic.'(43)

Reports from Italy in February 1944 that three British Generals (in fact two Generals and one Air Marshall) who were prisoners-of-war had escaped from the enemy had a special relevance for Hayle. In 1934 Lt Gen. Neame married Miss H. Alberta Drew of Hayle. They had three sons. (Lt Gen. Sir Phillip Neame VC was born 12th December 1888. He died 2nd September 1975).(44) He was captured with Lt Gen. Sir Richard O'Connor by Axis forces in the Libyan Desert on 6th April 1941.(45)

A indication of the imminent approach of D-Day could be inferred from the announcement that persons could be summonsed for being in a banned area without reasonable cause.(46)

One aspect of the Cornish diaspora was reflected in an item from America that Lt Jack Cocks was awarded the DFC (USA) for bravery in the Pacific. He had shot down two Zeros and sank a Japanese barge. He was the son of Mr and Mrs Jack Cocks of Morenci, Arizona. Jack Cocks (Sen.) was a native of Treglisson, Hayle. His wife was Miss Doreen Polkinghorne of Penpol Road, Hayle. She had been a teacher at Penpol School.(47) (Morenci, was, and still is, a famous copper mine in eastern Arizona very close to the Apache Reservation. It was a 'Hayle/Camborne' mine and many local men went out to this remote area to work in the mine.)

Ominous indications of great events soon to happen are contained in the announcement of 22nd March 1944 of the detailing of 'Coastal Protection Areas' effective from Saturday 1st April 1944. A coastal band ten miles in depth would be prohibited to anyone not resident on the 1st April.(48) This was the preliminary security preparation for the massive troop and equipment movements for D-Day. As one would expect howls of anguish arose from the hotel and holiday trade. The travel ban was lifted by the 20th July.

Strangely at the very time that the Allied armies were preparing to depart for the beaches of Normandy, with thousands of troops and vehicles crossing Cornwall to the departure ports, and the policemen at full stretch dealing with the activity, someone at the highest level in the administration of the County Constabulary decided to enforce, of all things, the dog licence laws. Presumably instructing many officers, regular and 'war specials,' to undertake this extra burden and conduct a wide sweep of unlicensed dogs, the owners of which were duly charged. On the 7th June 1944, the day after the D-Day landings sixteen cases came up before West Penwith Petty Sessions, the miscreants each being fined 7/6d (37½ p). Camborne Magistrates Court was packed with thirty-five cases, but the offenders were only fined 5/-(25p) each. Perhaps the Bench there was operating a discount-for-quantity policy.(49)

Civilian involvement in the war effort was highlighted in a report of the women meeting at Foundry Methodist Schoolroom who were making comforts for the Central Hospital Supply Services. Meeting weekly they had made 2,150 articles. Mrs Gregor and Mrs Turner were responsible for the issuing of materials and the collection and despatch of the finished articles.(50)

Leading Stoker L. Glanville of Hayle was on board the 'Hunt' class destroyer HMS *Blankney* which sank two submarines, destroyed three enemy aircraft and took the surrender of the Italian town of Pezzalo after a bombardment.(51) A Sgt Samuel

Woolcock of the USAAF paid a short visit to his sister at Copper Terrace, Hayle, after an absence of twenty-one years. He was the youngest son of the late Mr and Mrs John Woolcock of Bodriggy Street.(52)

Even the 'top drawer' of Hayle society were not immune from the activities of 'Harry' Turner, the Food Enforcement Officer. Eyebrows were raised in the town and no doubt mischievous nods and winks were gleefully exchanged across the machines on the factory floor when the Chairman of J & F Pool Ltd was charged and convicted for illegally possessing 2½ pounds of rationed butter.(53)

Another expatriate visiting Hayle at the time was Corporal Herbert Vivian Rowe of the American 8th Air Force, son of Mr George Rowe, Pontiac, Michigan and grandson of Mr George Rowe of Phillack.(54)

High excitement in the local press in September 1944. A headline read 'Hollywood in Cornwall'. This was a slight but understandable error – it was, in fact, a British-made film with British actors. The report went on, '*The Rake's Progress* filming in Portreath . . . owing to the large influx of visitors to Cornwall at this time several of the staff have to lodge at some distance from the location, a large number being at the White Hart at Hayle.'(55)

A follow-up on the 'Hollywood' story was written under the headline 'Film Stars at Phillack'. The story ran, 'During the making of part of the film *The Rake's Progress* by the Gainsborough Film Co, at Portreath, Phillack was thrilled to have Miss Lilli Palmer, her husband, Rex Harrison, Miss Margaret Johnson, and her husband Mr A. Parker staying with them at the New Inn. This very old place is down for reconstruction, but will retain its old atmosphere. It is now under the proprietorship of Mr & Mrs George Chandler, who gave the stars great satisfaction and a really enjoyable time.'(56) This last statement was confirmed some months later when the paper noted that 'Mr George Chandler of the New Inn, Phillack received two magnificent pewter tankards from Miss Margaret Johnson in appreciation of the hospitality she received when staying there during the filming of *The Rake's Progress*.'(57) No reported token of appreciation appears to have been forthcoming from Mr Rex Harrison or Lilli Palmer.

There were indications that peace was becoming uppermost in many minds. *The Cornishman* of the 19th October 1944 carried an advertisement by the Hoover company inviting the public to submit suggestions for improvements for post-war houses. Further signs of the relaxing of wartime sanctions came with the announcement that boating restrictions were lifted and that visitors could sail again.(58) The following week Cornwall Electric Power Company announced that restrictions on street lighting were to be lessened,(59) and in December came the welcome news from the Ministry of Home Defence that 'Blackout in Cornwall is "under review"'(60) Important news regarding employment in Hayle also came with the announcement in January 1945 by Cornwall Electric Power Company (Edmunsons Electric Corporation) of an extensive construction programme and extension of power lines throughout Cornwall, including an additional fifteen thousand kilowatts of new plant at Hayle.(61)

Also in January the Cornwall County Football Association held its first meeting since 1940 to discuss post-war football; and the 'Big Four' railway companies (*GWR, SR, LNER, and LMS*) announced that 'peacetime services would resume soon.'(62) In February 1945 Hayle Parish Council discussed a programme for the post-war years including the town's public lighting which was acknowledged to be 'the best in Cornwall.' In the same month the Gas Companies stated that they have 'Planned your post-war kitchen.'(63)

Mrs J. Linehan was notified of the news that her husband, missing in action since October 1944, was a prisoner-of-war in Germany.(64)

Excitement in March under the headline 'Stormy Scenes at WPRDC' when the robust defender of and stalwart campaigner for Hayle's rights, councillor R.A. Kevern objected to a report by the Clerk, Mr Caygil regarding administration by West Penwith in Hayle since de-urbanisation. Mr Kevern called the report 'lying and ridiculous' and he had to be restrained by others when he advanced on Mr A.F. Pool. Mr Kevern called the councillors 'a lot of hypocrites.' Mr Kevern declined to leave when asked by the Chairman, and the police were called, but Mr Kevern left before they arrived.(65)

Later in March came the news that Commander William C. Jenks of Hayle was missing in Italy, where he had a shore command.(66)

In April 1945 it was announced that Mr R.A. Kevern was to be the Chairman of the 'Hayle Welcome Home Fund.'(67)

The War in Europe ended on the 8th of May 1945 and with it all blackout restriction etc., but some regulations remained in force. In June 1945 the issue of new Ration Books took place at the Hayle P.E. Institute, Connor Downs WI, St Erth Parish Registry and Wall Methodist Schoolroom.(68)

The celebrations on the ending of the European war consisted of street dances throughout the town, and parties for children, and other festivities. In June the Hayle WI held a 'Fayre and Bazaar' at Point Garden (Permission of Mr and Mrs R.A. Kevern) with a dance in the evening on the lawns.(69) There was a dance at St Erth with music by 'Eric James and his Rhythm Rookies.' On the 7th July there was a VE parade by the children of St Erth through the village and on to Mr Eddy's field at Treloweth where they had a bun tea, a cup of ice cream and sixpence each.(70)

Finally, with the surrender of Japan in August 1945, the celebrations really got under way and the local reporters were out and about to describe them in full. The Hayle report read, 'Hayle greets Victory.'

> *'Last week will be long remembered at Hayle when everyone was full of joy and thankfulness. The bells from Phillack Church rang out across the Towans and Hayle Pool during the morning. In the evening there was a pilgrimage to the cenotaph. Clergy, ministers and officers of the Salvation Army joined in a service of thanksgiving. In the evening there were services in all places of worship. Later the lights went up and many walked in the twilight, revelling in the beauty of the night, enhanced by the flickering lights on the hillsides. Bonfires burned and rockets soared into the heavens, illuminating the country along the higher roads of Bodriggy, Clifton, Foundry Hill and High Lanes.*
>
> *At St Erth a huge bonfire was completed by 6pm on VJ Day, surmounted by an effigy of Hitler with his arm outstretched in the Nazi salute. The match was applied at 10pm and in a short time the fire was going merrily. An impressive feature of the conflagration was when the flames reached Hitler's outstretched arm and it began to drop slowly until the whole body was enveloped in fire. A free dance was held in the Club Room in the evening and music was supplied by Whear and Berry Radio.'*(71)

On the 25th August a revived Hayle Regatta and Carnival was held. This event was founded in 1838 and has been held continuously until the outbreak of the war. The Carnival Queen was Joan Philp with attendants Joan Williams and Sheila Pedlar. They were carried in an open landau driven by Mr Billie Grenfell.(72)

Early in September it was reported that one of the first prisoners-of-war to be released by the Japanese surrender was Capt. T.F. Ellis, a nephew of Col. J. Ellis of Penpol, Hayle, who had been held captive in Siam for three years.(73)

Victory celebrations continued in Hayle with a 'Party provided for all children under 18 residing in High Lanes and St Georges Road. There was a Punch & Judy show by Professor Edgar, plus tea and sports. Each child had a two shilling piece and a small prize. From 6 – 11pm dancing was held in the open in St Georges Road which had been floodlit. The music was supplied by Messrs Berry and Son. Mr J. Wills and Mr N. Quinn (of Hayle Merrymakers) rendered solos during the course of the evening. The tea and ice cream was generously provided by Mr A. Pool of The Beeches, St Georges road.'(74) Hayle's final VJ celebrations were held on Saturday 6th September. There were sports and shows in Mr John Matthews field together with a Punch & Judy show and music by Hayle Home Guard Band. More than 1000 children assembled with their parents and friends in the fair field in Copperhouse and marched through Brewery Lane to the field at Bodriggy. The weather was excellent.

Tea and saffron buns were served and there was a Tug-of-War contest. In the evening Hayle residents assembled in Foundry Square and danced the *Cornish Floral Dance*. From the Square the people went to the Recreation Ground where a bonfire was lit and there was a fireworks display after which there was an Al-Fresco dance until midnight. Approx. 5,000 people were present at the evening's events.(75) In December 1945 Hayle Grammar School proudly announced that its house journal, the *Hayle Wail* was back in print again. It had ceased publication in 1941, a victim of the wartime paper shortage. The new edition would cost 9d.(76)

The repercussions of war were still being felt, as highlighted by the announcement in January 1946, 'Portions of Hayle and Perranporth beaches will be closed to the public in the next few months. The reason for this is that the beaches are in the vicinity of minefields in adjoining sand dunes and the men of Southern Command are removing the mines. This extremely hazardous work should be completed before or during the summer.'(77)

In February 1946 came the welcome news that Hayle Cricket Club had restarted after six years of inactivity. The Officers were Mr H. Bond, Chairman; Mr P. Kemp, Vice-Chairman; Mr G. Dunn, Hon. Sec., and Mr S. Bond, Treasurer.(78) The results of the ending of hostilities and a new dawn were not entirely pleasant and positive. A report in February 1946 stated that there were 99 men out of work in Hayle.(79)

Chapter Twenty-Four:

AFTERMATH
The Break-Up of Ships

FOLLOWING THE CESSATION of wartime activities, a rapid close-down of facilities and the disposal of now unneeded vessels and aircraft was undertaken nationally. Hayle already had a pre-war history as a centre for the breaking-up of ex-naval and civilian shipping.

The main company that was involved in these disposals was the scrap metal business of Messers Thomas W. Ward, who had first come to Hayle in the early part of the century to demolish and dispose of Harvey & Co's foundry and were still represented in the town and were able to resume their dismantling undertaking with immediate effect. Ironically their first contract was to dispose of the two unfinished Boom Defence Vessels left standing on the stocks by Frank Curtis Ltd in the old Harvey shipyard. There then followed over the next few years a succession of redundant Royal Navy vessels brought into Hayle for breaking bringing much needed work to the town. This helped to allay the unemployment problem that followed the reduction of wartime industry.

A list (possibly incomplete) with some of their details is given below in chronological order.

Year	Name	Pennant	Type	Tonnage	Notes
1946	BDV101	—	(Boom Defence Vessel)	Not known	—
1946	HMS *Tedworth*	N32	(Hunt Class Minesweeping Sloop)	885 tons	launched 1917
1947	HMS *Burdock*	K126	(Flower Class Corvette)	1195 tons	built 1940/41
1947	HMS *Clarkia*	K88	(Flower Class Corvette)	1195 tons	built 1940
1947	LCT *1359*	—	(Landing Craft Tank Mk4)	200 tons	1947
1947	HMS *Sunflower*	K41	(Flower Class Corvette)	723 tons	built 1940
1947	HMCS *Vegreville*	J257	(Bangor Class Minesweeping Sloop)	673 tons	Royal Canadian Navy
1948	HMS *Fareham*	N89	(Old Hunt Class Minesweeping Sloop)	710 tons	built 1918
1948	Rhino Ferry	—	(Details unknown)	400 tons	built c1943 Hayle
1949	HMS *Aberdeen*	L97	(Escort Sloop)	990 tons	built 1936 Devonport
1949	HMS *Milford*	L51	(Falmouth Class Escort Sloop)	1060 tons	built 1936
1949	HMS *Unseen*	P51	(U Class Submarine)	730 tons	built 1942
1949	HMS *Uther*	P62	(U Class Submarine)	730 tons	built 1943
1950	HMS *Visigoth*	P76	(Modified U Class Submarine)	750 tons	built 1944
1950	*U-712*	—	(Kriegsmarine Type VII U-boat)	—	built 1942 Hamburg

Some of these vessels had interesting histories.

BDV101 was almost certainly one of the two Boom Defence Vessels almost completed, but never launched, in the old Harvey & Co shipyard and sold to T.W. Ward for breaking.

HMS *Burdock* on D-Day was an escort vessel for Assault Convoy G.13.

HMS *Clarkia* was involved in the award of a VC. In August 1943 a Liberator aircraft of No. 200 Squadron RAF sank a type VIIC U-boat *U-468* off West Africa. The aircraft was shot down by the submarine, and all the airmen killed. HMS *Clarkia* picked up seven survivors of the U-boat and landed them at Freetown. On the evidence given by the U-boat survivors, the pilot FO Lloyd Trigg was awarded a posthumous VC.(2) On D-Day HMS *Clarkia* was back in home waters and acted as one of the escorts for Assault Convoy J15.(3)

HMS *Sunflower* was part of the D-Day forces.

HMCS *Vegreville* served on D-Day as a dan layer and minesweeper in the 11th Flotilla as part of Assault Convoy UM2. She was off Utah Beach at 19.57 on the 5th June 1944.(4)

HMS *Aberdeen* when pristine-new took part in the Review of the Fleet at Spithead in May 1937.

U-boat *U-712* was built in Hamburg, and launched 10th August 1942. She ran aground on exercises in the Baltic on 28th October 1943, and did not go on operations, becoming a training craft. Surrendered in 1945 she became a Royal Navy vessel and was used for test purposes in 1946. She was scrapped at Hayle in 1950.(5)

HMS *Aberdeen* being broken up at Hayle in 1949 by T.W. Ward.

Photograph: the author

Chapter Twenty-Five:

'LEST WE FORGET'
1939 – 1945

ALL THAT IS written in this book – the incidents, the people involved in the happenings described – pales into insignificance when compared with the sacrifice made by the persons listed below. Taken from the Hayle War Memorial they are the names of the forty-three men who left their families and town never to return. They are listed here in alphabetical order. No ranks are given. In the sacrifice of their lives for their country all men are equal.

Greater love hath no man than this; that he lay down his life for his friends

E. Bagg	New Zealand Forces
A.W.E. Baker	Royal Navy
S. Barnes	Duke of Cornwall's Light Infantry
C. Bond	Royal Air Force
J.W. Burrows	Royal Air Force
H. Cook	Dorsetshire Regiment
A.W.I. Coombe	Royal Tank Regiment
O. Eddy	Royal Air Force
W.J. Eddy	Wiltshire Regiment
E. Ellis	Merchant Navy
R. Ellis	Merchant Navy
J. Gregor	Merchant Navy
R.E. Gregory	Merchant Navy
J. Hollow	Royal Air Force
E. Hosken	Royal Artillery
W. Hosking	Royal Air Force
R.G. Ingram	Royal Marines
R. James	Duke of Cornwall's Light Infantry
W.G. Jenks	Royal Navy
T.W. Jones	King's Own Yorkshire Light Infantry
O.H.G. Luke	Royal Air Force
H. Matthews	Queen's Royal Regiment
B.M. Mills	Merchant Navy
W.T. Mills	Merchant Navy
E.A. Monson	Royal Navy
L. Oliver	King's Own Regiment
W.O. Peerless	Royal Navy
W.G. Peters	Duke of Cornwall's Light Infantry
R. Polkinghorne	Merchant Navy
L. Radcliffe	Merchant Navy
T.G. Rail	Royal Artillery
I. Richards	Merchant Navy

A.P. Roberts	Merchant Navy
R. Roberts	Merchant Navy
F. Roskilly	Royal Sussex Regiment
E. Shepherd	Royal Electrical & Mechanical Engineers
S.H. Sullivan	Royal Artillery
V. Thomas	Queen's Royal Regiment
B.T. Virgin	Royal Navy
A.R. Williams	Royal Navy
C. Williams	Royal Army Service Corps
E.C. Williams	Royal Navy

APPENDIX I:

Chapter Notes & References

Chapter One – LACUNA
1   Reminiscences of the late Mr Bob Ellis and Mr Bill Rowe of Hayle.

Chapter Two – PRELUDE AND SITZKRIEG
1   *The Cornishman*, 10-7-1922.
2   Ibid, 24-7-1935.
3   Ibid, 6-7-1938.
4   Ibid, 18-8-1938.
5   Ibid, 5-9-1938.
6   Ibid, 17-8-1938.
7   Recollections of a former member of Penzance ATS.
8   *The Cornishman*, 30-8-1939.
9   Ibid, 31-8-1939.
10 Recollections of former member of the Royal Artillery.
11 *The Cornishman*, 6-9-1939.
12 Ibid, 21-2-1940.
13 Ibid.
14 Ibid, 28-2-1940.

Chapter Three
'WE SHALL FIGHT THEM ON THE BEACHES'
1   Personal recollection of the late Mr Percy Jacka, St Erth.
2   53rd (London) Medium Regt Royal Artillery (database).
3   *Harvey & Company Minute Book* 20th August 1940 and 20th August 1941 via John Higgans.
4   Colin Dobinson. *A.A. Command. Britain's Anti-Aircraft Defences of World War II.*(London 2001).
5   Arthur Fairhurst. *in litt*, 2002 and via the late Mr Thomas ICI employee.
6   Maj. Gen. Sir Frederick Pile.
    Ack-Ack. Britain's Defences Against Air Attack During the Second World War. London, 1949.
7   Chris Goss. *Luftwaffe Fighter-Bombers over Britain.* (Manchester 2003).
8   *Cornwall County Constabulary War Diary.*
9   Don MacGeorge, eye witness.
10 Author's recollection; *The Cornishman* 2nd September 1942,
    Cornwall County Constabulary War Diary.
11 Tom Clemence, ex-REME officer.
12 Vic Acheson. *The Sunday Independent* 14th December 1975.
13 Mrs Marion Peller, and author's recollection.
14 *Hayle Invasion Committee Minutes,* November 1942 – November 1944

Chapter Four
GARRISON TOWN
1   *The Cornishman*, 29-5-1940.
2   Ibid, 1-5-1941.
3   Ibid, 3-12-1941.
4   Ibid, 13-5-1942.
5   Ibid, 10-6-1942.
6   Ibid, 5-8-1942.
7   Ibid, 30-9-1942.
8   via Mr Michael Williams.
9   *The Cornishman*, 28-10-1942.
10 Ibid, 30-12-1942.
11 Ibid, 4-1-1945.
12 Ibid, 5-1-1944.

Chapter Five
THE HOME GUARD & THE AUXILIARY UNITS
1 John Warwicker, *With Britain in Mortal Danger*. (Bristol 2002).
2 John James, *The Paladins*.
3 *The Cornishman*, 15-5-1940.
4 Ibid, 22-5-1940.
5 Ibid, 29-5-1940.
6 Ibid, 10-9-1941.
7 Ibid, 1-10-1941.
8 Ibid, 19-8-1942.
9 Ibid, 10-6-1943.
10 Ibid, 8-7-1943.
11 *The Jubilee Booklet* (Associated Octel Company September 1988) via Arthur Fairhurst.
12 *The Cornishman*, 7-12-1944.
13 Author's personal recollections.
14 *The Cornishman*, 7-12-1944.
15 Ibid, 18-8-1944.
16 Ibid, 9-1-1944.
17 Ibid, 7-12-1944.
18 Ibid, 23-11-1944.
19 Ibid, 14-12-1944.
20 Ibid, 3-1-1946.
21 Ibid, 28-1-1943.
22 Ibid, 4-1-1945.
23 John Warwicker, *With Britain in Mortal Danger*. (Bristol, 2002).
24 David Campe, *The Last Ditch*. (via Gordon Stevens).
25 Ibid, p121

Chapter Six
CIVIL DEFENCE – A.R.P.
1 *Hayle Invasion Committee Minutes*.
2 *The Cornishman*, 18-2-1943.
3 Ibid, 3-9-1941.
4 Author's personal recollections.
5 *The Cornishman*, 26-11-1941.
6 Ibid.
7 Ibid, 24-12-1940.
8 via John Higgans.
9 via Gerald Williams, ex-employee.
10 *The Cornishman*, 26-2-1941.
11 Ibid, 2-4-1941.
12 Ibid, 27-8-1941.
13 Ibid, 3-9-1941.
14 Ibid.
15 Ibid.
16 Ibid, 17-2-1943.
17 Ibid, 8-9-1943.
18 Ibid, 3-11-1944.
19 Ibid.
20 Ibid, 15-9-1943.
21 Ibid, 8-2-1945.
22 Ibid, 12-7-1945.
23 Ibid, 1-11-1945.
24 Ibid, 15-11-1945.
25 Ibid, 26-10-1944.
26 Ibid, 22-2-1945.

Chapter Seven
THE FIREFIGHTERS – A.F.S. & N.F.S.
1 *The Cornishman*, 14-7-1940.
2 Ibid, 31-7-1940.
3 Ibid, 21-8-1940.

4   Ibid, 4-12-1940.
5   Ibid, 29-1-1941.
6   Ibid, 5-2-1941.
7   Ibid, 5-3-1941.
9   Ibid.
10 Ibid, 2-4-1941.
11 Ibid.
12 Ibid, 1-5-1941.
13 Ibid.
14 Ibid, 28-5-1941.
15 Ibid.
16 Ibid, 3-9-1941.
17 Ibid, 3-2-1943.
18 Ibid, 17-2-1943.
19 Ibid.
20 Ibid, 25-8-1943.
21 *Hayle Invasion Committee Minutes*.
22 *The Cornishman*, 10-5-1944.
23 Ibid, 1-11-1945.
24 Ibid.
25 Ibid, 6-12-1945.
26 Ibid, 10-1-1946.
27 *The West Briton*, 13-4-2004.

Chapter Eight
'STARFISH' & OTHER DECOYS
1   Dr R.V. Jones. *Most Secret War.*
2   Maj. Gen. Sir Frederic Pile.
    Ack-Ack, Britains Defences Against Air Attack in the Second World War. (London ,1949).
3   Huby Fairhead. *Colonel Turner's Department.* (Norwich,1997.)
4   Ibid.
5   Huby Fairhead, *in litt.*
6   Stephen Budiansky. *Air Power.* (London,2003)

Chapter Nine
BOMBS ON HAYLE & DISTRICT
1   *Cornwall County Constabulary Air Raid Report Books.*
2   *The Cornishman,* 11-9-1940.
3   *Cornwall County Constabulary Air Raid Report Books.*
4   *Cornwall ARP Records.*
5   *Cornwall County Constabulary Air Raid Report Books* and author's recollections.
6   *The Cornishman*, 15-11-1940.
7   Related by a former GWR ganger.
8   *Cornwall County Constabulary Air Raid Report Books.*
9   The late Mr J.C. Bowden.
10 *Cornwall County Constabulary Air Raid Report Books.*
11 Ibid.
12 Ibid.
13 Ibid. and author's recollection.
14 *The Cornishman*, 13-1-1943.
15 *Cornwall County Constabulary Air Raid Report Books.*
16 Author's recollections.

Chapter Ten
'SUFFER THE LITTLE CHILDREN' – The Evacuees
1   *The Cornishman*, 19- 6-1940.
2   Ibid.
3   Ibid, 18-5-1940.
4   Ibid, 6-3-1940.
5   Ibid, 8-5-1940.
6   Ibid, 5-6-1940.

7   Ibid, 19-6-1940.
8   Ibid.
9   Ibid, 15-5-1941.
10 Ibid, 26-7-1945.
11 Ibid, 19-6-1940.
12 Ibid, 1-4-1942.
13 Ibid, 16-9-1942.
14 Ibid, 10-11-1943.
15 Ibid, 20-8-1941.
16 Edward R. Murrow. *A Reporter Remembers. Volume 1, The War Years.* (1946).
17 *The Cornishman*, 20-7-1944 and 18-7-1946.
18 Ibid, 31-8-1944.
19 Ibid, 28-6-1945.
20 Ibid, 7-6-1945.
21 Ibid, 21-6-1945.
22 Ibid, 31-5-1945.
23 Ibid.
24 Ibid, 21-6-1945.
25 Ibid, 26-7-1945.
26 Ibid, 2-8-1945.

Chapter Eleven
THE *ROSSMORE & THE MARENA* – The Battle of the North Coast
1   *The Cornishman*, 2-4-1941.
2   R & B Lorn. *The Shipwreck Index of the British Isles. Volume 1.* (London 1997).
3   The late Mr Dai Trewartha (Rossmore survivor).
4   via the late Mr J.C. Bowden.
5   via Mr Raymond Trewartha.
6   Reminiscences of seamen involved and their families.
7   The late Mr Dai Trewartha.
8   David Donald. *Warplanes of the Luftwaffe.* (London, 1994).
9   *Cornwall County Constabulary War Diary* and Personal observation by the author.
10 via the late Mr Clive Carter.
11 Stephen Budiansky. *Air Power,* Viking (Penguin) (London,2003).

Chapter Twelve
THE RED DUSTER
1   Russel Plummer. *The Ships That Saved An Army.* (Wellingborough, 1990).
2   *Cornwall County Constabulary War Diary.*
3   *The Cornishman*, 30-8-1945.
4   Contemporary account, the late William Sullivan.
5   Author's personal recollections.
6   Information via Mr Dennis Hollow of Hayle.
7   The late Hughie Love, in conversation.
8   *The Cornishman*, 9-9-1942.

Chapter Thirteen
THE MYSTERY OF THE FRENCH CRABBER
1   Local residents' recollections and author's observations.
2   *The St Ives & Hayle Times,* 12-9-2003.
3   John McWilliams. (Lecture, Hayle 1st October 2004).

Chapter Fourteen
SOCIAL LIFE – The Light in the Darkness
1   *The Cornishman,* 25-9-1941.
2   Ibid, 4-1-1945.
3   Ibid, 9-2-1944.
4   Ibid, 6-12-1942.
5   Ibid, 10-12-1941.
6   Ibid, 5-3-1941.
7   Ibid, 30-12-1942.

8   Ibid, 16-12-1942.
9   Ibid, 28-1-1942.
10 Ibid, 14-1-1942.
11 Ibid, 10-6-1942.
12 Ibid, 5-8-1942.
13 Ibid, 21-4-1943.
14 Ibid, 11-8-1943.

Chapter Fifteen
AIR CRASHES
1   John Foreman. *The Forgotten Months*. (Air Research Publications).
    & *Cornwall County Constabulary War Diary*. (CC/Pol/68/1-2-3-4).
2   *Phillack Church Visitors Book*. (31-7-1989).
3   *Cornwall County Constabulary War Diary*.
4   Ibid.
5   Ibid.
6   *Operations Record Book*, 502 Squadron RAF St Eval.
7   *Cornwall County Constabulary War Diary*.
8   via Mr Michael Williams.
9   Author's personal observations.
10 Ibid.
11 *Cornwall County Constabulary War Diary*.
12 Ibid.
13 Ibid.
14 Information and documents via Mr Trevor Millett

Chapter Sixteen
The B-17 THAT DIDN'T QUITE GET TO THE WAR
1   Martin Bowman. *The Eighth Air Force at War*. (Sparkford, 1994).
2   Hawkins, Ian L., *B-17s Over Berlin*. (London, 1990).
3   Ms Lettice Curtis ex-ATA pilot, *in litt*.
4   *The Illustrated London News*, 1942.
5   USAAF *Report of Aircraft Accident*, 1943.
6   Ibid.

Chapter Seventeen
'THEY'RE JUST LIKE US'
1   Author's recollection.
2   *The Cornishman*, 3-5-1944.
3   Ibid.
4   Ibid, 23-5-1944.
5   Ibid, 1-6-1944.
6   Ibid, 14-6-1944.
7   Author's personal recollection.
8   *The Cornishman*, 22-3-1944.
9   via Capt George Hogg.
10 Robin Neilands. *The Battle for Normandy*.
11 Author's personal observation.
12 *The Cornishman*, 14-6-1944.
13 Ibid, 28-9-1944.
14 via David Chinn, Newlyn, Penzance.

Chapter Eighteen
'RHINOS' ON THE WEIR
1   Edwin P. Hoyt. *The Invasion Before Normandy*. (London 1987).
2   Lt Cdr Trevor Blore, RNVR. *Commissioned Barges*.
3   Author's recollections.
4   The late Mr Desmond Ferris, ex-Curtis employee.
5   via Mr Venn, Penzance.
6   Mr Alfred Williams, Hayle, ex-Curtis employee.
7   Ibid.

8   Ibid.
9   Author's recollection.
10 *The Cornishman*, 3-5-1944.
11 Ibid, 21-6-1944.
12 Mr Alfred Williams.
13 *The Cornishman,* 19-7-1945.
14 Ibid, 7-9-1944.
15 Ibid, 21-9-1944.
16 Ibid, 13-10-1944.
17 Ibid, 24-5-1945.
18 Ibid.
19 Ibid, 31-5-1945.
20 Ibid, 2-8-1945.

Chapter Nineteen
THE CADETS
1   *The Cornishman*, 1-3-1942.
2   Ibid, 1-7-1942.
3   Ibid, 5-11-1941.
4   Ibid, 3-12-1941.
5   Ibid, 24-6-1942.
6   *Hayle ATC Sports Day Programme*, 27-6-1942.
7   *The Cornishman*, 21-1-1943.
8   Ibid, 24-1-1943.
9   *Flypast* magazine, January 2003.
10 *The Cornishman*, 21-4-1943.
11 Ibid, 10-6-1943.
12 Ibid, 9-1-1943.
13 Ibid, 5-2-1944.
14 Ibid.
15 Ibid, 1-3-1945.
16 Ibid.
17 Ibid, 12-7-1945.
18 Author's recollection.
19 *The Cornishman*, 20-9-1945.
20 Ibid, 13-12-1945.
21 Ibid, 24-1-1943.
22 Ibid, 25-2-1943.
23 Ibid, 25-8-1943.
24 Ibid, 16-2-1944.
25 Ibid, 7-3-1946.
26 *The Cornishman*, 9-1-1944.
27 Ibid, 17-12-1941.
28 Ibid, 20-10-1943.
29 Ibid, 17-1-1943.

Chapter Twenty
NATIONAL SAVINGS
1   *The Cornishman*, 15-5-1940.
2   Ibid, 30-4-1941.
3   Author's recollections.
4   *The Cornishman*, 30-4-1941.
5   Ibid, 22-10-1941.
6   Ibid, 6-8-1941.
7   Ibid, 12-11-1941.
8   Bernard Ireland. *Jane's Naval History of World War Two, Volume 2.*(London,1998).
9   Roy Nesbit. *Aeroplane Magazine,* October. 2005.
10 *The Cornishman*, 26-8-1942.
11 Ibid, 5-2-1942.
12 Ibid, 22-4-1943.
13 Ibid, 19-5-1943.

14 *Chambers Biographical Dictionary.*
15 *The Cornishman,* 26-5-1943.
16 *Hayle 'Wings for Victory' Week, Official Programme,* 1943.
17 *The Cornishman,* 22-9-1943.
18 Ibid, 26-1-1944.
19 Ibid, 12-4-1944.
20 Ibid, 1-3-1945.
21 Ibid, 29-3-1945.
22 Ibid, 13-1-1943.
23 Nigel Parriss. *An Baner Kernewek.* November, 2005.
24 *The Cornishman,* 5-4-1944.
25 Ibid, 10-5-1944.
26 Ibid, 18-10-1944.

Chapter Twenty-One
THE BRITISH RESTAURANT
1 *The Cornishman,* 14-7-1943.
2 Ibid, 11-8-1943.
3 Ibid, 20-10-1943.
4 Ibid, 1-3-1944.
5 Ibid, 3-5-1944.
6 Ibid.
7 Ibid, 1-6-1944.
8 Ibid, 31-8-1944.

Chapter Twenty-Two
FLT LT MEYER DFC
1 Doug Richardson. *Classic Warplanes 2 - Boeing B-17.*
2 Steve Birdsell and Roger A. Freeman. *Claims to Fame B-17 Flying Fortress,* (London, 1994).
3 *The Cornishman,* 10-11-1941.
4 Ibid, 26-11-1941.
5 Ibid, 11-1-1945.

Chapter Twenty-Three
EVERYDAY LIFE IN WARTIME HAYLE
1 *The Cornishman,* 5-3-1941.
2 Ibid, 26-2-1941.
3 Ibid, 14-5-1941.
4 Ibid, 23-8-1941.
5 Ibid, 24-9-1941.
6 Ibid, 10-12-1941.
7 Ibid, 17-12-1941.
8 Ibid, 4-2-1942.
9 Ibid, 11-3-1942.
10 Ibid, 3-6-1942.
11 Ibid, 24-6-1942.
12 Ibid, 8-7-1942.
13 Ibid, 15-7-1942.
14 Ibid, 7-10-1942.
15 Ibid, 15-10-1942.
16 Ibid, 3-2-1943.
17 Ibid, 10-2-1943 and 17-2-1943.
18 Ibid, 10-3-1943.
19 Ibid, 24-3-1943.
20 Ibid.
21 Ibid, 31-3-1943.
22 Ibid.
23 Ibid, 26-5-1943.
24 Ibid, 9-6-1943.
25 Ibid, 18-8-1943.
26 Ibid.
27 Ibid.
28 Ibid.

29 Tony Lane. *The Merchant Seaman's War,* (Manchester,1990).
30 *The Cornishman*, 18-8-1943.
31 Ibid, 8-9-1943.
32 Ibid.
33 Ibid, 29-9-1943.
34 Ibid, 27-10-1943.
35 Ibid, 8-12-1943.
36 Ibid, 15-12-1943.
37 Ibid, 12-1-1944.
38 Ibid, 19-1-1944.
39 Ibid.
40 Ibid, 26-1-1944.
41 Ibid.
42 Ibid.
43 Ibid, 2-2-1944.
44 Ibid, 2-2-1944.
45 Ibid.
46 Ibid, 1-6-1944.
47 Ibid, 12-1-1944.
48 Ibid, 22-3-1944.
49 Ibid, 14-6-1944.
50 Ibid, 21-6-1944.
51 Ibid, 14-6-1944.
52 Ibid, 21-6-1944.
53 Ibid, 17-8-1944.
54 Ibid, 7-9-1944.
55 Ibid, 21-9-1944.
56 Ibid, 28-9-1944.
57 Ibid, 22-3-1945.
58 Ibid, 2-11-1944.
59 Ibid, 8-11-1944.
60 Ibid, 7-12-1944.
61 Ibid, 18-1-1945.
62 Ibid, 25-1-1945.
63 Ibid, 8-2-1945.
64 Ibid, 22-2-1945.
65 Ibid, 1-3-1945.
66 Ibid, 29-3-1945.
67 Ibid, 26-4-1945.
68 Ibid, 14-6-1945.
69 Ibid, 21-6-1945.
70 Ibid, 12-7-1945.
71 Ibid, 23-8-1945.
72 Ibid, 30-8-1945.
73 Ibid, 6-9-1945.
74 Ibid.
75 Ibid.
76 Ibid, 20-12-1945.
77 Ibid, 31-1-1946.
78 Ibid, 28-2-1946.
79 Ibid.

Chapter Twenty-Five
AFTERMATH – The Break-up of Ships
1 Basic list from T.W. Ward Ltd. Detailed data from other sources.
2 Bernard Ireland. *Jane's Naval History of World War 2.* (London 1998).
3 John D. Winser. *The D-Day Ships.* (Kendal 1994).
4 Ibid.
5 Wynn, Kenneth, *U-boat Operations of the Second War,* (Volume 2)

APPENDIX II:

Associated Octel

Historical Summary 1938 – 1974

THE HAYLE WORKS of the Associated Octel Company Ltd was established as the site for the extraction of bromine from seawater. This product was used in the subsequent production of octane boosters for aviation gasoline during the Second World War and afterwards in motor gasolines.

The factory itself was initially owned by the government (Ministry of Aircraft Production) but designed and operated by the British Ethyl Corporation on their behalf. This company was 50% ICI Alkali and 50% Associated Ethyl Co. Ltd.

Bromine was required for the war effort and the chosen site had to be secure from enemy action as well as meeting all the technical requirements. Warm water from the condensers of the adjacent power station was an important consideration.

Key Dates

1936	British Ethyl Corporation formed by ICI and Associated Ethyl.
Aug. '38	Building of anti-knock facilities sanctioned by Government.
Dec. '38	Hayle site surveyed by ICI Alkali division.
Jan. '39	Agreement reached with Dow Chemical Corp. (Midland, Michigan, USA) for rights to use their 'alkali' process to manufacture bromine from sea water.
Feb. '39	Hayle selected as the site for bromine production using land owned by Harvey & Co. on North Quay.
May '39	Agreement reached for British Ethyl to build and operate plants as required by the government. ICI Alkali undertook to construct and operate plants on behalf of the joint company.
Aug. '39	Site clearance began. Work undertaken by A.H. Dingle & Co.
Oct. '39	Work started on Carnsew tunnel.
July '40	Construction and commissioning complete. First bromine produced.
Jan. '41	Carnsew tunnel completed connecting Carnsew and power station water intake.
July '43	British Ethyl became wholly owned by Associated Ethyl.
Jan. '45	Plant and equipment purchased by Associated Ethyl from ministry of aircraft production.
Jan. '48	ICI Alkali ceased to operate the plant. Associated Ethyl assumes full responsibility for all activities.
1948 – '49	Sulphuric acid plant built. Commissioned July '49. Acid no longer imported but manufactured on site from solid sulphur.
Sept. '54	Liquid ethylene plant commissioned. External supply started, on-site production of ethylene ceased.
Oct. '54	Original 'alkali' process closed down. Conversion to 'acid' process started.

information via Mr Arthur Fairhurst

APPENDIX III:

Civil Defence

WEST PENWITH RURAL DISTRICT COUNCIL.

11, MORRAB ROAD,
PENZANCE,
11th January, 1939.

Dear Sir or Madam,

The Council have been requested by the Government to co-operate in plans which are being made for the protection of civilian life in the event of war.

Recent experience in other countries has shown that under the conditions of modern warfare the greatest loss of life is caused by bombardment from the air. This danger is most acute in crowded cities. It is to lessen this danger in case our own country were involved in war that arrangements are being made now to enable children to leave the crowded cities and be received in homes elsewhere. This protection can only be given with the co-operation of those like ourselves who live in the less congested towns or villages. We shall all agree that it is necessary for all of us to help in this plan for saving human life, and for safeguarding the rising generation who will eventually have the management of our country in their hands.

I am aware that some arrangements were made last September as a matter of emergency. These had perforce to be improvised and sometimes gave rise to points of criticism. But I am sure that in the light of the experience gained we shall be able to improve on these. The plans for this, as for other branches of civil defence, must be made in time of peace. We hope that it will never be necessary to put them into operation. But we shall all be happier to know that the plans have been made and that if ever they do have to be put in operation, the work will be done in an ordered manner, and that all will know their parts.

The Government has asked each local authority in the country to find out what housing accommodation would be available in case of emergency, and what homes would be suitable for those children who would be given the means of leaving the great cities. It is particularly important to know in which houses homes could be provided for the children, where they could be lodged, boarded and cared for. Payment would be made by the Government at the rate of 10s. 6d. a week where one child is taken, and 8s. 6d. for each child where more than one is taken.

A representative of the local authority will call upon you some time during the next month or so to find out how far you will be able to assist in this matter. He will produce to you a card showing that he is authorised to make these inquiries.

This note is sent to you now in order that you may be aware, in advance, of this enquiry and why it is being made.

I give you my assurance that the information supplied by you will not be used for any other purpose than that which I have described, and that it will not involve you in any work or responsibility unless and until an emergency arises. I feel that I can rely on the people of West Penwith to offer all the help they possibly can in this important branch of civil defence. It needs no words of mine to convey to you what that help will mean to children of the big cities.

Yours faithfully,

W. JEFFERY,
Chairman of the Council.

		Nos 8, 8A, 8
St Johns Street.	Seven	9, 10, 11, 12
Bodriggy Street	four	No 1, 2, 5, 5
Hill Crest Road.	one	
Trelawney Place.	ten	No 14, 14A, 15, 16B, 16c, 17, 18,
Commercial Road.	six	No 21, 22, 22A
Hayle Terrace. one at the Rear of the Institute	four	Nos 24, 25, 26,
Penpol Terrace.	Five	
Penpol Avenue.	one	
Chapel Terrace.	Two	
Foundry Square.	One	
Bay View Terrace.	One	
Harbour View	One	
West Terrace.	One	No 28
St Elwyns Place.	One	No 29
Clifton Terrace.	two	Nos 31, 32,
Mount Pleasant Shelters at Trelawney Place also available	two	No 20
Undercliffe & Pocket	one	No 30.
Penpol Council School.	For Children	
Bodriggy Council School.	do	
Copperhouse School.	do	
Grammar School	do	

A great many houses have Morrison Table Shelters.

Accommodation for app 2000 Adults & Children

List of public air raid shelters

Air Raid Wardens in the Hayle area

K3 WARDENS — COPPERHOUSE, PHILLACK & TOWANS AREA

H. Tremayn, (Senior Warden)	Loggans, Hayle.
S. Lander	Prospect Place.
C.S. Roscorla	42, Commercial Rd.
B. Wallis	Chycaren, The Towans.
O. Berrymen	7, Clifton Terrace.
J.G. Cartwright	25, Mount Pleasant.
H.B. Williams	Mexico, Phillack.
L.H. Golding	Poplar Villa, Penmare Terrace.
C.P. Pedlar	Ventonleague.
H. Rutter	Penmare Terrace.
L. McKee	Rose Cottage, Guildford.
W.S. Polkinhorne	Mexico, Phillack.
H.A. Nurdin	The Retreat, The Towans.

K4 WARDENS — FOUNDRY AREA, HIGHLANES, ETC.

C. Hewett, (Senior Warden)	Penpol Terrace.
G. Wilks	Mount Pleasant.
B.G. Smart	Arrol Villa, Highlanes.
W.J. Lapham	Penpol Terrace.
T.C. Burt	Penpol Terrace.
H. Simonson	The Laurels, Foundry Hill.
G.J.P. Dowrick	59, St John's Street.
P. Bennetts	2, Mount Pleasant.
J.H. Woolcock	18, Trelawney Place.
J. Ellis	The Haven.
W.J. Drew	8, Tolview.
H. Millett	7, Hayle Terrace.
D. Pearce	St Eia, Commercial Road.
N. Quinn	9, Chapel Terrace.
P. Jane	Bokiddiek, Highlanes.
W.H. Trevithick	Pentire, Chapel Terrace.
C. Runnalls	Treglissen.
W.J. Easterbrook	Tremeadow, Mount Pleasant.
T. Hocking	11, Mount Pleasant.
J.R. Rutter	Windance Farm.
L. Ellis, (Messenger)	Foundry Hill.
G. Hicks	Trelissick Terrace.

Hayle & District Warden's Posts

1. Gwithian – Gwinear, Connor Downs.
Senior Warden
V. Stephens, Carnell Green.   Phone no. Praze 263.
Other wardens with private phones:
Yates, Praze 32.   Shovel (Connor), Hayle 3257.
Giles, Leedstown 206.   Sara (Gwithian), Camborne 3280.

2. St Erth, Canonstown, Fraddam, St Erth-Praze, etc.
Senior Warden,
Mr H. Reynolds, Rose-an-Grouse.

3. Copperhouse, Towans, Angarrack, etc.
Senior Warden,
Mr H. Tremayne, Loggans.

4. Foundry, etc.
Senior Warden,
Mr Blewett, Hayle, 3105.

1. has nominally 4 Posts
Gwithian not working
Gwinear, Mr Stephens,   Phone no. Praze 263
Wall.
Women's Institute. Mr B. Carne.

2. has nominally 3 Posts
St Erth-Praze. Not Open.
St Erth, Mr Maddern.
Church Hall.
Mr Reynolds, Rose-an-Grouse.
Mr Daniel, Kiethen Wood has a phone, no. Leedstown 204

3. has nominally 4 Posts
Polkinghorne's Shop, Fore Street.
Mr Wallis's House, The Towans.   Phone no. 3184
Mr Tremayne's house.
Angarrack, not working.

4. has nominally 5 Posts
Mr Blackmore's House.   Phone no. 3162
2 in Foundry Square.   Phone no. 2254
Commercial Road (next Police Station).
Mr Smart's House.   Phone no. 2100

Hayle Rescue Squad members

J.L. Prisk	8, Foundry Hill
H. Ingram	Bar View
W. Hollow	5, Highlanes
H. Philp	Tremeadow Terrace
W. Hocking	26B Penpol Terrace
M. Hosking	Joppa
K. Lapham	Penpol Terrace
A. Cloke	30, Commercial Road
J. Temby	Trevose, Commercial Road
W. Phillips	Carnsew
V. Harvey	4, Foundry Hill

Hayle & District Decontamination Squad members

W.R. Trevithick	Pentire, Chapel Terrace, Phone 3197
W. Ostey	Highlanes
E.J. Ostey	5, Penpol Road
P. Bennetts	4 Mount Pleasant
S. Philp	Commercial Road
W.R. Christopher	Gwinear

Phone Praze 20
After 5p.m. Leedstown 245

APPENDIX IV:
Police

WHEN THE THREAT of invasion was a very real possibility the police were issued with instructions as to their role and duties should invasion be imminent. These instructions were as follows:

Police

(A) Brief description of their duties at Stand To and Action Stations.

On receipt of 'Stand To' instruction no operational action will be executed by the Police. A check will be made of arrangements made to put into effect instructions received to control the civil population, roads and notices, immobilisation of vehicles and petrol pumps, destruction of pigeons and lofts, closing of schools, places of entertainment and licensed premises. Display of E.L. Labels, liaison with the Military and Invasion Committee.

On receipt of 'Action Stations' such instruction will be passed to the Chairman, Invasion Committee and Food Executive Officer. Crash Invasion Barriers will be manned and steps taken to deal with the civil population who have neglected the policy of 'Stand Firm'. Barriers have been sited on the A30 road at Plough Inn, Collage and Berryman's Garage, Redruth, and Lanner Moor, Lanner. Persons endeavouring to evacuate will be turned back and directed to remain at their Home, Rest Centres or places where Slit Trenches have been provided.

If the Military consider the situation such that a number of persons should be passed out, such persons will be directed to avenues of safety and to scatter in fields and woods.

(B) Arrangements for closing roads and routing essential traffic.

All roads are subject to an order being made to close them except for Military, and perhaps, Essential traffic, and the roads to be made closed cannot be definitely fixed beforehand as military operations and enemy action may make any such arrangement impracticable or impossible.

Until the Military situation is known and the routes required are intimated to the Police the route for other traffic cannot be fixed.

(C) Steps to be taken to deal with refugees and enforce the 'Stand Firm' policy.

Arrangements have been made that where a large number of refugees are making towards the area they will be contacted and dispersed to Rest Centres or avenues of safety.

To enforce the 'Stand Firm' policy barriers are ready at the Sites and will be manned at 'Action Stations'. Persons will be turned back and advised to go to their homes, Rest Centres, Slit Trenches. If the police are unable to control the situation immediately appeal will be made to the Military for assistance to enforce the Policy of 'Stand Firm' by use of arms if necessary.

APPENDIX V:

Aid Posts and Nursing

HAYLE FIRST AID POST

FULLTIME STAFF

Miss J.M. Dempsey	Foundry Square
Miss P. Farthey	Chapel Road
Mr J.P. Fitzgerald	Commercial Road

VOLUNTARY PERSONNEL

Mrs E.C. Blackmore	Trethewa, Foundry Hill
Mrs W. Symons	Commercial Road
Mrs E.M. Smith	Glade, Pond Avenue
Mrs K. Galloway	Loggans
Mrs E.M. Webster	12, Penpol Road
Mrs J. Rogers	Penpol Terrace
Mrs M. Rendall	
Miss I. Symons	26, Penpol Road
Miss V. Love	5, West Terrace
Miss K. Baumbach	3, Undercliff
Miss E. Murphy	54, St John's Street
Miss H. Jones	Grammar School
Miss N. Orchard	Trelissick Terrace
Miss J. Bond	Penmare Terrace
Miss J. Oates	1, Penpol Terrace
Miss N. Hawkins	Mill Pond House
Miss P. Drew	Fore Street
Miss E.C. Honeyball	Penpol Terrace
Miss A. Clemence	38, Hayle Terrace
Mr Bridge	Chemist, Copperhouse
	(Local Gas Officer)

HAYLE NURSING DIVISION
S.J.A.B.

Name	Rank	Hospital Duties	C.N.R.	Munitions	F.A.P.	Services
Mrs H. Turner	Lady Div. Supt	Full Time	C.N.R.			
Miss West	L/Amb. Officer	Part Time	C.N.R.			
Mrs Blackmore	President	P/T Clinic	C.N.R.		Part Time	
Mrs E. Oats	Div. Sec.				Part Time	
Miss M. Tripp	Amb. Sister	Part Time	C.N.R.		Part Time	
Miss F. Bagg	Amb. Sister	Part Time	C.N.R.			
Miss V. Love	Amb. Sister	Full Time	C.N.R.			
Miss P. Farthey	Amb. Sister	Part Time	C.N.R.		Part Time	
Miss J. Bond	Amb. Sister		C.N.R.		Full Time	
Miss K. Baumbach	Amb. Sister		C.N.R.	Full Time		
Mrs K. Galloway	Amb. Sister		C.N.R.			W.L.A.
Miss Carvolth	Amb. Sister	Part Time	C.N.R.		Part Time	
Mrs N. Symons	Amb. Sister	Full Time	C.N.R.			
Miss I. Symons	Amb. Sister	Part Time	C.N.R.		Part Time	
Miss A. Matthews	Amb. Sister	Part Time			Part Time	
Mrs Webster	Amb. Sister	Full Time		Full Time		
Miss M. Ryan	Amb. Sister					Amb. Driver
Miss B. Ryan	Amb. Sister					Amb. Driver

HAYLE RED CROSS & ST JOHN WORK PARTY

Mr H. Turner	24, Penpol Terrace		Leader
Mrs Greever	31, Penpol Terrace		Assist. Leader
Mrs Orchard	Mellanear Road		
Mrs Brett	6, Clifton Terrace		Treasurer
Mrs Oliver	Bridge House		
Mrs Coombes	34, Commercial Road		
Mrs Coombe	59, Mount Pleasant		Secretary
Miss Veal	Commercial Road		
Miss Smitham	Commercial Road		
Mrs Clarke	Mellanear Road		
Mrs Opie	'Glencoe', Hayle Terrace		
Mrs Blight	'Eccola', Station Villas		
Mrs Grant	Penpol Terrace, (c/o Mrs Williams)		
Mrs Thomas	14, Tremeadow Terrace		
Mrs Burt	Penpol Terrace		
Mrs Hooper	Hollow's Terrace		
Mrs Rogers	Hollow's Terrace		
Miss Jenkin (May)	Bay View Terrace		
Miss Smith	'Trenower', Hayle Terrace		
Mrs Soray	30, Hayle Terrace		
Mrs Piper	Grammar School		

APPENDIX VI:

Fire Service & Water Supplies

LIST OF MEMBERS of the National Fire Service in Hayle during World War II

Bolitho, L.	10, Bodriggy Street
Bell, P.	Post Office
Bailey, D.	5, Trelawney Place
Casey, B.	1, Hayle Terrace
Care, F.	5, Church Street, St Erth
Dalton, H.	15, Mount Pleasant
Glanville, J.	4, Trelissick Terrace
Harvey, A.	24, Penpol Road
Hampson, P.	19, Penpol Road
Hollow, C.	Start, Hayle
Hosking, W.	Trevassack Court, Copperhouse Hill
Johns, B.	1, Guildford Viaduct
Jones, W.	Station Villas
Knight, A.	6, Tremeadow Terrace
Mitchell, A.	44, Mount Pleasant
Martin, C.	Ventonleague
Mills, E.	North View, Copperhouse
Polkinghorne, H.	Guildford
Pattle, J.	16, Bodriggy Street
Pascoe, I.	Barburton Cottage, Leathlean Towans
Roskilly, N.	13, Hayle Terrace
Roberts, W.	10, Commercial Road
Rusden, W.	1, Penpol Avenue
Richards, W.	1, Laity Villas, Ventonleague
Symons, J.	21, Penpol Road
Shelton, J.	34, Commercial Road
Sampson, W.	33, Penpol Road
Terrill, V.	Carnsew
Thomas, S.	Guildford Viaduct
Trenear, E.	7, Highlanes
Wilson, A.	9, Glebe Row
Wilkins, G.	85, St John's Street
Coombe, C.	St John's Street
Nicholas, T.	St John's Street

SUPPLEMENTARY WATER SUPPLIES
HAYLE

SITE	TANKS	OTHER SOURCES	MAP	REMARKS
1		Yachting Pool, Phillack	D4	6,500,000
2		Mill Pond, Copperhouse	D4	150,000
3		Fore Street	D4	tidal 1/3-½
4		Hayle Terrace	D5	tidal 1/3-½
5		West Terrace	D5	tidal 1/3-½
6		nr. Clifton Terrace	D5	25,000 GPM
7		Wharf, nr. Gas Works	D5	tidal 1/3-½
8		Wharf, opp. Penpol Terrace	D5	tidal avail. 1/3-½
9		Mill Pond	D6	375,000
10	13,000	Commercial Road	D4	
11	13,000	West Terrace	D5	
12	13,000	Penpol Terrace	D5	
13	13,000	Chapel Hill	D5	
14	13,000	Trelawney Place	D5	
15	13,000	Mount Pleasant	D5	
16	13,000	Foundry Hill	D6	
17		Connor Downs, Turnpike	E3	mill leat
18		Loggans Mill	E4	weir
19		Beatrice Terrace	D4	weir
20		Copperhouse Road	D4	weir
21		Upton Towans Pond	E3	656,000

APPENDIX VII:

After the War

The Passmore Edwards Institute with the three minute warning siren on the roof.

Photograph: the author

THE TENSIONS THAT had simmered below the surface between the main Allies during the war accelerated in the race to Berlin in 1945. These tensions led Prime Minster Winston Churchill to declare, during an address on March 5th 1946 at the Westminster College in Fulton, Missouri, that:

> *"From Stettin in the Baltic to Trieste in the Adriatic an "iron curtain" has descended across the Continent. Behind that line lie all the capitals of the ancient states of Central and Eastern Europe. Warsaw, Berlin, Prague, Vienna, Budapest, Belgrade, Bucharest and Sofia; all these famous cities and the populations around them lie in what I must call the Soviet sphere, and all are subject, in one form or another, not only to Soviet influence but to a very high and in some cases increasing measure of control from Moscow."*

While many may have seen Churchill's speech as warmongering – especially considering Russia was an Ally – his personal opinion of Stalin and his Government was borne out and the 'Iron Curtain effectively kept any warmth out of the relationship between the western allies and their former Eastern 'friend,' leading to a 'Cold War'.

In Hayle evidence of the fear over the possibility of a war between countries both now with nuclear weapons, was visible for many years.

Hayle's Passmore Edwards Institute during World War II had been the centre for the Hayle Invasion Committee as well as the committee rooms for the Hayle Parish Council. Now the Institute became the focus of new 'war' with a siren mounted on the roof to be sounded in the event of an imminent nuclear attack – the three minute warning siren.

INDEX

Admiralty, ... 19, 69, 70, 97, 98
    passes, ... 69, 70
Aircraft Crashes, ... 81-82
Air Raid Precautions (ARP), ... 13-14
Air Raid Wardens, ... 25
Air Training Corps (ATC), ... 99-103
    DHS Sqdn, ... 102
Ambulance Cadets, ... 99, 104
American soldiers, ... 89-92
Angarrack, ... 117
    Chapel, ... 79-89
    Inn, ... 90
Anti-Aircraft Defences (Hayle), ... 21
    Units: 8AA Division (later 3 AA Group), . . . 22
        137 Regt, ... 22
        462 Battery, ... 22
    Gunsites: Calais (Hayle), ... 21
        Clifton Terrace, ... 22
        Bodriggy Fields, ... 22
        Gwinear, ... 21
        Lelant Bend, ... 22
        Lelant Towans, ... 22
        Mexico Towans, ... 22
        Porth Kidney, ... 22
        Trevarrack, ... 21
        Gunwyn Farm, ... 21-22
        Hayle Towans, ... 22
Arcadian Dance Band, ... 14, 58
Area Fire Force Commander, ... 49
Army, British, ... 19, 20, 29-32
    Cadet Force, ... 19, 103
Atlantic, ... 83, 116
Auxiliary Fire Service (AFS), ... 13, 45-48
Auxiliary Territorial Service (ATS), . . . 13-14, 29
Auxiliary Units, ... 37-38
    British Resistance Battalion, ... 38
    203 South of England Unit, ... 38
Avonville, SS, ... 67

Baltimore, ... 89
Balloon tender, ... 67
Bands:
    American Band of the AEF, ... 78
    Arcadians Dance Band (Frances Andrew), . 75, 109
    Blue Rhythmics, ... 29
    Corona Dance Band, ... 75
    Cremona Dance Band, ... 75
    Crewenna Dance Band, ... 36, 75
    DCLI Regimental Band, ... 107
    Elite Dance Band, ... 75, 109
    Hayle Battalion Home Guard Band, ... 36,
        . . . . 122-19, 81, 88, 109
    King's Own Dance Band, ... 30, 75, 106
    Martlets Dance Orchestra, ... 75
    Nighthawks Dance Band (RAF), ... 75
    Riff-Raff Dance Band (RAF Portreath), . . . 105
    West Yorks Dance Band, ... 30
Baptist Church, ... 31
    Hall, ... 31

Barclays Bank Ltd, ... 106, 109
Barry Dock, ... 63-64
B A Swallow, ... 101, 103
Battle of Britain Day, ... 102
Berry & Son, ... 122
Bickford-Smith Ltd, ... 67
Black Bridge, ... 52
Black Houses, ... 95
Black-out, ... 73
Blewett's, ... 79
Blitzkrieg, ... 14
Bluff Hotel, ... 81, 56
Body bags, ... 41
Bodriggy Fields, ... 22
Bodriggy School, ... 59, 60
Boeing B-17, ... 82-87, 113-114
Bomber Command, ... 113
Bombs, ... 53 - 56
Booms, ... 19, 34
Boy Scouts, ... 104
Bristol, ... 49, 51, 56
    Channel, ... 67
Bridgewater, ... 32, 67
Britain, ... 15-37
British, ... 33
    agents, ... 74
British Purchasing Commission, ... 113
British Restaurant, ... 61, 111-11
    Committee, ... 111
Browning Automatic Rifle (BAR), ... 36
    Machine Gun, ... 36
'Bucket of Blood' (New Inn), ... 90, 120

Calais (Cornwall), ... 21
Camborne, ... 47, 48, 49, 61, 92
    Fire Service, ... 48, 49
    Magistrates Court, ... 119
    Station, ... 61
Camborne-Redruth Council, ... 59
Camouflage Nets, ... 80
Canadian Rifles, ... 33
Canonstown, ... 25, 38
Carbis Bay, ... 68
Carnsew, ... 91, 94, 98
    Spit, ... 94
Casualty Officer, ... 41
Casualty Service, ... 42
Caterpillar Cranes, ... 97
Causeway Garage, ... 48
Censorship, ... 10, 63
Central Hospital Supply Service, ... 119
Chief Fire Officer, ... 48
Christmas, ... 79-80
Chrysler Engines, ... 9
Church of The Holy Ghost, ... 31, 79
Church Street, ... 53
'Cisco', ... 90
Civil Defence, ... 39-44
Clifton Terrace, ... 19, 22, 121

Coastal convoys, ... 64, 67
Coastal Protection Area, ... 119
Coast Lines, Ltd, ... 67
Coffins, ... 41
Colonel Turner's Department, ... 51
Coloured American Singers, The, ... 89-90
Commercial Road, ... 39, 52, 111
Communist Party, ... 119
Concarnau, ... 71
Condor, Focke-Wulf, ... 64-65
Connor Downs, ... 13, 78
Construction Battalion (CBs, USN), ... 93, 97
Convoy B3, ... 91
Copperhouse, ... 11, 32, 47, 56, 91
    Chapel, ... 59, 79, 115
    Cutting, ... 55
    Pool, ... 52
    School (LCC Evacuee), ... 60, 78
Copper Terrace, ... 120
'The Cornishman', Newspaper, ... 10, 32, 34,
    . . . . 42, 46, 49, 53,
    . . . . 54, 57, 59, 61, 62, 70, 77,
    . . . . 101, 102, 113, 117, 118, 120
Cornwall:
    Agricultural Committee, ... 37, 77
    Constabulary, ... 92, 119
    County Council, ... 21, 39, 78
    County Architect, ... 40
    County Football Association, ... 120
    Education Committee, ... 60
    Emergency Committee, ... 41
Cornwall Electric Power Company, . 35, 43, 115, 120
Cornwall Troops Welfare Fund, ... 32
Cot Pool, ... 71, 72
Couch, Nicholas, ... 40
County Hall, ... 39
County of Cornwall Shipping Company, ... 63
Cove Café, ... 31

'Dad's Army', ... 33
'Daily Mirror', ... 82
Duke of Cornwall's Light Infantry (D.C.L.I.), . . . 34
D-Day, ... 90, 92, 93, 97, 119, 123-124
Decoys, ... 51
Demolition charges, ... 19
D.E.M.S. gunners, ... 67
Detroit, ... 94
Devonport High School (D.H.S.), . 58, 59, 60-62, 102
Devonshire Regiment, ... 30, 31
'Diver' Operation, ... 29
'Dog Green' Sector (Omaha Beach), ... 91
'Down By The Zuider Zee', ... 69
Drill Hall, Hayle, ... 14, 29, 99
Dunleary, SS, ... 67
Durham Light Infantry (D.L.I.), ... 31
Dutch seamen, ... 69

Eastcoaster, SS, ... 67
East Quay, ... 19
Edmunson's Electric Company, ... 120
8th Air Force (USA), ... 83, 116
8th Army, ... 29, 116

VIII Corps, ... 38
Emergency Committee, ... 43, 47
Emergency Medical Service, ... 77
Emergency water tanks, ... 18
Engineer Corps (US Army), ... 91, 92, 93, 94
Essential Works Order (1941), ... 118
Evacuees, ... 57-62

Farm Industries Ltd, ... 118
Falmouth, ... 36, 53, 56, 91
Ferry Command (USAAF), ... 84, 85
'Fighting Seabees', ... 93
Fire Force Area 19, ... 47
Fire Protection Officer, ... 46
Fire Services Act 1947, ... 49
Fire Services (Emergency Provisions) Bill, ... 47
Fire Station (Hayle), ... 47, 48
Fire Watching Order, ... 46
First Aid Post, ... 14, 40-42
'Flu' epidemic, ... 119
Food Enforcement Officer, ... 116, 77
Force 'B' (Follow-up), ... 91
Foresight, HMS, ... 106
Foundry Chapel, ... 60, 89, 100
Foundry School (LCC Evac.), ... 42, 59
Foundry Schoolroom, ... 95
Foundry Square, ... 39, 40, 53, 67, 122
Fowey, ... 91
Fraddam, ... 36, 42, 52
Fraddam – St Erth Praze FAP, ... 42
France, ... 13, 17, 33, 37, 45, 48, 57, 118
Frank Curtis Ltd, ... 94, 95, 109, 123
    Employees Benevolent Fund, ... 98
French Crabber, ... 71-72
French Navy, ... 25
Frythens Farm, ... 81

Gas masks, ... 14
Gas Works, (St Ives), ... 23
German, ... 37, 56
    Army, ... 13
    Bombers, ... 56
    Intelligence Services, ... 29
    Meteorological Service, ... 64
Germany, ... 13, 37
'G Is', ... 89, 90, 92, 95
Girls Training Corps, ... 99, 103-104
Globe Inn, ... 69
'GOC' Line, ... 33
Godrevy, ... 18, 34
    Light, ... 64
'Great Meat Muddle', ... 14-15
Great War, The, ... 13
Great Western Railway (GWR), ... 36, 55, 56,
    . . . . 92 37, 72, 73, 101
'Green Howards', ... 30, 82
Griggs Hill, ... 22
Guildford, (Hayle), ... 54
    Road, ... 53
    Viaduct, ... 49
Gulval, ... 34
Gun Defended Area ('GDA'), ... 21

Gunsites (AA), ... 21-22
Gunwalloe, ... 19
Gunwyn Farm, ... 21, 22
Gurnard's Head, ... 34
Gwinear, ... 21, 22, 36, 37, 57, 115
Gwithian, ... 13, 18, 26, 45, 81,115

Hamburg, ... 52
Hampden, Handley-Page, ... 81
Harbour View Terrace, ... 39
Harvey & Company, ... 11, 35, 40, 67,
. . . . 70, 71, 94, 12312ref, 18, 23,
. . . . 49, 50, 51, 53, 75, 78
Haven Holiday Camp, ... 54
Hayle, ... 11-13, 18, 19, 21, 22,
. . . 25, 29, 31, 32, 34, 36, 38, 39, 40-42, 44,
. . . 45, 46, 47, 48, 49, 51-54, 56, 57, 59, 60,
. . . 61, 63, 64, 66-69, 71, 72, 73, 75, 77, 80-82,
. . . 87, 89, 90-92, 94, 97, 99, 102, 106, 107,
. . . . 109–112, 115–119, 121, 122
    Ambulance Squad, ... 42
    Bar, ... 65
    Beach, ... 25, 87
    Carnival, ... 13
    Casualty Service, ... 42
    Demob Servicemen's Fund, ... 118
    Dramatic Society, ... 109
    Emergency Maternity Home, ... 77
    Fire Station, ... 47
    Grammar School, ... 39, 46, 78, 122
    Harbour, ... 25, 67, 69, 71, 94
    Harbour Office, ... 67, 71
    Horseshoe Club, ... 104
    Infant Welfare Committee, ... 77
    Invasion Committee, ... 26, 47
    Kindergarten & Preparatory School, ... 109
    Library, ... 48
    Merrymakers Concert Party, ... 73, 74, 122
    Parish Council, ... 40, 41, 42, 45, 48, 63,
    . . . . 105, 106, 109, 110, 115, 118
    Power Station, ... 26, 41, 45, 115
    Rescue Squad, ... 42
    Rifle Range, ... 99, 11
    Services Canteen, ... 15-31
    Soccer Club, ... 101
    South Quay, ... 56, 68
    Spitfire Fund, ... 106
    Station, ... 46, 109
    Troops' Welcome Home Fund, ... 32, 121
    Towans, . . . 19, 22, 25, 29, 30, 51, 54, 82, 89, 99
    Town Silver Band, ... 36
    Variety Orchestra, ... 75
    Xmas Gift Fund for the Services, ... 118
'Hayle Safe', ... 49
Heather Lane, ... 38
Helford, ... 91
Hell's Mouth, ... 52
Helston, ... 89
Highlanes Chapel, ... 104
Holocaust, ... 117
Home Guard, ... 33-37, 42, 80, 99, 101, 109
    Band, ... 36, 109, 122

Cadets, ... 99
    12th Land's End Battalion, ... 34
House, Mr C.R., ... 27
    Shop, ... 40
'HQ Line', ... 339
Hudson, Lockheed, ... 80, 82
Hyster Crane, ... 97

ICI Ltd (British Ethyl Corp), ... 118
ICI Bromine Factory, ... 18, 22, 26, 45, 67, 80
Ireland, ... 65
Italy, ... 29

Jagdgeschwader 2 (JG 2), ... 23

Kampfgeschwader 40 (KG40) 66
King George V Memorial Walk, . . . 95, 97, 115, 117
King's Own Royal Regiment, ... 30
    Dance band, ... 30

Labour Exchange, ... 111
Leedstown, ... 52
Lee-Enfield Rifle, ... 99
Lelant, ... 22, 25, 34, 35, 69, 71, 72
    Bend, ... 22
    Fire Guards, ... 48
    Golf Course, ... 22
    Quay, ... 22, 67, 68
    Towans, ... 22
Lello Bros, ... 54
Lewis Gun, ... 22, 36, 64
Local Defence Committee, ... 42
Local Defence Volunteers (LDV), ... 33
London, ... 33, 56, 58, 60, 61
London County Council (LCC), ... 59
Loggans Mill, ... 101
LSTs, ... 91, 93
Luftwaffe, ... 13, 17, 26, 56, 60, 83
    10 Staffel / Jagdgeschwader 2 (10/JG2), ... 23

Marazion, ... 19, 25, 35, 46
'Marena' SS, ... 63-67
Marrakesh, ... 83, 86
Maryland, ... 89
Masonic Hall, . . . 29, 47, 73, 92, 103, 104, 107, 109
Maternity Home, ... 42
Mellanear Smelting Works, ... 95
Memorial Hall Committee, ... 109
Merchant Curnow's Quay, ... 18
Merchant Navy, ... 116
Messerschmitt Bf109, ... 105
Methodist Chaplains (US Army), ... 89
Mexico Beach, ... 87
Mexico Towans, ... 22
Michigan, ... 94
'Michigan', ... 95
Military Cemetery (Illogan), ... 81
Military Police (US Army), ... 92
Minefield, ... 17
Ministry of Home Security, ... 40
Morrison Shelters, ... 39
Mount Pleasant, ... 39

Chapel, ... 90, 109
Mount Hawke, ... 78
Mousehole, ... 51
    Male Voice Choir, ... 107
Mulberry Harbour, ... 93

National Grid, ... 18, 26, 45
National Guard (USA), ... 89, 92
National Savings, ... 105-110, 116
Nazis, ... 56
Newlyn, ... 71
New Inn (The Bucket of Blood), ... 69, 90, 120
NFS, ... 48-49
    Benevolent Fund, ... 47
    2Z Division, ... 47
Nobel's Factory (Ardeer), ... 67
Normandy, ... 17, 23
Northover Projector, ... 37
North Quay, ... 18, 19, 26, 67, 71, 80, 100

Oerliken Gun, ... 67
Omaha Beach, ... 91
111th Naval Construction Battalion (US Navy), . . . 93
175th Combat Infantry Regiment
    (29th Div. US Army), ... 89, 91
    1st Battalion, ... 89
'Operation Steinbock', ... 56
Operational Bases ('OB's'), ... 38
'Oranje', MV, ... 68
'Overlord', ... 93
Overseas Forces Programme (BBC), ... 36

Paddington, ... 59, 92
Padstow, ... 19
Palace Cinema, ... 73, 90, 107
Parachute mine, ... 53
Passmore Edwards Institute, ... 39, 40, 41, 109, 121
Penmare Hotel, ... 17, 29, 89, 92
Penpol Avenue, ... 39
Penpol Road, ... 119
Penpol School, ... 39, 59, 60, 113, 118, 119
Penpol Terrace, ... 18, 39, 117
Penzance, ... 22, 25, 29, 30, 33, 34,
    . . . . 42, 46, 48, 51, 53, 56-58, 60-62,
    . . . . 89, 92, 94, 105, 106, 114, 116, 117
    Carnival, ... 13
    Council Welfare & Evacuation Committee, . 58, 59
    First Aid Post, ... 42
    Police, ... 92
    Police Station, ... 33
    Station, ... 14, 57
    Town Council, ... 59, 61, 62, 105
Phillack, ... 56, 120
    Church, ... 81, 116, 121
    Churchtown, ... 90
    Orchestra, ... 74
'Phoney War', ... 14
Pillboxes, ... 16, 17-18
Plymouth, ... 39, 56, 58, 62, 93, 97
Poison gas, ... 13
Police, ... 12, 53, 55, 56, 82, 87, 92, 115, 119, 143
Port Admiral (Falmouth), ... 98

Porth Kidney Sands, ... 22, 23
Porthleven, ... 19
Porthminster Point, ... 25, 35
'Port Lyauty' MV (Free French), ... 67
Portreath, ... 52, 63, 120
Portsmouth, ... 56
Pool, J & F Ltd, . . 19, 21, 36, 45, 48, 56, 75, 80, 106, 111
Power Station (Hayle),
    . 18, 26, 27, 35, 41, 43, 54, 67, 77, 103, 115
Praze an Beeble, ... 61
Predictors, ... 22
Primrose Dairy, ... 36, 106
Prisoners of War Fund, ... 32, 75
Prisoners of War:
    German, ... 95
    Italian, ... 31, 79, 95
Protected Area 19

'Queen Elizabeth' RMS, ... 89
'Queen Mary' RMS, ... 89
'Queen Mary' (RAF Truck), ... 82
Queens Hotel, (Penzance), ... 58

'The Rake's Progress', ... 120
'Ramleh', SS, ... 94
Rationing, ... 121
'Rat Week', ... 117
Recreation Ground, ... 95, 122
Redruth: 42, 61
    Hospital, ... 47
    Workhouse, ... 115
Regent Hotel, ... 36
Regional Commissioner, South West, ... 44
'Reiger' MV, ... 68
REME, ... 25
Rescue Party (ARP), ... 40
Rhino Ferries, ... 91, 93-97
'Rian' MV, ... 68
Richmond Methodist Church (Penzance), ... 62
'Rike' MV, ... 68
Riviere House, ... 17, 29, 89, 90, 92
RNAS St Merryn, ... 101
Road Blocks, ... 18
Rosevidney Farm, ... 81
Roseworthy, ... 13, 56
    Farm, ... 82
    Hammer Mill, ... 115
'Rossmore' SS, ... 63-65, 67
Rotterdam, ... 113
Royal Air Force (RAF), ... 56, 101, 107
Squadrons & other units:
    No 50 Sqdn, ... 81
    No 66 Sqdn, ... 81
    No 90 Sqdn, ... 113
    No 130 Sqdn, ... 81
    No 220 Sqdn, ... 81
    No 502 Sqdn, ... 81
    No 4 (Coastal) OTU, ... 101
    No 95 EGS, ... 102
Stations:
    Alness, ... 101

Davidstow,	82
Drytree (Goonhilly),	17
St Eval,	17, 81, 83
Mount Batten,	81
Nutt's Corner,	113
Pembroke Dock,	81
Perranporth,	17, 18, 102
Polebrook,	113
Portreath,	17, 18, 52, 53, 64, 81, 84, 104, 113
Predannack,	17, 81, 102, 107
Roborough,	17
Swinderby,	81
Trerew,	17
Royal Artillery,	13, 19, 21, 22, 29
Coastal Battery,	35
Searchlight Company,	13
203 battery HAA (TA),	13
Royal Engineers,	93
Royal Iniskilling Fusiliers,	31
Royal Navy,	106
Royale Hotel,	59, 102
'Ruja', MV,	68
St Agnes,	78
St Agnes Head,	64
St Austell,	56, 92, 118
St Elwyn's,	
Church,	79
Hall,	100
Place,	39, 109
St Erth,	25, 36, 40, 53, 78, 81, 118, 121
Horse & Pony Society,	78
Operatic Society,	75
School,	105
Station,	25, 36, 95
Working Party for Hospital Supplies,	14
St George's Road	115
St Hilary,	42
St Ives,	25, 35, 37, 42, 45, 47, 57, 61, 69, 70, 77, 81, 82, 84, 89, 94, 102
Archive Study Centre,	71
Fire Brigade,	46
First Aid Post,	42
Guildhall,	58
Harbour,	69
Pilots,	69
Town Council,	57
St Ives Bay,	25, 69, 70, 84, 97
St John Ambulance Brigade,	13, 145
Cadets,	42, 99, 104
St John's Hall,	30
St John's Street,	39, 32
St Joseph's Catholic Church (Hayle),	31
St Just,	60, 105, 106, 110
St Lo,	91
St Michael's Hospital,	41, 42, 59, 76, 77, 78, 90, 97, 99, 117
Contributory Scheme,	77
X-Ray Fund,	77
'Salute The Soldier Week',	105, 109
Salvation Army,	42, 121
Scouts,	104, 118
Savings Weeks,	105
'Schuyts',	67-68
Scotland,	67
'Seahorse', Tug,	97
Secretary of State,	49
Shelters,	39-41
Signals Section (HG),	35
Siren,	41-42
'Sitzkrieg',	13
Slapton Sands,	91
South Quay,	68
Spain,	39, 84
Spigot Mortar,	37
Spitfire, Supermarine,	64, 109
'Starfish',	51-52
'QL',	51
Station Villas,	109
Stavanger,	64
Steam Packet Inn,	39
Sten Gun,	37
Stevens Fish & Chip Shop,	37
Stop Lines,	33
String vests,	80
Swing Bridge,	19
Task Force,	126-124, 91
'Taycraig', SS,	69
Taylor's Tea Rooms,	17, 89
Tempest Depot,	18, 48
Territorial Army,	89, 116
35th Division (US Army),	91, 92
Thompson Sub-Machine Gun,	95
Tolroy Garage,	95
'Tongshan' SS,	94
Totnes,	94
Towans (Hayle),	22, 29
Towans Stores & Cafe,	82
Townshend,	53
Trailer pumps,	45-48
Trebah,	91
Tredrea,	53
Treglisson,	119
Treglistian Farm (Lower),	56
Trelawney Place,	39
Treloweth Manor,	121
Trevarrack,	21
Trevassack,	55
Cricket Ground,	101, 109
Trevega Farm,	53
Trevessa Farm,	81
Trewinnard Manor,	53
Trinity House Pilots,	69
'Triumph' HMS,	115
Truro,	46, 49, 51, 56, 92
'Twente' MV,	68
25th US Naval Construction Regiment (25th NCR),	93
29th Division (US Army),	89, 92
Twin Towers,	117
Undercliff,	39
Union Hotel,	58
United Kingdom (UK),	83

United States (USA), ... 95
   Army, ... 29
   Army Air Corps, ... 92
   Army Air Force, ... 56, 83
   Navy, ... 93

V1, ... 29, 60
Ventonlegue, ... 53, 55, 89
   Prize Male Voice Choir, ... 76, 107
Vickers Machine Gun, ... 36
Virginia, ... 89

Wall, ... 121
War Office, ... 92
'Warships Week', ... 105, 106
'War Weapons Week', ... 105
'Wasp' USS, ... 85
Weir, The, ... 93
Wermacht, ... 33
West Cornwall, ... 44, 57
West Cornwall Hospital, ... 62
West Penwith Area, ... 33
West Penwith Petty Sessions, ... 97

West Penwith Rural District Council (WPRDC), . 13, 39,
   . . . . 40, 42-49, 57, 105, 106,
   . . . . 109-111, 116, 118, 121
   Finance Committee, ... 48
   Food Control Committee, ... 48
West Terrace, ... 39, 118
West Yorkshire Regiment, ... 30
'Westcoaster', MV, ... 67
Western Hotel, ... 58
Wheal Merth Mine, ... 38
White Hart Hotel, ... 90, 120
Whitecross Bend, ... 25
Whitley, Armstrong Whitworth, ... 81-82, 83
Wilhelmshaven, ... 113
Wilson's Pool, ... 18
'Wings for Victory' Queen, ... 103
'Wings for Victory' Week, ... 103, 105-109, 117
'Witch' HMS, ... 106
Women's Voluntary Service (WVS), ... 42-43

'Yanks', ... 29